Mexico under Mi

MW01596168

Mexicans and those who follow Mexican affairs were optimistic in 2000 when the country experienced its first alternation in government (from the Partido Revolucionario Institucional—PRI—to the Partido Acción Nacional—PAN) in more than 70 years. Moreover, the Mexican economy had been restructured in a more open, market-led direction in the course of the 1980s and 1990s. The outcomes of these dual transitions were expected to create a new type of politics that were representative and accountable to citizens, and an economy that would grow rapidly, as it was forced to modernize by facing international competition.

Some two decades later, views about Mexico are much less sanguine, and for many the country continues to follow a bipolar politico-economic trajectory characterized by periods of enthusiasm and mania which are followed by crisis and depression. This book presents a new analytical framework and reviews in detail Mexico's political and economic history since the 1980s. The explanation offered is based on the idea of 'misplaced monopolies'—i.e. an open political regime but a weak, fragmented state, and an internationally open economy, but highly concentrated economic sectors and activity in the domestic sphere. Accordingly, sown in the course of the crisis-ridden 1980s and 1990s, misplaced monopolies grew roots and became core features of Mexico's political economy in the 2000s and 2010s. The end result has been great concentration of wealth in a small number of hands, and the dramatic growth in brutal violence in many parts of the country. From this perspective, unless 'misplaced monopolies' are reversed, conditions will remain prone to crisis, polarization, and conflict in Mexico. This volume concludes by extrapolating the framework and placing Mexico in comparative perspective, alongside internationally important countries such as Brazil, China, India, and Russia.

This is a highly original investigation that will interest people who follow Mexico's politics and its economy. The analytical framework will be of use to analysts, scholars, and students of comparative political economy, democratization studies, market reforms, and security and conflict studies.

Francisco E. González is an Associate Professor of International Political Economy specialized in Latin American countries at the Paul H. Nitze School of Advanced International Studies (SAIS) of the Johns Hopkins University, in Washington, DC, USA. Professor González is also the author of *Dual Transitions from Authoritarian Rule* (2008) and *Creative Destruction? Economic Crises and Democracy in Latin America* (2012), both published by Johns Hopkins University Press.

Europa Emerging Economies

The Europa Emerging Economies series from Routledge, edited by Robert E. Looney, examines a wide range of contemporary economic, political, developmental and social issues as they affect emerging economies throughout the world. Complementing the *Europa Regional Surveys of the World series and the Handbook of Emerging Economies,* which was also edited by Professor Looney, the volumes in the *Europa Emerging Economies series* will be a valuable resource for academics, students, researchers, policy-makers, professionals, and anyone with an interest in issues regarding emerging economies in the wider context of current world affairs.

There will be individual volumes in the series which provide in-depth country studies, and others which examine issues and concepts; all are written or edited by specialists in their field. Volumes in the series are not constrained by any particular template, but may explore economic, political, governance, international relations, defence, or other issues in order to increase the understanding of emerging economies and their importance to the world economy.

Robert E. Looney is a Distinguished Professor at the Naval Postgraduate School, Monterey, California, who specializes in issues relating to economic development in the Middle East, East Asia, South Asia and Latin America. He has published over 20 books and 250 journal articles, and has worked widely as a consultant to national governments and international agencies.

The Islamic Republic of Iran: Reflections on an emerging economy
Jahangir Amuzegar

Argentina's Economic Reforms of the 1990s in Contemporary and Historical Perspective
Domingo Felipe Cavallo and Sonia Cavallo Runde

Handbook of Small States: Economic, Social and Environmental Issues
Edited by Lino Briguglio

The Political Economy of Financial Transformation in Turkey
Edited by Galip L. Yalman, Thomas Marois and Ali Rıza Güngen

Mexico under Misplaced Monopolies: Concentrated Wealth and Growing Violence from the 1980s to the Present
Francisco E. González

Mexico under Misplaced Monopolies

Concentrated Wealth and Growing
Violence from the 1980s to the Present

Francisco E. González

Routledge
Taylor & Francis Group

LONDON AND NEW YORK

First published 2019
by Routledge
2 Park Square, Milton Park, Abingdon, Oxon OX14 4RN

and by Routledge
711 Third Avenue, New York, NY 10017

Routledge is an imprint of the Taylor & Francis Group, an informa business

© 2019 Francisco E. González; Chapter 6 © Francisco E. González and Albert 'Jim' Marckwardt

The right of Francisco E. González to be identified as the author of this work and of Francisco E. González and Albert 'Jim' Marckwardt to be identified as the authors of Chapter 6 has been asserted by them in accordance with sections 77 and 78 of the Copyright, Designs and Patents Act 1988.

All rights reserved. No part of this book may be reprinted or reproduced or utilised in any form or by any electronic, mechanical, or other means, now known or hereafter invented, including photocopying and recording, or in any information storage or retrieval system, without permission in writing from the publishers.

Trademark notice: Product or corporate names may be trademarks or registered trademarks, and are used only for identification and explanation without intent to infringe.

by Taylor & Francis Books

Europa Commissioning Editor: Cathy Hartley

Editorial Assistant: Eleanor Catchpole Simmons

British Library Cataloguing in Publication Data
A catalogue record for this book is available from the British Library

Library of Congress Cataloging in Publication Data
Names: Gonzâalez Gonzâalez, Francisco Enrique, 1970- author.
Title: Mexico under misplaced monopolies : concentrated wealth and
   growing violence from the 1980s to the present / Francisco E. Gonzâalez.
Description: 1 Edition. | New York : Routledge, 2018. | Series: Europa
   emerging economies
Identifiers: LCCN 2018015596 (print) | LCCN 2018026725 (ebook) |
   ISBN 9781351046756 (master ebook) | ISBN 9781351046749 (webPDF) |
   ISBN 9781351046732 (epub) | ISBN 9781351046725 (mobi/kindle) | ISBN
   9781857439656 (hardback) | ISBN 9781351046756 (ebk)
Subjects: LCSH: Wealth–Mexico. | Monopolies–Mexico. | Violence–Mexico.
   | Mexico–Economic conditions–21st century.
Classification: LCC HC140.W4 (ebook) | LCC HC140.W4 .G66 2018 (
   print) | DDC 338.972–dc23
LC record available at https://lccn.loc.gov/2018015596

ISBN: 978-1-857-43965-6 (hbk)
ISBN: 978-1-351-04675-6 (ebk)

Typeset in Times New Roman
by Taylor & Francis Books

Dedicado a mis hijos, Francisco y Tomás, //también mexicanos. // A mi Amy, por no serlo. // A mis padres, Laura y Francisco, // llanto, auxilio, y consuelo mexicanos. // A mi tío Enrique y mi primo Pedro, // por el México que se nos fue; // que nunca existió; // y, sin embargo, // pulsa en // nosotros.

Contents

Illustrations

Figures

Table

Preface and Acknowledgments

In 2008–09 I was doing research about the political consequences of the global financial-economic crisis. I ended up writing a comparative history book about the major effects of the worst economic crises between the Great Depression (early 1930s) and the Great Recession (2008–10) on political regimes, democratic or authoritarian, in the Southern Cone countries of Argentina, Chile, and Uruguay.

Despite the battering it took during the 2008–10 global economic crisis, Mexico did not feature in that book. However, as a Mexican who also studies that country's politics and economic policy, I kept getting requests to comment about not just this terrible economic crisis, but the many others my country was suffering.

Among other things, colleagues in academia, graduate students, think tanks, and the media wanted me to discuss the origins, consequences, and severity of Mexico's breakdown of order and stability, and the proliferation of barbaric violence since the early 2000s. They wanted to know about the effects of President Felipe Calderón's official declaration of a 'war on drugs' in December 2006; about the Mexican economy, which had joined the USA and Canada in the North American Free Trade Agreement (NAFTA) in 1994, but had, none the less, chronically underperformed, at least according to the expectations of many professional economists, investors, and businessmen, not to mention rural Mexican farmers, small and medium-sized business owners in the country, and the millions of underemployed workers in the country's vast informal economy.

Likewise, why had Mexico finally given in and asked for US support (monetary, intelligence, hardware, training, and highly specialized agents on the ground) to contain the spiraling violence in its territory after many decades of jealous safeguarding of national sovereignty and self-determination? And later on, once the Partido Revolucionario Institucional (PRI—which had ruled uninterrupted during 1929–2000) returned to power in 2012 under President Enrique Peña Nieto, was it likely that there could be light at the end of the tunnel and Mexico could regain order and stability, as well as a fast-growing, competitive economy? Oh, and what about the election of Donald Trump, who called Mexicans 'rapists and criminals,' and promised to build a wall between the USA and Mexico, during the campaign that brought him victory and made him the 45th President of the United States of America in January 2017?

As a result, I have devoted a significant amount of my working time studying the country where I was born and grew up. I have gone back home more frequently than I used to. I have talked with scholars, politicians, technocrats, journalists, non-governmental organization workers, family members, friends, acquaintances, and people in the streets of cities and towns in the states of Morelos, Coahuila, Guerrero, and Michoacán, as well as Mexico City. I also want to acknowledge the help and support of several institutions and individuals. The School of Advanced International Studies (SAIS) of The Johns Hopkins University, where I work, was a great forum where I presented different parts of the manuscript on several occasions. I am particularly indebted to the graduate students who took my Mexico course between 2009 and 2017. I am also indebted to Tulane University, in particular Dr. Ludovico Feoli, and El Colegio de México, particularly former President Javier García-Diego and President Silvia Giorguli for invitations to participate in two 'Mexico-US' conferences, in New Orleans in November 2011, and in Washington, DC (thank you to the Inter-American Dialogue for hosting this event) in February 2018. Material that constitutes part of the book was also presented at the SAIS Bologna Center; St. Antony's College, University of Oxford; and Boston College, as well as in conferences convened by the Red de Economía Política de América Latina in the Universidad Católica de Chile in Santiago in 2014 and at the Massachusetts Institute of Technology in 2016. Some material was presented in Latin American Studies Association meetings in Washington, DC in 2013 and in Chicago in 2014. I received very good feedback from many colleagues among whom I would like to make special mention of Ben Ross Schneider, Juan Pablo Luna, Robert Kaufman, Alan Knight, Laurence Whitehead, Steven Levitsky, Carlos Elizondo Mayer-Serra, and Gustavo Flores Macías. Special thanks to Albert 'Jim' Marckwardt, who co-wrote chapter 6 with me. My gratitude goes to my mother and father, who offered moral support and kept encouraging me to see the project through to completion. My greatest debt, gratitude, and love are for my family: my wife, Amy, and our boys, Francisco and Tomás, for making me want to keep living a meaningful life.

By the way, I did not get definitive answers to many of the questions I was motivated to explore. However, I saw and heard many things that justified the general sense of dread felt by many Mexicans and foreigners who are interested in, follow, or have links with Mexico. Some of the questions were answered by facts on the ground: no, Mexico did not regain order and stability and did not grow at 5 per cent or more annually after the return of the PRI to power; the 'war on drugs' led to a fragmentation of organized criminal groups, many of which operate in niches of expertise—extortion, kidnapping, trafficking in humans, narcotics, and weapons, among others; many of the leading figures of the large, traditional cartels operate and make astounding profits from the sale of narcotics, mainly in the USA. The tragic opioid abuse epidemic raging in that country since the 2000s has more than compensated for traffickers' profits arising from falling sales of imported cannabis, which have been partly substituted by a combination of US-grown strains and legalization of the drug in several US states, as well as a gradual reduction in the demand for cocaine. In the legal economy, some manufacturing sectors have done well as a consequence of NAFTA, while primary activities like the farming of staple crops have not; and yes, the surprising electoral triumph of Donald Trump made not only Mexico but the entire globe a more uncertain and dangerous place to live in than before.

In order to try to understand Mexico's political economy during the last couple of decades, I thought it sensible to take a longer-term perspective. This decision was the result of my belief that some of the main factors that have characterized the country, such as extreme wealth concentration and a weakening, fragmented state, which lost its monopoly on the legitimate use of persuasion, force, and coercion throughout its territory in the course of the 2000s and 2010s, were sown in the crisis-ridden 1980s. Therefore, I have tried to identify, trace, and analyze the interaction of political and economic factors since then, and have summarized them in an explanation according to which Mexico's main economic and political problems have been the result of 'misplaced monopolies.'

This concept is explained in detail in chapter 1. Here I summarize it as a case of a country that has undergone long, uneven processes of economic and political liberalization since the 1980s and 1990s. The outcomes of these processes have been mixed: on the one hand, Mexico has been considered an open economy and an electoral democracy since around 2000, while on the other, it has ended up becoming a country characterized by great concentration of wealth in a small number of hands (which was the case before the transition) and little economic competition, and by weak, fragmented political authorities incapable of enforcing law and order against non-state actors (which was not the case at least during the years of PRI hegemony), particularly organized criminal groups which in some cases became the *de facto* rulers of the territories where they operate.

While pessimistic, my diagnosis does not imply that Mexico is condemned to continue on this trajectory. Contingent factors such as leadership, collective action, foreign affairs, international economic trends, and luck, among others, can change countries in relatively short periods of time. The question is: will the intervention of these factors help to improve or undermine the dignity and quality of life in Mexico? This question applies to everyone in Mexico, but particularly to the vast majority who cannot improve their lot through personal connections or networking, nor earn enough through legal means, to avoid economic precariousness and, in some cases, risk to their personal security.

Introduction

Mexico is a large emerging market which by 2020 will have more than 130 million inhabitants; its economy will be one among fewer than 20 around the world whose size in terms of gross domestic product (GDP) is larger than US $1,000,000m., while its GDP per capita will hover around $8,000–10,000. This range of income per head will place Mexico among a large group of developing economies which the World Bank considers as 'middle income.'

Mexico's recent history has been characterized by alternate cheering and booing from the international community, and many Mexicans themselves. The country was structured by a strong, centralized state (despite its federal framework) that helped to guarantee relative social peace, political stability, and a protected, inward-looking economy that on average delivered high growth and low inflation between the 1940s and the 1960s (6–7 percent annual growth and single-digit annual inflation, on average) under the umbrella of authoritarian rule by an hegemonic party, the Partido Revolucionario Institucional (PRI). Despite holding regular elections at the three levels of government (federal, state, and municipal), this party remained in power uninterruptedly between 1929 and 2000. Elections were not considered free or fair, but Mexico was not a one-party state. It allowed right-wing and left-wing parties to compete, and granted them token victories in some places, even though the PRI maintained presidential control at all times.

The record of high growth and low inflation, and relative social peace and political stability started being questioned in the second half of the 1960s. Particularly, starting in the 1970s, Mexico followed what can only be described as a bipolar trajectory, with phases of manic optimism invariably succeeded by collapse and depression; recuperation, in turn, followed again by downturns (see figure i.1).

Inflation took off into double-digits starting in the early 1970s and continued almost without interruption—and with two significant spikes into triple-digit inflation in the 1980s—until the end of the 20th century. It was not until the early 2000s that the annual rate of inflation stabilized into single-digits. In turn, the high rates of annual growth seen between the 1940s and 1960s continued until 1980–81, albeit through monetary and fiscal expansionism, which created the inflationary problem in the first place. Moreover,

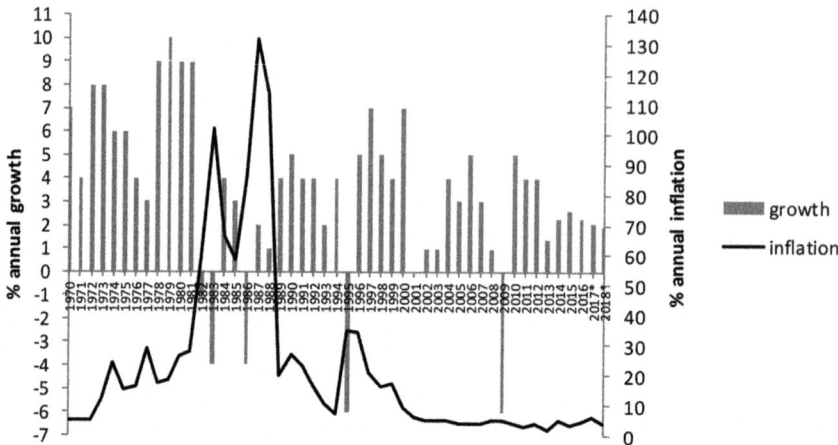

Figure i.1. Mexico's Jagged Macroeconomic Performance, 1970–2018
Source: Elaborated by the author from data in World Bank (WB), *World Development Indicators*, http://data.worldbank.org/country/mexico, accessed 23 December 2017; *forecasts for 2017 and 2018 from International Monetary Fund (IMF), *World Economic Outlook*, October 2017, https://www.imf.org/en/Publications/WEO/Issues/2017/09/19/world-economic-outlook-october-2017, chapter 1, p. 65.

four successive end-of-presidential-term financial crises (1976, 1982, 1987–88, and 1994–95) broke the trend of sustained growth rates of the previous three decades. Thus, the growth rates depicted in figure 1.1 exemplify the typical 'boom and bust' type of economic activity that shortens political and economic actors' capacity to plan activities such as consumption and investment in the short and medium term.

It is also noticeable that the growth spurs of the 1990s, 2000s, and 2010s have occurred at increasingly lower rates, compared with the preceding decade, although they have been accompanied by single-digit annual inflation, as was the case during the good, stable period (1940s–1960s) and unlike the period of great economic instability (1970s–1980s and mid-1990s). Therefore, real growth in terms of purchasing power for the average citizen has probably been higher since the late 1990s than during the high-growth but double or triple-digit inflation eras of the 1970s, 1980s, and the inflationary spike after the 1994–95 economic bust (the so-called 'tequila crisis,' which rattled financial markets across the world).

It is also important to note that successive Mexican governments' adoption of strict, conservative fiscal and monetary policy since the second half of the 1990s has not been enough to stop the onset of economic recessions (as in 2001–02, and the much more aggressive financial crisis of 2008–09). These have been imported as a consequence of external shocks—mainly, recessions and crises in the USA due to Mexico's deep integration and dependence on

US economic performance, particularly since the North American Free Trade Agreement (NAFTA) came into force at the beginning of 1994.

In the political sphere, the years of high inflation, economic contraction, and prolonged austerity led to fast weakening state capacity after Miguel de la Madrid (1982–88) inherited the presidency from José López Portillo (1976–82), who effectively bankrupted the country. From the early 1980s on the Mexican state became unable to retain a monopoly on power throughout the country's territory, a necessary condition to keep social cohesion. Deteriorating living conditions for a majority of Mexicans during those years chipped away slowly but continuously at the social contract and cohesion that had allowed the PRI to monopolize power in exchange for gradual, sustained socioeconomic improvement among the organized population, and in particular those with ties to the party. The PRI was finally ousted from power peacefully in the 2000 elections.

The conservative Partido Acción Nacional (PAN) took over and held the presidency for two consecutive terms (2000–12). During these years, power and authority continued to fragment, the economy underperformed, and the country ended up being compared with countries that have traditionally had weak central authority and a proliferation of organized violence fueled by the extremely high profits narcotics trade, as in Colombia in the 1980s–1990s. An analysis by the US Joint Forces Command of 2008 put Mexico alongside Pakistan as the "worst-case scenarios [in the world] for the Joint Force [if they faced] a rapid and sudden collapse."[1] The Mexican state was characterized as "under sustained assault and pressure by criminal gangs and drug cartels... Any descent by the [sic.] Mexico into chaos would demand an American response based on the serious implications for homeland security alone."[2]

The US governments led by George W. Bush (2001–09) and Barack Obama (2009–17) gave aid to Mexico through the so-called Mérida Initiative, which starting in 2008 disbursed around US $1,400m. in hardware, training, logistics, communications and other means to help propup the Mexican government in its attempt to defeat the main organized criminal groups.

Scholars, analysts, pundits, and the mass media in the USA continued to stoke the flames of this debate.[3] Mexico-baiting in fact became widespread and paid handsomely in the US presidential election of 2016, after Republican candidate Donald Trump singled out Mexicans throughout the campaign trail, characterizing Mexican immigrants in some instances as 'rapists and criminals.' He also declared that he would revoke NAFTA, which has integrated Mexico with the economies of the USA and Canada since 1994. Trump called this trade agreement 'the worst in history,' in the knowledge that it had been signed and started operating during the presidency of Bill Clinton (1993–2001), husband of his rival for the US presidency in the 2016 election, former Secretary of State and First Lady, Hillary Clinton. Trump also promised to build a wall that would physically separate the entire 3,140 km (1,951 miles) land border that the two countries share. In many mass rallies, particularly in the south, Midwest and northeast rustbelt states, the chant "Build the wall!" energized Trump's campaign.

It would be a gross exaggeration to say that Mexico-baiting on its own won Trump the presidency in November 2016, followed by his inauguration as the 45th President of the USA in January 2017. But Mexico, or what the country represents in the mind of many in 'Middle America' became a proxy for stagnant wages, illegal immigration, crowded public services, and the so-called 'war on drugs.' And the average US voter chose to support these issues in many states where the presidential race was a close call.

The perception of heightened alert and concern quoted above by the top brass in the US military, alongside intelligence and diplomatic personnel stationed in Mexico, as well as US businessmen and tourists who visited the country in the course of the presidencies of Vicente Fox (2000–06), Felipe Calderón (2006–12), and Enrique Peña Nieto (2012–18) is worrying. In and of itself, it does not validate Trump's often racist, bigoted views because it is, in turn, the product of perceptions rather than everyday reality throughout the Mexican territory. Yes, there are hot spots where high-intensity, systemic violence has become a matter of regular occurrence in Mexico since the early and mid-2000s. However, most of the country's territory remains as it was before the formal declaration of a 'war on drugs' by President Calderón in December 2006.

That is to say, most of Mexico is not under siege or beset by civil war-like violence. Rather, it remains a middle-income country with high levels of socioeconomic inequality, significant petty crime, and violence, due to ineffective government, low capacity to generate formal sector jobs, and a majority of the population who entertain hopes about a better future at the beginning of each presidency, at least since President Carlos Salinas de Gortari's government (1988–94), but who have become disillusioned, cynical, and pessimistic in the face of promises about economic and social improvement which, time and again, have gone unmet.

To understand the alarming problem of the rise and dissemination of daily acts of barbaric violence in some parts of Mexico since the early 2000s one has to consider the proliferation of organized criminal groups, whose great influence and power is fuelled by the extremely high profits that the narcotics trade creates, due to its prohibition. At the crux of the problem lie the intimate links through co-optation and collusion between these organized criminal groups and the state (i.e. authorities, particularly the forces of law-and-order at the three levels of government–federal, state, and municipal). The resulting turf wars and spiral into anarchy in areas that became hot spots of violence, are supported by metrics such as the number of homicides per 100,000 inhabitants; the number of special operations by the state to go after kingpins; the disturbance of the peace in the heart of cities, towns, and villages due to gunfights among organized criminal bands or some of those bands and the state; or state forces that work for one criminal group and state forces that work for another. Likewise, the growth of other criminal activities such as kidnapping, extortion, and human- and weapons-trafficking speaks volumes about the fragmentation and ineffectiveness of the state in Mexico in the last two decades.

In summary, the economic and political evolution, main changes, conflicts, challenges, and opportunities that Mexico has faced since the 1980s, covered in greater detail in Chapters 3 to 6 of this book, suggest a political economy that has undergone a dramatic transformation: from a relatively closed, protected, state-led economy, guided by a disciplined, authoritarian political regime under hegemonic party (PRI) rule, which crashed in 1982 and was forced to stabilize, undergo seven or eight years of austerity (the so-called 'lost decade' of growth and development), and restructure. The result has been an open economy, dependent to a significant degree on US economic growth, and a multiparty electoral democracy where power became fragmented, where no single party could rule by fiat, and where social cohesion—weakened after the 1982 crisis and the subsequent recessions and crises of the 1990s and the 2000s, unravelled in the form of growing lawlessness fuelled by petty and organized crime, corrupt government authorities, and daily incidents of barbaric violence, as various criminal organizations vied for more control of illicit activities that bring them mega-profits. Lastly, on July 1, 2018 Mexico had a general election in which the left, led by charismatic Andrés Manuel López Obrador or AMLO and his Movimiento de Regeneración Nacional or MORENA, won a resounding victory. AMLO's diagnosis about what has gone wrong in Mexico is quite similar to the idea of 'misplaced monopolies': on the one hand, a weak state captured by vested interests, engaged in grand corruption, and used to apply its powers to reward and protect its friends while punishing anyone and everyone who disagrees with its actions; on the other hand, an open economy that grows at low rates, whose main sectors are highly concentrated in few hands, where inequality is very high and economic opportunity is skewed to those with connections. This is the first time that the left will govern at the national level in Mexico. The Mexican population is right in believing that the problem of misplaced monopolies was created by the PRI and the PAN (or as many started calling the two parties' close cooperation between 1988 and 2018, the 'PRIAN'). Can the left reverse such deep-seated structural problems?

Notes

1 United States Joint Forces Command, *The Joint Operating Environment 2008: Challenges and Implications for the Future Joint Force*, Norfolk, VA, 2008, p. 36.
2 Ibid.
3 Luis V. Nevaer, "Mexico and the Myth of the 'Failed State'," New America Media, 9 July 2011, http://newamericamedia.org/2011/07/mexico-and-the-myth-of-the-failed-state.php, Accessed 8 November 2014.

1 Wealth and Violence: Untangling a Complex Relationship

The main political problems that scholars and analysts have had to grapple with when studying Mexico since the 1980s have been the many effects of the country's long, gradual transition from an authoritarian, hegemonic-party based regime to an electoral, democratic one. The transition to democracy has produced many effects. Of particular importance in my view is that any analyst who wants to understand this complex process properly has to place at the center of analysis the changes in the way that individuals and groups that exercise power or domination (i.e. power in its basic connotation of being able to force one's will against another's, if necessary through different degrees of force and violence), relate to one another.

In Mexico, a cottage industry of very good research devoted to studying the origins, trends, and likely development of violence in society took off in the 2000s, and this can be seen as a reflection of the prominence of this growing phenomenon since then.[1] It has to be remembered too that even if it is true that Mexico has experienced a big increase in public shows of extreme violence since the early 2000s, social decomposition and higher violence and criminality—particularly professional, organized crime—can be traced back at least to the 1980s and the growing profile of drug cartels and their interaction and penetration of the Mexican state.[2]

It is therefore fundamental to observe the changing ways that power and violence have been exercised, and particularly the contrast between the years of hegemony of the Partido Revolucionario Institucional (PRI), which ruled during 1929–2000, and those of Mexico's young democracy. The earlier years were characterized by the control and hegemonic use of power by the PRI and its network of *caciques*.[3] This system allowed a high degree of centralization of the exercise of at least visible coercion and violence in a way that was dictated from above, and more often than not requiring compliance from below. Still, the system remained less centralized and more subject to negotiations by regional leaders with successive presidents than the simplistic idea of 'an imperial presidency,'[4] suggests.

  i Diversity: Mexico has remained, in the view of many observers, from Justo Sierra in the last third of the 19th century to early 21st-century scholars and analysts, a vast and highly diverse country. A common characterization of Mexico has been that of an archipelago[5] made up of regions, sub-regions, localities, states, and municipalities where, even though people would self-identify as Mexican, they would refer first to more palpable identities in their everyday lives like the sub-regional (or *patria chica*) or ethnic (for example, Zapoteco, Mixteco, or Mayan) or state or municipal identities.[6]

ii Federalism: an issue connected with the previous question, relating to the change in the use and exercise of violence in Mexico; but also covering more broadly issues of different jurisdictions, political competition, public policy and public management, and the creation of subnational centers of power and dispensation of political and economic favors, is the fragmentation of authority, given Mexico's federalist framework. Similar to the USA and other federal countries, this type of framework creates three levels of government, with their own jurisdictions, police forces, and basic social services that they deliver, such as public health, housing, and education. Subject to varying degrees of free and fair electoral competition (lower barriers to entry) since the 1990s, this system has decentralized power, created pluralistic representation, and likewise has engendered conflicts, lobbying, horse-trading, often leading to certain parties threatening to veto measures they oppose, to the point of stalemate (but also capacity for significant structural reforms as between 2012 and 2014).

iii Weak Rule of Law: lastly, the fragmentation of authority and power, given Mexican federalism, has been increasingly problematic because the long, gradual transition to democracy in Mexico unfolded under state institutions whose daily practice, norms, and underlying values were not only not in accordance with the rule of law and the basic principle of legality (i.e. the same public, *ex ante* laws that apply equally to all individuals, irrespective of any social, economic, or political attributes); this is a very damaging problem and one that will not be easy to fix. On the contrary, the state institutions built under and developed by the hegemonic party regime system that the PRI ran quite successfully—so much so that it stayed in power for seven decades without interruption, and at least on paper allowed plural, regular elections to be held—created a system of political rule and domination that was self-serving: whoever is in charge orders everyone else around; creates opportunities to grow his or her political group's influence, money, power, and future opportunities; and then steps down, given the golden rule of no re-election to public office (see below for the constitutional changes that allow for the re-election of legislators and mayors, and their potential effects after 2018). Furthermore, participants seek to "*haber amarrado*" or "*obtenido hueso*" (to 'tie up' a position or 'secure' a [no doubt juicy] 'bone' to gnaw on—a revenue stream from public resources—in Mexican political class parlance), given the dense network of favors and counter-favors that keep at least this part of the political sphere quite competitive, with all the vices and virtues that this creates: parties have to convince citizens to vote for them so elected politicians have to care more about their track record in a competitive system than in a non-competitive system; there are proper checks-and-balances on the executive branch—which often went unused during the years of PRI hegemony—given active legislatures and courts; but there has also been a proliferation of graft, malfeasance, grand corruption, and what is worse, given the absence of a legal system where the rule of law operates, impunity via bribes, collusion, threats, or the naked use of power, violence and murder, which carry the day more often than not when it comes to the resolution of conflicts. In addition, and to make matters worse, Mexico's main left wing and conservative parties, the Partido de la Revolución Democrática (PRD) and the Partido Acción Nacional (PAN), respectively, which vehemently criticized the PRI for its rent-seeking, corrupt, client-based system when they were in opposition, ended up copying the system once they started gaining power and establishing areas of influence and their own politico-electoral machines, particularly at the state and municipal levels.

From the main political analyses about Mexico's transition to democracy and its main effects, I underline the importance given to the changing role in the use of power and violence; the federalist institutional framework which creates a multiplicity of power centers under democracy, and which is very different from the years when authoritarianism under PRI hegemony held sway; and the changing non-state organizations that took away the state's monopoly on the use of violence as barriers to entry fell since the 1982 economic crisis, but accelerated after the 'tequila' crisis (1994–95).The background to all these political changes was a state characterized by a weak rule of law because the long period of PRI hegemony (from the 1940s to the early 1990s) was based on an overlap between the state, the regime, the hegemonic party, and successive governments.

The main rationale of this institutional arrangement was control, negotiation, and selective repression rather than the impersonal dispensation of justice, given the individual rights and the framework laid out in the 1917 Constitution for, at least on paper, a 'liberal democracy,' where state action is constrained by general rules that protect individuals from official or private harm against them and their interests, irrespective of their socioeconomic status or political connections.

Therefore, my aim in this work is to present a general explanation about the general effects of Mexico's dual transition on specific sectors, actors, and institutions. In particular, I offer a general explanation about the effect of Mexico's dual transition as it grew into a situation of what I refer to as 'misplaced monopolies' on freedom. Freedom in this context means a continuum that encompasses both different degrees of physical security, and economic opportunity, to develop one's potential.[7]

The aim of this type of work is to try to generalize by accounting for a complex politico-economic process in a way that one is able to summarize and include in a consistent manner the many explanations offered for more narrowly-defined, specific problems derived from the general problem studied—in this case Mexico's process of dual transitions since the mid-1980s.

The 'Violence and Social Orders' Framework as Starting Point for Analysis

The recognition of the centrality of violence in any human society (and therefore its role in economic and political development), and, given its growing role and influence in Mexico since the 1990s—which has led to the rate of violent deaths per 100,000 inhabitants tripling since the mid-2000s until today—attracted me to an influential study on 'violence and social orders' which prominent economic historians and political scientists published in 2009.[8] More recently, the World Bank commissioned the 'testing' of this theory through the elaboration of case studies in countries in East Asia, South Asia, Latin America, and Africa, the results of which were published in 2013.[9] Therefore, the 'violence and social orders' framework has not been confined to the small and hyper-specialized debates that characterize academia, but have instead influenced the world of international policymaking, and been implemented via institutions such as the World Bank. This real-life application of the framework makes it even more prominent in discussions about political and economic development in most middle-income and poor countries around the world.

North, Wallis, and Weingast, authors of the original study, identify two types of politics used to mediate and suspend violence (the authors remind readers early in their text that violence is always latent in human interaction) in order that economic exchange, production, and consumption can take place. According to them, the first type of political model, referred to as 'limited access order or natural state,' applies in the early 21st century to around 175 countries and 85 percent of the world's population.[10] The great majority of human beings in the 2010s live in such 'limited access' orders. The second type comprises what are popularly known as advanced economies. These authors refer to them as 'open access societies.' They estimated that the citizens of around 25 countries (15 percent of the world's population) live in such 'open' social orders.[11]

The authors contend that the main distinction between these two different types or ways of doing politics is based on the extent to which the leaders of the most powerful organizations in a given society create a 'dominant coalition' which in turn is able to limit to different degrees the freedom that individuals outside that coalition have to create political and economic organizations that protect and pursue their own interests—which can, and more often than not do, clash or at least create permanent frictions—with the dominant coalition's interests.[12]

This limitation of freedom of organization creates rents for the leaders of the main organizations in the dominant coalition, inasmuch as limitations to competition increase net benefits for them at the expense of those left out of the 'racket' that comprises the dominant coalition.[13] This is predicated on the general principle that a larger degree of constraints to competition produces the type of monopoly organization, which either in the economic or in the political spheres or in fact in both, and usually in a self-reinforcing manner, will tend to under-produce and over-charge, in the absence of competition.

In summary, the 'violence and social orders' framework is basically concerned with establishing how such different types of politics turned 'orders' as distinctive groups of institutions (i.e. basic laws and rules), organizations (i.e. groups of individuals pursuing some similar purpose), and élites (the leaders of such organizations and those closest to them), their interactions, and their capacity to keep their own rank-and-file under control so that the system of buying off violence produces sufficient rents that leaders and the rank-and-file of participating organizations alike, decide that the benefits of co-operation outweigh the costs of exiting, going rogue and trying to gain advantage independently of the dominant coalition, which raises the risk of violence.[14]

One of the innovations of this analysis is that it highlights the limitation of the neoclassical economics/public choice analysis that has dominated the literature about 'market' and 'government' failures as prerequisites for productive activity, and therefore economic growth. Whereas for the neoclassical paradigm 'rents' are first and foremost about 'rent-seeking' (i.e. "The socially costly pursuits of wealth transfers."[15]), for the authors of the 'violence and social orders' theory, rents act as the glue of social orders and are 'rent creating' (at least for élites) too, given that their creation and distribution among the members of the dominant coalition generate the conditions that make the benefits of keeping the *status quo* outweigh the costs of defecting, and trying to gain rents by opposing the dominant coalition by resorting to violence.

In other words, in both 'limited' and 'open' access orders, to different degrees politics is organized and used to generate rents for élites, but these are not necessarily so socially costly, once the constant negotiation of latent violence in human interaction is factored in. From this perspective, rents are part and parcel of preserving the peace, although the decision about the allocation and control of such rents is more personalized and therefore more uncertain and likely negative in 'limited access orders' compared with 'open access orders' (i.e. the English-speaking countries, a majority of European Union countries, Japan, and more recently South Korea and maybe Chile[16]), according to the authors.[17]

Another of the strengths of this analysis is that it is not teleological: that is, a type of analysis where events in a process move toward a more or less predetermined outcome. On the contrary, the theory of violence and social orders lead the authors, on the one hand, to the creation of a typology of natural or limited access (from the weakest, which is identified as 'fragile', to an intermediary model, labelled 'basic', to the most advanced, known as 'mature') orders, in which any number of given countries may find themselves at a given point in time, amid the basic circumstances to be able to transition into an open access order. On the other hand, the authors allow their 'stages model' to go in both directions, which allows for improvement as much as for deterioration or decay.[18]

The 'Violence and Social Orders' Framework and the Case of Mexico

The chapter in the case studies volume devoted to Mexico by Alberto Díaz-Cayeros is an excellent essay that helps to understand the prevalence of economic and political privilege and lack of fairness in the country's political economy, due to the formation and continuation of what he refers to as 'entrenched insiders.'[19] The author highlights four aspects of Mexico's political economy (1. land reform and assets; 2. access to stock markets; 3. monopolistic regulation of firms and labor; and 4. oil rents and low public revenue yield[20]) "that can shed light on the social arrangements that awards insiders huge advantages that prevent mobility, economic dynamism, and political accountability."[21]

I highlight two factors from Díaz-Cayeros's analysis which I in turn use in my own framework. First, this explanation sheds light particularly on to the domestic structural arrangements that have allowed Mexico's political economy to remain dominated by a small number of personalized interests which include high-ranking politicians, businessmen, and bankers, as well as trade union leaders and leaders of other social organizations, effectively preventing a transition to an 'open access order.'

Second, in terms of violence control, the analysis recognizes the contrast between on the one hand the golden years of PRI hegemony, which the author equates with the "Stabilizing Development period from 1958 to 1970," and which were characterized by relative stability "punctuated, however, by mass mobilizations…which the state countered with its own displays of force."[22] And on the other hand, a rise in violence and in the state's incapacity to retain its relative monopoly on the use of force and violence, although the author does not put it in these words and my analysis emphasizes this aspect.

I agree with Díaz-Cayeros about expressing doubts that the start of the slippery slope towards the proliferation of private violence—that is, violence carried out not by public authorities but by non-state actors, from petty thieves and thugs to sophisticated criminal syndicates and kingpins—in many parts of Mexico coincided with the transition to democracy (since the second half of the 1990s). I support his contention that "violence … did not quite disappear in Mexico, and in fact witnessed an upsurge during the 1980s and 1990s [as] banditry, in the form of robbery, burglary, kidnappings, and murders."[23] Moreover, the author also agrees that violence got much worse since 2007 after the adoption of a 'war on drugs' policy—the label later changed to a 'war on organized crime' by President Felipe Calderón (2006–12) shortly after he assumed office.

My Contribution to the Debate: Barriers to Entry and Misplaced Monopolies

Rather than referring to 'social orders' and how 'open' or 'limited' access enables or thwarts the free organization of political and economic groups' existence and their capacity to operate, I use the classic idea of 'barriers to entry.' In broad terms, this concept of classical political economy refers to the same process that North, Wallis, Weingast and their collaborators use. However, it is an even more general category (i.e. it contains within it different degrees of limited and open access to the social orders these authors refer to).

My aim is to build theoretical and empirical knowledge based on the 'violence and social orders' by highlighting two refinements to this approach, which means that I qualify it rather than disprove or reject it.

The Political Sphere: State and Regime

The first qualification comes from the literature about comparative democratization since the 1970s and 1980s.[24] This literature from Anglo-American political science highlights the distinction in the political sphere of, on the one hand the 'state' and, on the other, the 'regime.' North, Wallis and Weingast do not make this distinction explicit. They identify 'open access orders' with those where barriers to entry into the free formation of political and economic organizations are low, compared with the different degrees of limitations to access: that is, higher barriers to entry in 'limited' access orders.

Because the difference between the state and the political regime is not highlighted in the authors' analysis of the political sphere, their general prescription, according to which the transition from a limited to an open access order happens merely by lowering barriers to entry (in general), contains important differences about what this means for the state, as opposed to the political regime, and creates problems for their analysis. Do we want barriers to entry to fall for the free and fair competition for public office as much as for the state's monopoly on the legitimate use of persuasion/force/coercion in the territory it claims jurisdiction over?

One the one hand, supporters of limited government via liberal democracy desire low barriers to entry in the political regime, where competition, regulation, and a frequent change of those in public office occurs (i.e. free and fair participation and contestation, in Robert Dahl's classic formula: a lively, rules-bound party system and regular elections with effective enforcements of the said rules).

On the other hand, however, supporters of limited democracy via liberal democracy do not want to see a lowering of barriers to entry in the state. They do not want private individuals and groups to be able to challenge the state in its supposed monopoly control over the legitimate means of force and violence in the territory over which a given state claims jurisdiction. If actors other than the state are able to start using persuasion/force/violence against other private parties or against the state itself, a cornerstone of classic liberalism—namely, the effective protection of basic individual rights—can easily be overwhelmed, and therefore create an increasingly disaffected society, given the big gaps between formally written laws and everyday practice and their implementation.

This problem is not due to the authors' omission of the figure of the state from their analysis *per se*. In fact, their construction of the spectrum that contains the main categories of their typology of cases—from a 'fragile limited access order' at one end to an 'open access order' at the other, includes the concept of the state. In the original volume the authors explicitly refer to the presence of the state as part of their second out of three "doorstep conditions" for countries before they can transition from a limited to an open access order.[25] Likewise, in the case studies volume, the authors refer to the state explicitly (but only once) in the table that summarizes their typology of access orders and their main characteristics.[26]

At the end of the original volume the authors acknowledge they "ducked the problem of defining the state" and provide a couple of pages on "acknowledging the difference between the state and the government..."[27]

The problem in my view is related to the authors' failure to distinguish, from the outset of their analysis, the state from the political regime (not between the state and the government) in their characterization of the political sphere. When one introduces this distinction it becomes patently obvious that the lowering of barriers to entry that they identify in the political sphere, as helping to establish doorstep conditions to transition from a limited to an open access order, should not apply *tout court* (across-the-board).

At least prescriptively, when we separate out the political sphere into the state and the regime, what is desirable is the maintenance or creation of high barriers to entry so that the state monopolizes the legitimate use of force and violence in the territory it claims jurisdiction over, and of low barriers to entry so that the regime is open to relatively free and fair participation and contestation in the formation, regulation, and change of publicly elected authorities (see Figure 3.1 below).

The Economic Sphere: Domestic and International

The second qualification to the 'violence and social orders' theory I introduce in this analysis is, like the previous one, based on the disaggregation of a general category. As with the political sphere, which I subdivided into the state and the regime, I disaggregate the general economic sphere identified by North, Wallis and Weingast. Thus, I differentiate the 'domestic' from the 'international' components of a given economy, and within each I also identify producers and consumers. Such a disaggregation allows for a more detailed (although still general) lens of observation that can help to understand better the benefits and costs that members of a given dominant coalition face as time passes. Furthermore, different rent-creation as well as rent-seeking opportunities and challenges from both domestic and international forces present themselves to the leaders of the main organizations of the said dominant coalition, as well as to their opponents.

The introduction of these categories would, for example, have allowed Díaz-Cayeros's analysis of the Mexican case not only to be mostly concerned with domestic conditions, given that some of the components of those conditions (like stock markets and oil[28]) have a significant international component that is, in turn, defined and redefined constantly by the interaction of foreign actors, rules, and resources with domestic political and economic realms.

My Hypothesis

Based on the disaggregation that I propose for the general 'economic' and 'political' spheres that the authors of the 'violence and social orders' and their collaborators propose, I return to classic works in political sociology and political economy on the effects of monopolies (i.e. barriers to entry) and their different degrees of dominance as main building blocks for analysis.[29]

I argue that the misplaced[30] combination of a weakened state, which lost the monopoly on the allocation of authoritative value through the deployment of persuasion/force/coercion, and a domestic economic structure that remained heavily concentrated and dominated by monopolies and oligopolies, despite low barriers to entry in the international economy (i.e. trade and financial flows) and, likewise, low barriers to entry in the political regime (i.e. competition for public office), have created significantly fewer winners than losers in Mexico's political economy since the 1990s.

In turn, this condition of suffering from 'misplaced monopolies' can be seen as a new explanation based on an analytical narrative that helps to account for Mexico's economic underperformance and growing socio-political conflict and violence since the 1990s.

My claim goes against the positive results that both agents and observers of Mexico's twin processes of economic and political liberalization (also known as 'dual transitions') have expected since the 1980s.[31] Opening up the economy was supposed to enhance efficiency and productivity, raising growth rates without inflationary pressures and accelerating the generation of formal employment. Figure 1.1, above, showed that inflation was tamed in the 2000s after two decades of runaway price increases in the light of macroeconomic mismanagement.

However, growth remained volatile, and despite conservative monetary and fiscal management from the mid-1990s[32] Mexico suffered externally-induced shocks, given contagion from recessions in the USA, which produced growth of zero percent in 2001 and −6.5 percent in 2009. Likewise, the country's record in generating formal employment has remained dismal despite or because of Mexico's membership of the North American Free Trade Area (NAFTA). Informal workers have continued growing as a proportion of the total employed population. Whereas this is not just a problem in Mexico, as the average for informal employment in Latin America has been and remains very high (more than 56 percent of the economically active population), Mexico's average is higher than the region's.[33]Informal employment, while bringing food to the table of such workers, does not contribute to the public purse and therefore creates a problem of a dependent population who do not seek to enter employment themselves. Furthermore, a large informal employment sector kicks the can further along the road regarding the future health, housing, and educational needs of these individuals and their families.

In the political sphere, in turn, liberalizing and ultimately democratizing the regime was supposed to eradicate the authoritarian exercise of power by enhancing checks-and-balances among the three branches of government at both the federal and state levels, as well as by making the political class accountable to citizens through electoral competition and the effective exercise of the rule of law. Checks and balances have been strengthened particularly at the federal level and a measure of accountability/transparency has grown thanks to the passage of a freedom of information law (which created the IFAI) during Vicente Fox's presidency (2000–06), for example.

However, the political class remains on the whole unaccountable. Rather than just having PRI members using and abusing the privileges of the exercise of power as was the case during the years of its hegemonic rule, the current democratic system has widened and deepened such practices by giving similar prerogatives to the members of the PAN and the PRD, to Andrés Manuel López Obrador's populist Movimiento de Regeneración Nacional (MORENA) and to several smaller parties which hold public office, and in the process receive many legal as well as illegal resources to operate and represent their backers' interests in the process of law-making in Congress and policy formulation and implementation in the executive branch, and its growing number of agencies. In turn, the governors of the 31 federal states, plus the mayor of Mexico City, have become in some ways a law unto themselves, particularly where their party controls the state legislature, leading some analysts to dub the current territorial allocation and use of power as a case of 'feudalism,' in allusion to the feudal lords and the fragmentation of power that characterized Europe in the Middle Ages.[34]

In the rest of this chapter I explore how the misplaced monopolies developed from Mexico's dual transitions, and how such configuration of the political and economic spheres led to the country's economic underperformance and encouraged the growth of social and political conflict and violence.

My Conceptual Framework

This analysis follows what is known in comparative politics as a 'middle-range' focus. The aim of this type of analysis is to find the main similarities and differences in *small n* comparisons (i.e. a small number of cases in great detail rather than many cases in a given number of statistical markers). The logic is inductive and generalizes by contrasting specific facts from a given place and time with similar facts from other times and places. At best, such comparative analysis can help to make cautious, non-sweeping generalizations informed by empirical evidence and held together by a framework of concepts and expected relations put together *before* or *ex ante* the systematic analysis of evidence is carried out. Usually, the aggregation of empirical evidence tends to end up qualifying the extent to which one can generalize or assume that some of the posited relationships are caused by some of the factors contained in the conceptual framework.[35]

The conceptual framework I have constructed is typical of studies of comparative politics and comparative political economy that proceed through searching for, ordering, and analyzing information in a qualitative rather than a quantitative way. It is closest to what is known in comparative political analysis as 'historical institutionalism.'[36]

My framework is made up of two spheres and four main factors, which are the building blocks for analysis: the spheres are the political and the economic, and the factors of analysis are, for the political sphere, the state and the political regime, while for the economic sphere they are the international and the domestic economies as shown in Table 1.1

These are the building blocks of the analysis but the author is well aware that the 'political' and the 'economic' are inextricably linked in complex ways that help to explain why things happened the way they did rather than in myriad other potential ways in accordance with the analytical lens used to analyze information. Although artificial, the division into 'political' and 'economic' spheres is meant to aid the aggregation of information into systematic categories for analytical purposes, which in turn helps to establish the

Table 1.1 Building Blocks of the Analysis

Spheres	Factors	Time 0	Time 1
Political	1) State	Monopoly	Fragmented
	2) Regime	Monopoly	Open
Economic	3) International	Closed	Open
	4) Domestic	Closed	Concentrated

Source: Elaborated by the author

yardsticks that help the author explain why he believes that the so-called "misplaced monopolies" in Mexico have led to "freedom for few" rather than many since the 1990s and despite economic and political liberalization.

I am aware that the proposition I have put forward by juxtaposing general claims made by Weber and Smith is normative. Neither a perfect monopoly on the use of force and coercion, nor perfect economic competition in a given territory, exists in the real world. They are and remain ideal types. Moreover, even if such ideal conditions could be put in place in different empirical contexts, they might not always translate into the best results in the sense of, on average, basic physical security and economic opportunity for individuals on the ground.

Such ideal interaction of the political and economic spheres is a construct of social science, which unlike some general propositions in the natural sciences, is far from ever aspiring to become a universal law. Nonetheless, what can be done is to contrast such ideal conditions by assuming that they produce the positive outcomes these authors posited with the real, historical, changing empirical conditions for the case of Mexico's political and economic spheres, and then assess how close or far away events on the ground, and the trends they have produced, are from the said ideal conditions.

The analysis of misplaced monopolies according to the passage of time and in the realms of politics and the economy can also be presented in diagram form. This representation has the advantage of showing a graphic representation of monopolies or their degrees of relative dominance or absence thereof in the face of competition (i.e. the existence of continuous or punctuated lines depict the high or low barriers to entry) in both the political and economic spheres.

t0 (time zero) in both the political (upper left hand side box and circles) and economic spheres (lower left hand side box and circles) represents the period of classic PRI hegemony (1940s to early 1990s although the economy started liberalization in 1985-6)) whereby a strong state capable of monopolizing the exercise of force, strengthened by an authoritarian regime that permitted only token electoral competition but ensured PRI hegemony, unquestionably dominated in Mexico. Such domination was augmented by state-led stewardship and development in the economy. Both the international and domestic economies were characterized by strong state protection, which allowed for the development of inefficient, rent-seeking monopolies and oligopolies, and both foreign as well as domestic firms, living off their rents from the exploitation of a protected, captive market where they could under-produce and overcharge. Together, the political and economic monopolies produced a political economy that was able to grow in the context of the post-Second World War years, created some social mobility, and delivered regime stability, albeit one characterized by authoritarian rule under the hegemonic dominance of the PRI.

In turn, t1 (time one) in both the political and economic spheres exhibits significant changes compared with previous conditions. On the economic

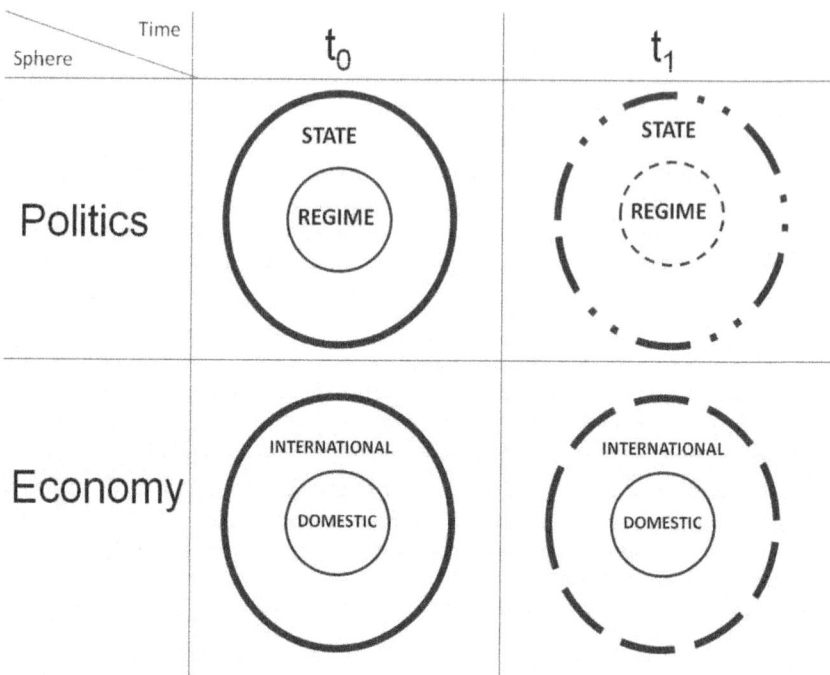

Figure 1.1 From Political and Economic Monopolies to Misplaced Monopolies
Source: Elaborated by the author.

front, in the aftermath of the 1982 external debt crisis the Mexican government was forced to open up its economy to international forces (lower right hand box, outer circle) during a gradual process that started in 1985–86, and which continues to date, with Mexican officials having signed up to the Alianza del Pacífico and promoting the Trans-Pacific Partnership (TPP), despite the withdrawal from the bloc soon after Donald Trump was inaugurated as US President in January 2017.

In great contrast, the domestic economy (lower right hand box, inner circle) has remained, at least until now, relatively protected and impermeable. Monopolies and oligopolies, which have led to under-production, over-pricing, and a rentier mentality for the captains of industry have only now—since President Enrique Peña Nieto's structural reforms of 2012–14—been shaken up.

However, the system, in the words of Díaz Cayeros, remains one of entrenched insiders, and the main beneficiaries of the structural reforms (see chapter 5) implemented under Peña Nieto will remain individuals and firms connected with and influential in power circles. It is too early to tell what the consequences of these latest structural reforms will be. I anticipate gradual change rather than a radical transformation. Moreover, the underlying logic for such reforms has not been the public interest but rather politico-economic gain for the current group in power and its business and political allies (see below section on the Domestic Economy). Yes, there might be more economic competition in Mexico in the 2020s, but it will remain tied to insiders. Therefore, Mexico will remain a glaring case of crony capitalism, whereby the top players who can apply political and economic power scratch each other's backs at the expense of all non-insiders (i.e. the vast majority of domestic and foreign producers and consumers).

In turn, looking at changes in the political sphere at t1 (upper right hand box), the Mexican state has suffered a significant and growing weakening and fragmentation of its authority and capacity to retain the monopoly on the use of force over its territory since the 1980s economic crises. Such a dramatic change was related to many factors: weak public finances after a decade of exporting capital to pay interest and principal on the external debt; personalization of power during the presidency of Carlos Salinas (1988–94) at the same time in which institutions such as the Instituto Federal Electoral, Comisión Nacional de Derechos Humanos, and Centro de Investigación y Seguridad Nacional were created to manage civil, political and electoral conflict; the 1994–95 financial crisis which led to a significant flight by police and military personnel into the illegal economy, either by becoming drug cartel enforcers or by creating their own small organizations that gave way to the rise of what came to be known as 'la industria del secuestro y la extorsión' (i.e. the kidnapping and extortion industries).

The outer circle made up of dash-and-dots in the upper right hand box is meant to illustrate the fragmentation and weakening of federal authority. It is different from the dashed outer circle in the box below regarding the international economy, because changes in the latter were planned, decreed, and executed by neoliberal technocrats as clear-cut economic policy actions (i.e. to liberalize trade or open up the capital account or manage monetary policy).

In contrast, the dash-and-dots denoting state weakening suggest a much less orderly and some would even say chaotic process, whereby some forces within the state wanted to weaken it, while others wanted to keep it strong at the same time that growing, powerful private groups capable of exercising professional, lethal violence came to the fore and challenged the state successfully in different parts of the Mexican territory to take charge and earn the rents that used to accrue to the previous dominant coalition (i.e. the state and its allies).

Lastly, the dashed inner circle in the upper right hand box represents the opening of the political regime. It represents first and foremost the weakening of PRI hegemony and its eventual demise, given successive electoral reforms that gave the opposition more chances to win elections in exchange for not rocking the boat, particularly after each of the financial crises between the mid-1970s and the mid-1990s. The current political regime still contains some barriers to entry (parties have to gain a minimum of 3 percent of the national vote to keep their registry and gain representation), and there remains general criticism about '*partidocracia*' (i.e. rule by the leaders of the main parties).

In my view, the concept of *partidocracia* is more appropriate for systems in which two main parties divide the spoils of voting, as in Colombia or Venezuela during the years of élite pacts in those countries between the late 1950s and the 1970s. In Mexico, there are three well-established parties and at least three or four others that act like swing voters and make the creation of cozy and predictable legislative outcomes much harder to call than in *partidocracia* systems. Moreover, since the latest electoral reforms of 2013–14, independents have been allowed to run. And to the surprise of many seasoned analysts and commentators, in the 2015 mid-term elections in Mexico one of them (although with a long, previous record under the PRI) won the governorship of the wealthy, industrial, border state of Nuevo León; an independent was also elected for federal deputy in the influential state of Jalisco. This steady growth in the representation of 'independents' will no doubt keep growing as one successful case encourage others, particularly disaffected politicians who already have an established following in one of the three main parties plus the rise of MORENA.

Still, in my view some of the criticisms of *partidocracia* are valid as the Mexican electoral system is made up of closed lists, so party leaders decide who is and who is not in the ballot. However, the electoral reform of 2013–14, which allowed re-election for legislators and mayors (and has come into full force starting with the 2018 elections) will no doubt lead to significant changes to the system of democratic representation in Mexico. For the purpose of this work, the main point to highlight is the relatively free and fair alternation of power at the three levels of government for executive and legislative posts of representation around the country since the late 1990s—a big change compared to the years of PRI hegemony.

In the next subsections I elaborate in more detail the main changes in the four factors of analysis that produced the misplaced monopolies in Mexico.

1 The State

The state is supposed to be the guarantor of freedom from violence by any private party against another or by the state itself against a private party if the former does not have the backing of the law to carry out so-called legal-rational domination over transgressors of the law. At t0 (i.e. Mexico in the years of PRI hegemony, 1940s to early 1990s-) the Mexican state possessed a relatively cohesive monopoly on the use of force. Such official force flowed from the figure of the President of the Republic to his cabinet collaborators and to the governors of the country's 31 states plus the capital city (Distrito Federal or CDMX). However, as mentioned above, the Weberian perspective regarding the modern state and its capacity to monopolize the legitimate use of force in a given territory is a normative construct. For the case of Mexico, the state during the years of PRI hegemony (1940s to early 1990s) did not exercise this monopoly through the use of what Weber refers to as "legal-rational domination."

Instead, I follow historians and anthropologists of Mexican politics who have studied the micro-foundations of domination, given institutions such as '*caciquismo*' and '*caudillismo*', and have concluded that the PRI hegemonic regime managed to carry out more or less effectively a monopoly on the use of force through 'rational but not legal domination'.[37] It would be a stretch of the imagination to say that the state monopoly on the use of force in Mexico was based on and adhered to the law. The law might be invoked but not always. Many times it was not invoked or charges could be based on false accusations. The bottom line remained a top arbiter, or the 'cacique of caciques' (i.e. *capo di tutti capi*), the boss of all bosses in Mexico, the President of the Republic, on whose hands the future political careers of everyone in public service depended (given the no-re-election rule).

'Principal-agent' problems were minimized under this system as vertical command-and-control was highly effective given all players' future material well-being depended on a supreme and unassailable, though changing (every six years) president. Relative circulation of political élites (i.e. the capacity of rank-and-file individuals to improve gradually their power position and potentially end up at the apex of the pyramid) in this system allowed its resilience through accommodation and relative inclusiveness of the best organized stakeholders.[38] Every new president between the 1940s and the 1990s restored equilibrium and social peace after conflicts flared up, through the strategic use of carrots and sticks.

In contrast, at t1 the state lost the capacity to retain the monopoly on the use of force in the country's territory. There are different opinions as to when this happened, but there is rough agreement about the weakening of the federal government and the proliferation of new centers for deploying force even against the wishes of central authorities since the second half of the 1990s. Crime and violence grew significantly between then and the mid-2000s, by which time President Calderón tried to recentralize power. His signature policy was to do this through militarization and a declaration of a 'war against drugs,' less than two weeks after he assumed office on 1 December 2012. The 'war' was later re-dubbed against 'organized crime,' as, paradoxically, narcotics groups' profits from such sales were squeezed, and they split and diversified their portfolio of business activities into extortion, kidnapping, migrant-smuggling into the USA, military weaponry bought in the USA and imported into Mexico, prostitution rings, and more broadly, the 'entertainment industry' (i.e. tourism, sports, music, media, and the internet).

The unintended consequences of this 'war' was more than 80,000 dead and more than 20,000 disappeared by the time Calderón stepped down on 1 December 2012. The administration of President Peña Nieto of the PRI who took office then promised to introduce sweeping changes in this most fundamental area of state activity. Police, intelligence, the attorney general, and military commanders were made dependent again on the overall strategy put together by the Secretaría de Gobernación (Segob—Ministry of Interior), which, having been the key institution for monitoring and guaranteeing political stability and social peace during the authoritarian years of PRI rule, was weakened systematically between the 1990s and the 2000s, in many cases on purpose (see chapter 6 on governors, caciques, and cartels). Did this change help to reconfigure a federal state with the capacity to re-possess the monopoly on the use of force?

No. Peña Nieto's strategy did not in fact change much from Calderón's. There were definitely changes in how the government handled the issue by giving it much less exposure in its communications. Rather than just talk about the war on organized crime, like President Calderón did every single day and at every opportunity he had, the government of President Peña Nieto tried to turn the page by talking little about it (the President hardly referred to the problem unless public controversies in the domestic and international media forced him to (see below, for example, the cases of official massacres or collusion with organized crime in the cases of Tlatlaya and Ayotzinapa).

Peña Nieto's government simply stuck to its script, which was 'selling Mexico' abroad by talking about the significant structural reforms (further liberalization of the Mexican economy) it managed to secure in 2012–14, while minimizing the plight of many Mexicans, trapped in the pervasive and uncontrolled use of intimidation, force, and violence by both organized criminal groups and many official forces of the state (municipal, state, and federal).

And like Sisyphus, the federal government under Peña Nieto continued a repetitive cycle of low-profile (in terms of media exposure) but equally violent and bloody confrontation with many organized criminal syndicates, some of them quite formidable. While lawful official efforts to try to put a stop to barbaric violence continued, Mexico's federal executive was far from able to regain its monopoly on the use of force in many parts of the country's territory. Alliances between the three levels of Mexican government and organized crime (and its enormous profits) continued to come to light; the rate of violent deaths per 100,000 of the population fell (but it already had before Peña Nieto took office in 2012) until around 2016, after which it started rising again, and by late 2017 the monthly toll of violent deaths linked to organized crime had surpassed the high point under Calderón in 2010–11. By the time Peña Nieto stepped down in December 2018, the figure had grown to around 200,000 killed and more than 30,000 disappeared in the so-called war against organized crime.

The most pernicious element regarding the weakened monopoly of the state on the use of force is the absence of the rule of law in Mexico, at least for everyone except the élites who can buy justice.[39] But this is not a new problem, which means that a diagnosis regarding weakened state capacity cannot be based on a presence of the rule of law at t0 and its absence at t1.

The rule of law has probably never existed in Mexico because it has always been a function of personal connections, privileged access, and lopsided regulation and policies which have benefited the few powerful, rich, and influential at the expense of the vast majority of citizens who have not enjoyed any of these benefits.[40]

During the years of PRI hegemony, the use and abuse of power tended to be centralized under the President and his lieutenants, the state governors. Such centralization did not guarantee fair policing or adjudication of justice, but it contained abuses within a range of possible outcomes, inasmuch as the PRI's hegemonic legitimacy depended not only on good economic performance, but also on keeping relative social peace and political stability. If cases of flagrant abuse of power by state officials or high-visibility criminality by private parties became national news, the President forced the governor of the state where such actions had taken place, to resign. Instances of such cases happened dozens of times throughout the country and the ritual of governors' heads rolling at the same time that new ones were installed, in an effort to at least initially focus on solving the problems that had brought national attention to the disgraced governor, was a strong incentive for state executives to manage issues of law and order within common parameters set by the center.

The end of PRI hegemony and the pluralization of power in the federation is a good thing in terms of democratic contestation and potential accountability. However, the loss of a central agent with the capacity to impose parameters of law and order (even if they are not based on the rule of law) on the chief executives of the states, has translated into a much broader distribution of outcomes that have damaged very significantly basic security for the average citizen, social peace, and the credibility of authorities, whichever party they emanate from.

The criminal justice system and all its elements, despite undergoing a reform put in place in 2008 which was supposed to be complete throughout Mexican territory by 2016, has remained patchy, dysfunctional, and subject to resistance from vested interests in different states by 2018. In particular, the myriad police forces in the Mexican federal framework are mired in corruption and collusion with organized crime. Public prosecutors and judges tend to respond more often than not to bribes and/or calls from above (politicians or politically connected individuals), rather than to due process and evidence to make their verdicts.[41] Under the current system, citizens are not generally granted a fair, public, or timely trial. For example, often defendants cannot access government documents, trials are carried out in secret, and key witnesses are coerced. According to a Human Rights Watch report, "over 40 percent of prisoners in Mexico have never been convicted of a crime. Rather, they are held in pretrial detention, often waiting years for trial."[42] Other studies have suggested that nearly 75 percent of defendants lack defense attorneys and 71 percent of convicted defendants were sentenced without seeing a judge.[43] Unfortunately the current system is such that an estimated 47 percent of prisoners in Mexico City are in prison for stealing less than US $20, while professional criminals who can afford high-quality attorneys often walk free.[44] As one study noted, "inmates are generally not the most dangerous criminals, but they are the poorest...The proportion of inmates incarcerated for serious crimes is very low, and evidence shows that criminals who commit major crimes frequently manage to avoid prosecution."[45] The institutionalization of corruption remains the key weakness of Mexico's law enforcement system. Impunity for corrupt officials is rampant. Recent studies show that organized crime is making this problem worse by channelling enormous amounts of money toward the bribery of officials, which, according to Edgardo Buscaglia, affects 72 percent of the nation's municipalities.[46]

2 The Political Regime

The political regime is made up of the institutions and processes that help to regulate who gains power how, and when, and how that power is regulated. This level of analysis is the model that academics use when they refer to democratic, authoritarian, or totalitarian regimes. In each of these different regimes accession, holding of power, and change of individuals in power occur in very different ways. In Mexico alternation in power has been allowed by the 1917 Constitution, but for seven decades the PRI regime controlled the process of elections, and therefore competition and pluralism were limited. There was opposition representation in the federal Congress, in state legislatures, and in some mayoralties around the country, but they were minimal and in fact helped to legitimize the regime by showing that Mexico was not a 'one-party' state; elections occurred regularly and the opposition won in some places; and therefore Mexico was far away from the totalitarian regimes in the Soviet orbit. Thanks to the golden rule of the system, i.e. no consecutive re-election for any public position whatever, there was significant mobility, and the key measure was that every single president, having served his six-year term, stepped down.

Therefore, the inner circle of the upper right hand box in Figure 3.1 at t1 is not meant to represent a sudden or single instance of regime change. In fact, the opening of the regime (i.e. the breakdown of the monopoly on accession to public office) was a gradual affair with different dates cited for a variety of electoral reforms which granted more representation to the opposition in exchange for not rocking the boat, given successive financial and economic crises in 1977; 1987; 1990; 1993; 1994; and 1996. The end result of the 1996 electoral reform was free and fair competition. Mexico, in effect, became an electoral democracy, with all the advantages and shortcomings of this type of political regime. The bottom line was that effective contestation and participation have translated into changes in power, which have swung from one to another of the main three parties—the PRD on the traditional left; MORENA on the revitalized left led by AMLO; the PRI in the center; and the PAN on the right—and smaller parties at the three levels of government (federal, state, and municipal) or coalitions thereof. The breakdown of this monopoly, enjoyed by the PRI during seven decades, was salutary for democratic representation, although important problems such as the 'rule by party leaders' or the abuse of power by public office holders of all parties, given the absence of rule of law, remains a pressing problem throughout Mexico.

In summary, the analysis of the political sphere (both the state and the regime levels of analysis) shows a significant deterioration in the state's capacity to perform its core function of monopolizing the use of force throughout the country's territory. The rise of organized crime, including collusion by criminals with authorities at all three levels of government, and a significant fragmentation of power after the demise of what a once influential constitutional scholar and reluctant politician, Jorge Carpizo, called Mexico's "'meta-constitutional' strong presidency,"[47] created myriad situations in which basic citizen security and social peace have disappeared, and private groups—from drug cartels to criminal cells specialized in kidnapping and extortion or human trafficking, to self-defense groups that have taken up arms in states like Michoacán and Guerrero to reclaim their families' basic dignity and security, given 'anything-goes' activity by criminal groups behaving with impunity—compete with the state to be in charge.

In turn, the political regime experienced an opening that has allowed relatively free and fair contestation and participation in regular elections. Power alternation is becoming standard practice, which should help to establish mechanisms of vertical accountability that may empower the citizenry vis-à-vis power-holders. However, criticism about 'rule by party leaders' or systemic abuse of power by public office holders, thanks to the immunity the law grants them and the networks of influence they have in order to avoid punishment, remain sore points for the quality of Mexico's young electoral democracy. Likewise, and more worrisome, are the financial arrangements to run elections. Each party is guilty of illegal financing from illicit sources, and whoever runs the federal government transfers resources to its allies to contest and try to win elections at all levels of government. Of utmost concern are the resources that flow from organized crime to electoral campaigns, from poor, isolated municipal contests to the most important, federal elections. Does this mean that Mexico is a narco-democracy? Nobody can tell for sure, but the likelihood of this becoming the case is high.

3 The International Economy

At t0, Mexico's economy was protected from international market forces—between the 1940s and the early 1980s through import-substitution industrialization. During these decades, the hegemonic PRI regime worked informally with industrialists to create the backbone of urban-based, industrial economic activity. The Mexican business class was promoted and helped, if not created, although in many instances this was the case, by the PRI system itself. The 1982 external debt crisis endangered the viability of the import-substitution industrialization model and despite attempts to stabilize and adjust the economy gradually, it became clear in around 1985–86 that in order for the country to be able to surmount the debt crisis, and reignite sustained growth, major changes were needed.

Thus, t1 does not represent a single instance of change, but rather a process which started with Mexico joining the General Agreement on Tariffs and Trade in 1985–86. This international process committed the country to multilateral trade liberalization and some early experiments with privatizing small and medium-sized state enterprises. Mexico became further integrated into the international economy in the early 1990s, as the capital account was liberalized to attract foreign direct investment, and President Carlos Salinas (1988–1994) proceeded with an aggressive strategy to market Mexico abroad and, particularly, to integrate the economy with the USA and Canada through NAFTA. The second half of the presidency of De la Madrid and the presidencies of Salinas and of Ernesto Zedillo (1994–2000) can be considered a first wave of liberalization and privatization.

Since then, the international economy has been a source of some strengths (high-end manufacturing and exports of cars, trucks, and electronic goods) and some weaknesses (China's accession to the World Trade Organization in 2001 and its cost advantages, which took away from Mexico some of its market share of the US consumer market on which Mexico has historically been so dependent). On balance, the way the Mexican economy became integrated globally through its opening up and forging of links through free trade with the USA and Canada has yielded a mixed record. Comparatively, in contrast to many other large emerging economies in the world, Mexico's economy underperformed significantly during the 2000s.

There is an area where the embrace of liberalization has probably accrued tangible benefits for the many. Thanks to trade liberalization, consumption patterns have improved on average across Latin America. Previously protected markets that benefited domestic producers who tended to under-produce and over-charge, opened up, and mass consumption was the result. Therefore, it is plausible to suggest like Andy Baker did by looking at the case of Brazil, that Latin American citizens have not rejected all neoliberal policies. Thus, public opinion polls show support for trade liberalization—the rationale being cheaper access to more and better goods—particularly among popular rather than rich sectors, at the same time that there is a general rejection of privatization, given perceived corruption, price increases, and no improvements in goods or services pre- and post-privatization.[48] Therefore, at least from the perspective of citizens as consumers, opening up the economy in Mexico might have benefited many sectors, although at the same time it also weakened and in many cases destroyed firms and domestic-oriented sectors that could not compete with cheaper imports.

4 The Domestic Economy

In contrast to the aggressive opening of the Mexican economy to international forces, President Salinas engineered a wholesale process of privatization of large state-owned firms, many of which were left as monopolists or operating in highly concentrated oligopolistic markets. The typical example is the country's telephone company, Telmex, which was sold to Carlos Slim in the early 1990s, who became the richest man in the world. Banks were also privatized, and colluded against competition. Likewise, visual media remained very concentrated, as did many other industries that had operated in concentrated sectors even before Salinas's industrial reorganization—cement and glass producers, flour, bread, and tortilla producers. A 2011 study by CIDAC, a Mexican think tank, contrasted the levels of market concentration in some of the main sectors of the Mexican and the US economies. The higher the number in the Herfindahl-Hirschmann index, the more concentrated economic activity is in a given sector. If a measure of 2,500 or more indicates highly concentrated economic activity, then of those sectors taken into consideration for the study, the oil industry, electricity, telecoms, media, and land transportation were the main offenders in Mexico.[49] The presidents who emanated from the PAN,—Fox and Calderón —paid lip service to the idea that the Mexican economy required more competition to raise total factor productivity and therefore raise the growth rate, which compared to other big emerging economies was very mediocre in the 2000s. In the case of Fox, all his attempts to pass structural reforms failed due to PRI and PRD opposition in Congress. In the case of Calderón, a shrewder strategy of negotiation with Congress allowed him to pass mild reforms of the fiscal system, energy (i.e. just state-run hydrocarbons company Pemex, rather than the whole sector), and labor. In Díaz-Cayeros's formulation, even since economic liberalization under President Salinas, "monopolistic regulation of firms and labor" continued.[50] The end result was state capture by powerful and affluent organized interests, both on the side of employers, like Carlos Slim, as well as trade union leaders, such as Elba Esther Gordillo, and their coteries.[51]

In summary, the analysis of the economic sphere (both domestic and international factors) suggests that it would be incorrect to adopt an all-or-nothing perspective, according to which either all or none of the promises of such systemic changes have been realized. Opening the economy helped to tame the high inflation that plagued the country in the 1970s and 1980s, created affordable mass consumption of basic goods, and also brought into the economy significant amounts of foreign capital investment required for production and growth. At the same time, organized capital and labor remained heavily concentrated, producing hefty rents for a few politically connected tycoons and trade union leaders, rather than spilling over and spurring the growth and dynamism of small and medium sized enterprises, which are the main creators of formal employment in the country. Likewise, Mexico's place in the so-called global economy, while shifting the country's external sector away from reliance on oil exports and into manufactures via NAFTA, also produced concentrated gains for a few sectors (textiles and apparel; some microelectronics; auto and auto parts; and more recently aerospace), while undermining subsistence agriculture as well as manufacturers who supplied the domestic market.

Change to Misplaced Monopolies? Reforms under President Peña Nieto

One of the innovations of this analysis is that it includes an assessment of the process of formulation and early implementation of far-fetched structural reforms under President Peña Nieto. As the PRI returned to power in 2012 promising far-fetched structural reform, Peña Nieto presided over the most far-reaching reforms since President Salinas's term in office. Salinas, furthermore, became Peña Nieto's closest elder statesman, unofficially. The style of governance, therefore, was similar (although Salinas was always an astute, clever political operator, whereas his pupil was not).

The main reforms have been to education, telecoms and media, taxation, the financial sector, and crucially, energy. The possibility of lower barriers to entry in core sectors of the economy for the long-term economic growth trajectory of the country should not be dismissed as simple public relations exercises.

The controversy about the net results that these reforms will produce shall linger well into the 2020s. Progressive observers criticize the government by saying that these reforms were not disinterested actions taken with a hypothetical public interest as the top priority. Rather, in their view, such changes have been guided by a politico-economic logic that will prioritize the material interests, power, and influence of the political leadership that implemented the reforms and their domestic and foreign business partners, in an effort to cement a new power bloc in the country (not unlike the attempt carried out by President Salinas himself and what, apparently, Peña Nieto did as governor of Estado de México between 2005 and 2011[52]). The process, observed as Peña Nieto's government drew to a close, reeked of cronyism. Yes, there has been significant economic liberalization, but it has been implemented through special access and information to the government's main contractors, domestic, like Higa, as well as international operators, such as OHL from Spain.

In contrast, pro-globalization institutions, scholars, and analysts from journals such as *The Economist* spoke, naively, about 'Mexico's moment' or the 'Aztec tiger,' and expressed a positive view of the reforms started by Peña Nieto.[53] The reforms might lead to unintended consequences which their authors cannot foresee. Still, the political culture under which they were carried out was dictated not by the pursuit of the general interest, but rather the enrichment and strengthening of the vested interests surrounding Peña Nieto, the so-called 'new PRI' (a misnomer), and their allies, who came from both the conservative PAN, as well as the left-wing PRD in the 'Pacto for Mexico.' From the vantage point of 2018, this could be referred to as the Pacto for enrichment of those who participated in the selective opening of the many policy spheres under Peña Nieto.

It is impossible to know who is right, because it takes more than a decade of evidence to assess properly the costs and benefits of structural reforms such as those carried out in Mexico in 2013–14. I posit that unintended consequences loom large whenever big-scale politico-economic change is undertaken, just like the chaotic end to Salinas's *sexenio* and the subsequent implosion of Mexico's financial sector (the 'tequila' crisis, 1994–95) were the final nails in the coffin of the continuation of PRI hegemony. Therefore, from this work's perspective, a necessary though not sufficient condition to reverse the 'misplaced monopolies' condition is opening up competition in the domestic economy in a transparent, fair way.

Fat chance. From the vantage point of 2018 this did not happen. However, it was not a surprise, given the culture in the upper echelons of politico-economic leadership. The commanding heights of Mexico's economy have been and continue to be dominated by cronyism: economic titans and political honchos scratch each other's backs. A virtuous process would entail level playing fields, whereby neutral, non-partisan regulators as well as a distanced central authority from the areas opened up to new activity prevailed: this is far from the reality in Mexico. This has been next to impossible. And Mexico is far from being in a class of its own regarding partiality, favoritism, and cronyism. It happens around the world, in rich advanced economies as well as in middle-income ones and, even more often, in poor ones. Want is a jealous and prickly mistress: the higher the want on average in a given country, the easier it is to buy-off cheaply such basic wants and get at least temporary support for what comes across as revolutionary change.

Progressive observers see in these dynamics the imposition of the opposite: namely, counter-revolutionary change, which enriches and strengthens those close to power as well as power-holders. And the growth of progressive political representation in the legislative and potentially the executive branches of federal government in Mexico after 2018 makes at least a stop or partial reversal of this 30-year-plus inertia not impossible, although even López Obrador and the leaders of MORENA have been part of the system of favoritism, cronyism, and impunity, because a majority of them, including López Obrador himself, were at some point members of the PRI, or even if they were not, they knew how to operate in that system of informal politico-economic alliances which concentrated and used for their own benefit economic and political power.

The bottom line is that, so far, neither neoliberals nor left-wingers operate by prioritizing impersonal rules in Mexico. Therefore, the best social outcomes, of which the probability of panning out is low, would be if whoever is in power managed to adhere to and enforce impersonal, transparent processes in the main policy spheres. If this was the case (a low probability in the foreseeable future, no matter who is in the presidency), these pillars of policy, production, and consumption in Mexico would surely fare better, inasmuch as effective allocation of resources (i.e. non-partisan, and adhering to the maxim that the best possible outcome starts by raising the bottom end of income and wealth distribution without affecting the upper levels—a very hard exercise which, nonetheless, a number of countries in Europe and the Far East have managed) end up with more and better-quality production at more affordable prices and, crucially, stimulate the generation of more formal sector jobs—an area in which Mexico, given the current structure, has been woefully weak.

Likewise, Peña Nieto offered to strengthen the state without having to resort to the large-scale militarization that his predecessor, Calderón, used. No strong evidence of a change of strategy was detected to restore a measure of order and stability, particularly in 'hot spots', where both drug-trafficking as well as mugging, kidnapping, and widespread extortion took root. The attempt made to strengthen the Segob, which used to be the 'cockpit' if not of 'law and order', at least of relative 'order' during the years of PRI hegemony, helped to strengthen connections between the center and the states, which had been lost. The price was the renewed imposition of media censorship, harassment of legitimate opposition, and withdrawal of resources to states where, particularly, opposition governors denounced corruption, repression, and the return of past PRI authoritarian practices. Worst of all, organized crime, which apparently had been less lethal in 2013–15 than during the Calderón years, reached record heights in 2017–18. To all intents and purposes, Mexico remained a weak and fragmented state with incredible variations: from relatively safe and prosperous states to lawless, lethal, and economically stagnant ones.

Likewise, the reform of the criminal justice system, which was introduced in 2008 and which was intended to be operational throughout the country's 31 states and the capital city by 2016, was over-ambitious. Its obvious failure drained credibility from the entire and crucially important intention to reform, but it might if effectively implemented throughout Mexican territory at some point in the 2020s, create a measure of rule of law beyond the élites. The probability of this happening is low.

Finally, electoral reform will allow for the first time in close to a century, the consecutive re-election of legislators and mayors, starting in 2018. This is a reform that will reconfigure the balance of power in Mexico. Will this reconfiguration be better or worse for a majority of the population? It is very hard to tell. The 'no re-election' rule strengthened the federal executive and ensured that the President and his closest associates decided the allocation of all public offices.

Conclusion

The Western version of liberal democracy and capitalism tends to associate changes from authoritarian to democratic rule and from protected, inward-looking economies to open ones with more freedom for individuals in the country or countries that undergo these dual transition processes. Mexico underwent these changes, but the results so far have been disappointing. The break-up of the political monopoly enjoyed by the PRI during its years of hegemonic rule and the opening of Mexico to the international economy have created 'misplaced monopolies.' Instead of the combination that classic social science posits for producing effective governance and growth (i.e. a monopoly by the state in the use of force in its territory, and significant competition in the economic sphere), Mexico has so far ended up with the opposite combination: an absence of monopoly by the state in the use of force, and significant concentration characterized by monopolies and oligopolies in the economy.

These outcomes are by no means definitive. Time continues its relentless march and these outcomes can either become more entrenched or alternatively they can be modified in the—at least normatively—desired direction, or there can be periods of stasis followed by ruptures or more gradual change. As I have said from the start of this chapter, it remains an empirical question the extent to which these normative social science prescriptions in fact produce the best results. My understanding is that sometimes they do, but at other times they do not. One needs to specify why one or the other apply at a given place and time. For the case of Mexico, the systemic political and economic changes of the last three decades have, on average, checked rather than advanced the freedom (i.e. physical security and economic opportunity) of its people. Admittedly, these changes have created some big winners in both the political and economic spheres. But the majority of Mexicans have been made worse off by the prevalence of misplaced monopolies. At the same time, the return of the PRI to power under President Peña Nieto led to the largest-scale policy changes to Mexico's political economy since at least President Salinas's term. At the end of Peña Nieto's government the condition identified as 'misplaced monopolies' remained, and its main corollary was freedom for the few. Can this condition, detrimental to a majority of Mexicans, improve under the presidency of López Obrador?

Notes

1 The work of analysts such as Luis Astorga, Alejandro Hope, Edgardo Buscaglia, Eduardo Guerrero; of journalists like Anabel Hernández, Francisco Cruz, Ricardo Ravelo, José Reveles and countless others, many of them executed or disappeared by organized criminals or state agents; and of civil society organizations that have been created usually by the loved ones of violence victims, and earlier to promote human rights in Mexico, such as the Academia Mexicana de losDerechos Humanos, Centro de Derechos Humanos Miguel Agustín Pro Juárez (Prodh), Colectivo contra la Tortura y la Impunidad (CCTI), Equis: Justicia para las Mujeres, Instituto Mexicano de Derechos Humanos y Democracia (IMDHD), México Unido contra la Delincuencia, Red Retoño, and the umbrella organization Red Nacional de Organismos Civiles de Derechos Humanos "Todoslos Derechos Humanos – para Todas y Todos", among others, attest to the birth and growth of civil society-based resistance to the violence, crime, and impunity that has characterized Mexico since the 1980s in general and more brutal, intense, and lawless since 2000.

2 See Luis Astorga, *El siglo de las drogas: del Porfiriato al nuevo milenio*, 3rd edition, Mexico, Penguin Random House, 2016; Anabel Hernández, *Los señores del narco*, Mexico, Grijalbo Mondadori, 2010; José Reveles, *Las historias más negras: de narco, impunidad y corrupción en México*, México, Grijalbo, 2009; Ricardo Ravelo, *Narcomex: Historia e Historias de una Guerra*, Mexico, Vintage, 2012; J. Jesús Esquivel, *La CIA, Camarena y Caro Quintero: la historia secreta*, Mexico, Penguin Random House, 2014; and two excellent outsider perspectives: Alfredo Corchado, *Midnight in Mexico: a Reporter's Journey through a Country's Descent into Darkness*, New York, Penguin, 2014; Ioan Grillo, *El Narco: Inside Mexico's Criminal Insurgency*, New York, Bloomsbury, 2012.

3 Alan Knight and Wil Pansters, eds., *Caciquismo in Twentieth Century Mexico*, London: Institute for the Study of the Americas, 2005.

4 This historical perspective about the golden years of PRI hegemony was put forward by Enrique Krauze, *La presidencia imperial*, Barcelona y México: Tusquets, 1997.

5 See for example Edward L. Gibson, *Boundary Control: Subnational Authoritarianism in Federal Democracies*, Cambridge: Cambridge University Press, 2012, p. 113. This author took this image from Wayne A. Cornelius of the University of California at San Diego (UCSD). The image of the 'archipelago' has been used and is well known in political and policy circles in Mexico since the 19th century.

6 Justo Sierra, *The Political Evolution of the Mexican People*, Austin: University of Texas Press, 1969 [1900–1902];

7 This perspective associated with Amartya Sen view of freedom, which is connected with development through the elimination of obstacles in order that individuals can develop capabilities to the best of their ability. See Amartya Sen, *Development as Freedom*, New York: Oxford University Press, 1999.

8 Douglass C. North, John Joseph Wallis, and Barry R. Weingast, *Violence and Social Orders*, New York and Cambridge: Cambridge University Press, 2009.

9 Douglass C. North, John Joseph Wallis, Steven B. Webb, and Barry R. Weingast, eds., *In the Shadow of Violence: Politics, Economics, and the Problems of Development*, New York and Cambridge: Cambridge University Press, 2013.

10 North, Wallis, and Weingast, 2009, xii.

11 Ibid.

12 The permanent frictions between the returns to capital (dividends) and labor (wages) in long-run economic growth and its socioeconomic consequences have been summarized and achieved great media and readership visibility in Thomas Piketty, *Capital in the Twenty-First Century*, Cambridge, MA: Harvard University Press, 2013.

13 For an influential perspective about the state as the result of 'organized crime' principles see Charles Tilly, "War Making and State Making as Organized Crime," in Peter Evans, Dietrich Rueschemeyer, and Theda Skocpol, eds., *Bringing the State Back In*, Cambridge: Cambridge University Press, 1985.

14 North, Wallis, and Weingast, 2009, pp. 16–17; North, Wallis, Webb, and Weingast, eds., 2013, pp. 8–9.

15 Robert D. Tollison, "Rent Seeking," *The Encyclopedia of Public Choice*, 2004, 820–24, 820, http://link.springer.com/chapter/10.1007/978-0-306-47828-4_179, accessed 11 November 2014. This is the thrust of the general analyses by classics like Olson (1965, 1982), Krueger (1974, 1990), Buchanan, Tollison, and Tullock (1980), Bhagwati (1982).

16 North, Wallis, Weingast, 2009. These are the "25 or so countries and 15 percent of the world's population" that these authors identify as 'open access order,' p. xii.

17 Ibid., pp. 18–25.

18 North, Wallis, Webb, and Weingast, 2013, eds., pp. 10–19. Social scientists have used extensively 'stages models' to explain varying degrees of political and economic development around the world at least since the rise to prominence of 'modernization theory.' See Simon Kuznets, *Economic Growth of Nations: Total Output and Production Structure*, Cambridge MA, Harvard University Press, 1971.

19 Alberto Díaz-Cayeros, "Entrenched Insiders: Limited Access Order in Mexico", North, Wallis, Webb, and Weingast, eds., 2013, pp. 233–260.

20 Ibid., pp. 234–235.

21 Ibid., p. 233.

22 Ibid., p. 258.

23 Ibid.

24 The most important collaborative projects that helped to define this literature were Juan J. Linz, *The Breakdown of Democratic Regimes: Crisis, Breakdown, and Reequilibration*, Baltimore: Johns Hopkins University Press, 1978; Juan J. Linz and Alfred Stepan, eds. *The Breakdown of Democratic Regimes*, 4 vols. Baltimore: Johns Hopkins University Press, 1978; Guillermo O'Donnell, Philippe Schmitter, and Laurence Whitehead, eds. *Transitions from Authoritarian Rule*, 4 vols. Baltimore: Johns Hopkins University Press, 1986; Juan J., and Alfred Stepan. *Problems of Democratic Transition and Consolidation: Southern Europe, South America, and Post-Communist Europe*, Baltimore: Johns Hopkins University Press, 1996.

25 North, Wallis, and Weingast, 2009, p. 26.

26 North, Wallis, Webb, Weingast, 2013, p. 14.

27 North, Wallis, Weingast, 2009, p. 268.

28 Alberto Díaz-Cayeros, "Entrenched Insiders: Limited Access Order in Mexico", North, Wallis, Webb, and Weingast, eds., 2013, pp. 234–235.

29 The classic work in political sociology is Max Weber's "Politics as a Vocation," published originally as a lecture in Munich in 1921 and translated and edited by H.H. Gerth and C. Wright Mills, *From Max Weber: Essays in Sociology*, New York: Oxford University Press, 1946, 77–128; the classic work in economics is Adam Smith, *An Inquiry into the Nature and Causes of the Wealth of Nations*, first published in 1776, Vol. II, Books IV and V of The Glasgow Edition of the Works and Correspondence of Adam Smith, edited by R.H. Campbell and A.S. Skinner. Oxford: Oxford University Press, 1976; a more recent review about development in monopoly/oligopoly writings can be found in Avinash Dixit, "Recent Developments in Oligopoly Theory," in *The American Economic Review*, 72, 2, 1982, 12–17.

30 I use the word 'misplaced' to convey the idea that the monopolies or absence thereof I observe in Mexico go against what mainstream social science has taught us as effective ways of social organization to promote and enhance individual security and opportunity. Such effective ways entail, politically, an organization—the state—that monopolizes the use of force and coercion in a given territory and, economically, some degree of free play of market forces, given that organizations that compete to produce cheaper and better goods and services than their competitors. Mexico at least since the mid-1990s moved in the opposite direction: fragmentation of authority and entry of many private individuals and groups into the exercise of force and coercion against others, and monopolies and oligopolies that stifled the possibility of economic competition, innovation, and a less unequal distribution of income and wealth in the country.

31 In Mexico the work of analysts including Luis Rubio and the think-tank CIDAC and of Luis de la Calle, of Juan Pardinas and the think-tank IMCO are associated with the promotion of liberalization policies.

32 For some economists, the exceedingly orthodox—that is, conservative (i.e. contractionary)—macroeconomic management adopted since the mid-1990s is the main factor behind disappointing economic growth in Mexico during the last two decades. See Ros Bosch, *supra*, ft. 1.

33 Andrés Fernández, Luca Flabbi, Juan David Herreño, "Reformas laborales para impulsar el crecimiento económico", 21 March 2013, http://vox.lacea.org/?q= reformas_laborales_para_crecimiento_2013, Accessed23 January 2018. Informal employment is a big phenomenon throughout Latin America, and therefore there must be cross-country structural reasons behind it so that Mexico-only characteristics do not explain its abundance.

34 Héctor Aguilar Camín y Jorge G. Castañeda, *Una agenda para México*, México: Punto de Lectura, 2012.

35 For seminal pieces on the make-up and operation of this type of analysis in comparative politics, see Peter Gourevitch, *Politics in Hard Times: Comparative*

Responses to International Economic Crises, Ithaca: Cornell University Press, 1986; Sven Steinmo, Kathleen Thelen, and Frank Longstreth, eds., Historical Institutionalism in Comparative Analysis, Cambridge: Cambridge University Press, 1992; Kathleen Thelen, "Historical Institutionalism in Comparative Politics,"*Annual Review of Political Science*, 2 (June 1999, 369–404); James Mahoney and Dietrich Rueschemeyer, eds., *Comparative Historical Analysis in the Social Sciences*, Cambridge: Cambridge University Press, 2003.

36 Kathleen Thelen, "Historical Institutionalism in Comparative Politics,"*Annual Review of Political Science*, 2 (June 1999, 369–404).

37 Alan Knight and Wil Pansters, eds., *Caciquismo in Twentieth Century Mexico*, London: Institute for the Study of the Americas, 2005, pp. 13–14.

38 See the excellent account by Magaloni, *supra*, ft. 2.

39 Díaz-Cayeros, p. 233.

40 *Ibid.*, p. 235.

41 A gruesome portrait about a framed and wrongfully convicted young man and his nightmare in the labyrinth of the putrid Mexican criminal justice system grabbed headlines and went viral in the mainstream media as well as social media around the time the criminal justice system reform was formulated and passed into law in 2008. See the film *Presunto Culpable*, directed by Roberto Hernández and Geoffrey Smith, first shown in a documentary festival in Amsterdam in 2008.

42 Human Rights Watch, "Mexico,"*World Report 2011*, http://www.hrw.org/en/world-report-2011/mexico.

43 Hector Tobar, "Judicial Overhaul in Mexico OKd,"*Los Angeles Times,*7 March 2008, http://articles.latimes.com/2008/mar/07/world/fg-mexjustice7.

44 *Ibid.* Also see "Índice de Incidencia Delictiva y Violencia 2009," Centro de Investigación para el Desarrollo A.C., 2009, p. 10.

45 Elena Azaola and Marcelo Bergman, "The Mexican Prison System," in *Reforming the Administration of Justice in Mexico*, p. 112.

46 Joel Millman and Jose de Cordoba, "Drug-Cartel Links Haunt an Election South of the Border,"*Wall Street Journal*, 3 July 2009, http://online.wsj.com/article/SB124657442789989017.html.

47 See Jorge Carpizo, *El presidencialismo mexicano*, México: Siglo xxi, 16th ed., 2002 [1st ed., 1978].

48 See Andy Baker, *The Market and the Masses in Latin America: Policy Reform and Consumption in Liberalizing Economies*, New York and Cambridge: Cambridge University Press, 2009.

49 Jaime Serra Puche, "Openness and Growth in Mexico," Keynote Address, Conference "Mexico at the Crossroads: Learning from History, Facing the Future," 17–18 November 2011, Tulane University, New Orleans.

50 Díaz-Cayeros, p. 235.

51 The author is grateful to Gustavo Flores-Macias for reminding me about the key role of anti-competitive labor practices in helping to keep the monopolistic or oligopolistic structure of the Mexican economy rather than an over-emphasis on the captains of industry and banking.

52 See Francisco Cruz and Jorge Toribio Montiel, *Negocios de familia: Biografía no autorizada de Enrique Peña Nieto y el grupo Atlacomulco*, Mexico: Temas de Hoy, 2009.

53 See Mexico Institute, Wilson Center for International Scholars, "Mexico: Aztec Tiger – Mexico Institute in the News" in http://www.wilsoncenter.org/article/mexico-aztec-tiger-mexico-institute-the-news; Adam Thomson, "Aztec tiger begins to sharpen its claws"*Financial Times*, 27 June 2013; Peterson Institute for International Economics, "Mexico and the United States: Building on the Benefits of NAFTA", conference, 15 July 2014, Washington, DC.

2 Historical Evolution of Political and Economic Monopolies in Mexico, Antiquity to the 1980s

I Great Wealth Inequality and Violence have been the Norm since the Beginning

Political power and wealth produced in the territory that today comprises Mexico was concentrated in very few hands long before Europeans arrived in the continental Americas in the early 16th century. Rigid socioeconomic pyramids characterized the strongest and most advanced Amerindian civilizations like the Mayans in the southeast, the Aztecs and before them the Toltecs in what today is central Mexico, and other older civilizations like the Zapotec and Mixtecs in Oaxaca, and the Olmecs in Veracruz and Tabasco.[1]

Such primeval inequality was accentuated after the Spanish conquest. The Aztecs' capital Tenochtitlán fell on 13 August 1521 and by the 1560s, despite some resistance in western, and southeast areas, Europeans had appropriated most of the wealth of the territory they baptized as 'la Nueva España' (New Spain). The rigid socioeconomic pyramids from pre-Columbian times were reconfigured. At the top were the Spanish-born (*peninsulares*) and under them were Europeans born in the Americas (*criollos*). In turn, the growing mixed population (children of Spaniards and Amerindians, the *mestizos*) were under the white Europeans, while other mixed populations (Amerindians and Africans imported as slaves) were further below. At the bottom were the vast majority of Amerindians (some of the élites from before the Conquest assimilated into the new Spanish-led élite) and Africans. The Spanish in charge of this system of social stratification explicitly called it 'las castas' (i.e. a caste system, which included more than 20 different groups depending on the race/ethnicity of their ancestors).[2]

Two points are worth emphasizing for the purpose of this analysis. First, the populations of what today is Mexico have been highly unequal for millennia, as archaeological and later on written texts attest.[3] Second, the *castas* system, while officially abolished when Mexico declared its independence from Spain in 1810 (although independence was not finally achieved until 1821), continued to operate in a *de facto* way. An individual's life chances were structured significantly, given their racial/ethnic background, their facial and bodily features, the way they spoke, and the region of the country from which they came.[4] Due to these irreconcilable differences, inventing a proto-typical Mexican became a long-term process in nation-building, whose modern roots lie in the 19th century.[5]

Educated foreigners who visited Mexico in the 19th century noted very quickly that the country was highly unequal, and that such inequality followed the lines of these racial/ethnic differences.[6] These conditions still pertain in the 21st century. The areas where extreme poverty is concentrated are over-represented by Amerindian groups and communities. The élites tend to live in the country's largest cities such as Mexico City, Guadalajara, and Monterrey, and they are invariably light-skinned. Mexicans themselves reinforce this strati-fication system by bestowing high social status on light-skinned people (even if they are not rich); by showing deference to them (at the same time that they rightly feel resentful about the *status quo*); and by aspiring to whiteness, if not for them at least for their descendants, due to the many unwritten but real privileges that a light-skinned physiognomy bestows on individuals in Mexico.[7]

Therefore, a first conclusion from the historical record is that networks, access to influence, power, and resources in Mexico since Europeans conquered the Amerindians have been tied, in general, to race/ethnicity. In the words of the 'violence and social orders' framework of analysis which I have adopted as a starting point to test Mexico's economic and political development, it could be said that barriers to entry have been higher the darker a person's skin is; the farther away they have been from decision-making centers; and the more at odds their everyday lives (*usos y costumbres*) are, compared with the lighter-skinned élites in the largest Mexican cities.

II A Nation State and Capitalism Take Off in Mexico

Mexicans lived under a state of semi-permanent anarchy during the first half-century after their independence from Spain. The eleven year war of independence (1810–21) destroyed a significant number of productive assets. The new-born country found itself bankrupt and in need of foreign financial assistance (mostly provided by British banks in the first half of the 19th century). Economic destruction was compounded by political fragmentation and competition among regional leaders.[8] Mexico suffered acutely from the Iberian phenomenon of *caudillismo* [9] (i.e. military leaders, usually, who fought other peers and tried to establish their hegemony—a typical phenomenon associated with state-building[10]). The end result was constant bickering for power among the *caudillos*; short-lived governments; instability and uncertainty regarding the short-term future; and, as a con-sequence, stagnation and lack of economic and political development.

After US and French invasions and occupations (between the 1830s and the 1860s) on top of the semi-permanent state of civil war among the Mexican political class, led by liberals and conservatives, there is agreement among historians that the birth of the modern Mexican nation-state hap-pened during the presidencies of Benito Juárez (1858–72) and Porfirio Díaz

(1876–80 and 1884–1911). During Díaz's years in power Mexico managed to create a modern capitalist economy. Juárez and to a greater extent Díaz reversed political fragmentation and centralized the state. This process helped to impose (relative) stability and order in Mexico's territory. Political and economic actors' time horizons lengthened and the benefits of integrating what up until then had been a collection of regional markets into a country with significant wealth in natural resources, population, and geographic location (just south of the growing power of the USA with ports on both Atlantic and Pacific oceans and just north of the geopolitically globally important Central American isthmus and the myriad Caribbean islands), created the conditions for a process of modernization spearheaded by railways, roads, incipient industrial activity, and mass migration from rural to urban areas. The establishment of property rights, legal codes, and effective enforcement (in and by economic institutions) in turn produced credible commitment for investors to allocate resources into what by the 1880s had become a robust, high-growth economy.[11]

From this perspective it can be said that barriers to entry were raised in the political sphere as the nation state was consolidated and fewer *caudillos*, regional strongmen, bandits, and robbers could use force and coercion to pursue their aims. Exercise of that prerogative (i.e. use of institutionalized force and coercion), became relatively monopolized by the central state and its peripheral agents (Don Porfirio's *jefes políticos*).

In turn, in the economic sphere regional markets were integrated and as infrastructure and other investments grew, barriers to entry fell, allowing more producers to be in touch with consumers. However, in a now classical work of historical political economy, Haber, Razo, and Maurer argued that barriers to entry remained high, due to their selectivity and personalization. The group in power and its foreign and domestic capitalist allies organized in what they refer to as 'vertical political integration—VPI'.[12] This concept entails a given government and a subgroup of asset holders who can create an economic system where property rights accrue to those inside the beneficiary group (members of the government and capitalists) as private goods—in other words, property rights are bestowed selectively on politico-economic allies. A third group, a 'support group', joins the insiders through the receipt of rents from the asset holders, at the same time that it provides basic political support for the government.[13] In my view, these authors rightly conclude that Díaz and his close collaborators created a viable political system, as well as a growing system of capital accumulation.

By abandoning the goal of protecting property rights globally, Díaz instead specified and protected the property rights of a select group of asset-holders and used the rents generated from this selective protection to subdue or seduce his political opponents. Díaz's mix of carrots and sticks—*pan o palo* in Spanish—to get his way meant that he had to engage in a very delicate balancing act.[14]

The end result was a highly centralized, authoritarian state personified by Díaz, his close collaborators (known as the *científicos*) and their domestic and foreign capitalist partners. Barriers to entry in both the political and the economic sphere were high. The system was dependent on personalized networks of politicians, businessmen, and middlemen (a growing complaint became how dominant foreign business—US, British, French, and German—and their domestic partners dominated and enriched themselves to the detriment of anyone who was not a member of these networks). For the group in power and its foreign and domestic allies, their task became to co-ordinate their activities to integrate the country, raise its output, modernize the economy, and provide token measures akin to charity to keep a large though highly dispersed and unco-ordinated segment of the population acting as the passive support group of this oligarchic system.

III The Mexican Revolution: Birth of a New System

There is a cottage industry of academics who debate why the Mexican Revolution happened, its basic dynamics, trajectory, and its consequences.[15] As this analysis focuses on barriers to entry into the political and economic spheres of social organization, I shall only highlight its main components for this transformational period. There is no doubt that, in particular 1910–20—and with particular virulence during 1913–17—saw a lowering of barriers to entry in political and economic activity in Mexico. Social revolutions tend to allow previously excluded groups to claim rights and access to resources and activities that were previously out of bounds.

In Mexico the new political and economic framework that was created was framed by the 1917 Constitution. This remains the highest law of the land more than a hundred years later. Judged by the time it was written, the document was indeed transformational. It managed to mix civil, political, and social rights in a way considered highly progressive at the time.[16] Therefore, if we stick with the formal reading of the Constitution, there is no doubt that, compared with the previous constitution (1857) that applied in Mexico, the 1917 version lowered barriers to entry in both the political regime (full suffrage for males) and the state (there was significant circulation of élites—leaders of different political, economic, and social groups who could access power and move up the social ladder over time—as well as creation of new law-and-order groups that assumed the role of maintaining social order from the *porfirista* state). Likewise, the Constitution lowered barriers to entry in the economic sphere, as access to land for the landless peasantry (the creation of *ejidos*), the capacity for collective organization of workers to demand fair working conditions, and the empowerment of the state to become more involved in economic activity, destroyed the bases upon which the *porfirista* oligarchy had managed to operate and grow successfully.

IV Creation of a Corporatist State and Concentration of Economic Activity

In the course of the 1920s and 1930s, the state created by the 1917 Constitution evolved in a direction that was authoritarian rather than democratic, and economic activity, despite its fruits being less unequally distributed than during the

Porfiriato, remained heavily concentrated among networks of new insiders (i.e. the victors from the Revolution). Indeed, as in Haber, Razo, and Maurer's work, it is possible to identify the return of VPI after the fragmentation and decentralization that the Revolution produced.

If we concentrate only on the outcomes of the Revolution, for the majority of Mexicans the facts suggest that, at least in terms of barriers to entry, there was no real transformation. Instead, what happened was a war accompanied by the circulation of élites, massacres, compromises, and new political and economic institutions. These institutions ended up evolving in practice thanks to the VPI forged in the 1920s and 1930s. Such VPI favored new insiders, their political and economic partners, and the masses, who acted as passive or, if needed, active supporters (in mass rallies, strikes, and shows of force in favor of the revolutionary leaders).

The new élite and its close partners organized a political system around a dominant party (founded in 1929 by Plutarco Elías Calles—president in 1924–28—as the Partido Nacional Revolucionario) which was redesigned later as a corporatist party (renamed as the Partido de la Revolución Mexicana in 1938 by president Lázaro Cárdenas del Río, who served as president in 1934–40) and, finally, was re-formed again to ensure civilian dominance over the military and to pursue a capitalist rather than a socialist development path (renamed as the Partido Revolucionario Institucional—PRI—in 1946 by Ávila Camacho). The party changed from a dominant into a hegemonic party in the course of the 1930s.

Hegemony entails absolute domination in elections, which in turn created a political system ruled by the prominent members of the hegemonic party with only token representation for other parties which, nonetheless, were accepted or in fact encouraged to participate in elections to show that the Mexican system was not a single-party state, like the Union of Soviet Socialist Republics (USSR) and some of its satellite allies. Mexico was ruled by an authoritarian political regime, not a totalitarian one.

In turn, in the economic sphere the state gradually took over different sectors of the economy. The system was never a command economy (i.e. a system where the state monopolizes activity and prohibits any private economic activity—as was the case in the USSR and its allies). Rather, it was a state-led economic system. The state promoted the creation of a new industrial and commercial bourgeoisie and therefore partnered informally with this new capitalist class in the promotion of economic growth.

V. 'The Mexican Miracle': Hegemonic Rule by the PRI, 1940s–1960s

The post-revolutionary settlement again raised barriers to entry for the average Mexican citizen in both the political and economic sphere. While the new system was not an oligarchy like the *porfiriato*, political and economic power and resources were recentralized. Participation in the system required navigation of relatively narrow channels structured by, for example, membership or close acquaintance with members of the hegemonic PRI and its main sectors (i.e. organized labor, the peasant sector, and the popular sector, composed mainly of public sector workers). Likewise, in the economy, despite no formal alliance between the PRI and the new capitalist class, there was tacit understanding among them that allowed a mixed economy to grow and flourish, particularly between the 1940s and the late 1960s.

These years (known as *el milagro mexicano*) were characterized by high economic growth rates (an annual average of some 6–8 percent) accompanied by low inflation (in the low single digits). Mexico became a less rural, more urban and industrialized country. On average, its population became more educated, attained higher life expectancy, and there was significant growth of the middle classes. In short, Mexico underwent a spell of rapid modernization. This process of economic transformation was guided by the hegemonic PRI, which means that the political underpinnings of strong economic performance remained narrow, selective, vertical, and authoritarian. As long as individuals complied with these rules of the game, their chances of being better off than their parents or grandparents (except for the small members of the *porfirista* oligarchy who either exiled themselves, or remained and had to learn to play a new game, in which they were not the undisputed leaders and bosses of the system) were higher than in the past. Active allegiance or at least passive acquiescence to PRI rule was very important to gain opportunities for personal, family, and community improvement.

Barriers to entry were high. In politics the period between the 1940s and 1960s has been described by historians as the years of *la presidencia imperial* (the imperial presidency). All manner of good things accrued to those who followed the strict chain of command emanating from *Los Pinos* (equivalent to the White House in the USA or 10 Downing Street in the United Kingdom)—the mansion where the President and his family lived. Other parties were allowed to compete and won token representation in federal, state, or municipal governments, but they were never allowed to aspire to capture an important office like a governorship or the mayor's office of an important city, let alone the presidency. The Communist Party of Mexico was outlawed. The hegemony of the PRI favored offering carrots before using sticks. Co-optation of dissidence was tried first, although the system openly engaged in coercion and repression when the opposition persisted in challenging the PRI's hegemony, such as during elections, industrial action, or land takeovers by organized peasants.

In the economy barriers to entry were likewise high. Mexico embraced the strategy of import-substitution industrialization, which purported to transform rural into urban landscape and agricultural into industrial economic activity through a variety of protectionist policies such as high tariffs and taxes to imports; subsidized credit to local producers; licenses, quotas, and production permits; and a tacit alliance between the state, which favored domestic industrialists, their foreign (multinational corporations) partners, and organized labor, the last of which was controlled by the state. The end result was high growth during the early stages of adoption of this growth and development strategy.

This period can be summed up as one characterized by high barriers to entry in all the realms identified in the analytical framework of this work:

- In the political sphere:

  i   A strong, centralized state based in Mexico City (in spite of the federalist framework established in the Constitution) with a relative monopoly over the use of persuasion/force/coercion;

  ii a relatively closed political regime characterized by regular elections, no re-election for any public office, undisputed domination by the hegemonic PRI, and token representation for left- and right-wing opposition parties;

  iii PRI leaders frequently asserted in public that Mexico was not a single-party state like the USSR and its allies; representation by the opposition showed this to be the case.

- In turn, in the economic sphere:

  i   In the foreign sector, an inward-looking economy protected by and propelled during several decades by import-substitution industrialization, which shunned export-oriented growth and tried to achieve success through concentration on development of the domestic consumer and producer markets;

  ii In the domestic sector, a mixed economy with growing state participation and key partnerships with domestic and foreign corporations, whose aim was not just economic growth but also the establishment and perpetuation of a politico-economic block of support for the PRI, and whose main characteristic was heavy concentration of production in most sectors of the economy, which in turn led to monopolies, duopolies, or oligopolies; in short, a lack of competition and concomitant advantages for producers and disadvantages for consumers.

VI. Overreach: Seeds of the Weakening and Demise of the Political Economy Dominated by the PRI and its Allies, 1968–88

The period of hegemonic domination by the PRI did not come to an abrupt end. The process of weakening and demise of this politico-economic system lasted for around three decades, and it was pinpointed by very visible episodes of political violence (massacres) perpetrated by the state against different groups of Mexican society; by successive financial and economic crises during the last year in office of four presidents—1976, 1982, 1987–88, and 1994–95; and finally by the electoral defeat of the PRI in the presidential elections of 2000, and the peaceful transfer of power to the conservative Partido Acción Nacional (PAN).

The setbacks suffered by the Mexican state and the PRI regime as a consequence of the highly visible episodes of state violence and repression led to a lowering of barriers to entry into the political sphere. Starting with the infamous massacres of students on 2 October 1968 in Tlatelolco and on Corpus Christi Thursday in 1971 by soldiers and police, the state found itself having to explain why it was killing the children of the revolution the PRI had created, and in theory still represented. As a consequence of state violence, some actors among the fringe left-wing opposition became radicalized, and created or joined small guerrilla groups. The PRI's answer was to co-opt (and use coercion if co-optation failed) these individuals, groups, and their growing number of sympathizers, particularly in universities. Thus, the government of President Luis Echeverría (1970–76) co-opted thousands of young university graduates into the federal bureaucracy to pursue, in theory at least, development and social justice inside, rather than outside, the system. In turn his successor President José López Portillo (1976–82) enacted an important electoral reform in 1977 which introduced a mixed system of representation (combining first-past-the-post and proportional representation), as well as a government amnesty to bring guerrillas back into institutionalized politics.

In contrast, in the economic sphere the years 1970 to 1982 saw a significant rise in nationalization of economic activity and state-led growth. It can be argued that barriers to entry remained high or increased. The state did not necessarily crowd out private participation in the economy. In many instances it bailed out failing private economic activity by acquiring it to protect employment, which yielded politico-electoral dividends. As a consequence, politically connected businessmen and workers had easy access to sources of rents. In contrast, the vast majority of economic actors without such connections continued to face high barriers to entry. Rent-seeking by those connected to the hegemonic party system continued to rule the roost, and as a consequence entrepreneurship and innovation remained weak and sparse.

The turning-point against the PRI regime happened in 1982, when, as a consequence of grand corruption, presidential megalomania, and external shocks (rising interest rates and lowering oil prices) the highly indebted (in US dollars) Mexican economy forced the government to declare a moratorium on external debt payments, thus sparking not only a depression in Mexico itself but also the so-called 'lost decade' in economic growth and development throughout Latin America.

The cohesive coalition that had been in power—PRI leaders, insider capitalists and their foreign partners, and organized workers, peasants and middle class individuals dependent on the PRI—since the 1940s weakened and in some cases unravelled and created a stronger opposition both to the left and to the right of the hegemonic party during Echeverría and López Portillo's presidencies and legacies.

Key examples of the weakening of the ruling coalition included:

i) President Echeverría's embrace of left-wing populist discourse to chastise industrialists and co-opt workers, students, and young professionals (while at the same time as Minister of Interior and then as President he was the direct executioner of the 1968 Tlatelolco and June 1971 Corpus Christi massacres, respectively); deciding that Mexico's economy would be ruled from *Los Pinos*; flirting with 'third world causes' and showing support for left-wing leaders whom Washington, DC considered enemies—from Fidel Castro in Cuba to Salvador Allende in Chile; giving carrots in order to tame trade unions, while repressing more assertive ones; the kidnapping and murder under his watch (although he was not involved, but certainly knew about plans to commit violence) of Mexico's most representative symbol of the country's big capitalist class: Monterrey-based Eugenio Garza Sada, in 1973, among others.

ii) President López Portillo's gambling with billions of dollars to try to put Mexico in the big league of world oil producers, while all the work and infrastructure that went on to try to make this dream come true went through the President's personal favorite contractors, or directly in bribes to secure a share of the business throughout the PRI's political class most connected to the energy (oil) and banking sectors; the entire political class but particularly the president and his circle earned billions of dollars in kickbacks and direct theft, and some of them exhibited and showed off their new wealth in very public ways—mansions, bodyguards for family members who could get away with anything they wanted to do in restaurants, shops, schools, and universities—which after the 1982 economic collapse backfired spectacularly; López Portillo also supported the Sandinista left-wing revolution in Nicaragua in 1981–82 against the explicit wishes of the US Government during the early years of Ronald Reagan's presidency; the final straw was the President's nationalization of the private banking system after he claimed that the bankers were responsible for the 1982 financial and economic collapse; this last point severed the remaining trust that the majority of large domestic and foreign capitalist players had toward the PRI regime. Private business looked to the right and found in the PAN a highly effective vehicle to start competing for real in elections, in order to control not only economic but also political power.

The inheritor of this economic disaster, President Miguel de la Madrid (1982–88), tried to contain the reversal of fortune that the PRI, and through it Mexico as a whole, had undergone. From the beginning of his period in office, the major issue he had to contend with was the country's external debt and its consequences—severe economic contraction, a rise in political dissent and strong opposition showings in municipal, state, and federal elections. De la Madrid seems to have presided over an economy in a state of coma, and his major contribution was to keep the patient alive.

Likewise, an incredibly potent change—a generational change in leadership—took place during his presidency in the PRI. Among several contending groups that wanted to inherit power, the youngest one (its leading members were in their late thirties and early forties), led by Secretary of Planning and Budgeting, Carlos Salinas, were in favor of a pro-US solution (i.e. liberalization of prices, rolling back of state intervention, and the free movement of capital) to the external debt crisis.

However, this generational and ideological change in the PRI's direction and promises to the people also produced a split of the party in 1987–88. This event can be seen in retrospect as a watershed moment or a critical juncture: future events became influenced and co-shaped by the new politico-economic conditions which forced the PRI to face a credible, winning opposition not only to its right—as had been the case with the PAN since the 1982 banking nationalization—but also to its left.

The departure of Cuauhtémoc Cárdenas from the PRI (son of arguably the most popular and left-wing Mexican president of the 20th century, Lázaro Cárdenas del Río), and other 'progressive' party grandees in 1987, in order to challenge the apparent takeover of the PRI by a younger generation educated in US universities and in favor of what came to be known as a 'neoliberal' orientation (i.e. a preference for free market allocation of resources, small government, light regulation, and other pro-business policies) ended with a bang, not a whimper.

President De la Madrid's record on elections was already bad. There were documented allegations of electoral fraud by PRI operatives in the mid-term elections of 1985. The 1986 governorship elections in Chihuahua, Mexico's biggest state, which shares a long border with the US states of Texas and New Mexico, allowed not only Mexican media but also the US media and public opinion to witness first-hand accounts of electoral fraud by the PRI to keep the governorship from falling to the PAN. However, these episodes of blatant illegality paled in comparison with the fraud perpetrated under his watch in the forthcoming presidential elections.

On that day, 6 July 1988, competition was fierce, due to the fact that Cuauhtémoc Cárdenas, having left the PRI, managed to create a broad, credible progressive front of the main left-wing parties and movements in the country—the National Democratic Front. Early vote-counting showed Cárdenas and Salinas neck and neck in the heart of the country (Mexico City, México state, and Morelos state) and the presidency, through the Ministry of Interior, sabotaged the elections. The ruse was an apparent 'collapse of the computing system' counting votes. This statement was announced by the Minister of Interior himself, Manuel Bartlett Díaz, and was followed, several days later by the declaration of Salinas as the winner of that election.

Despite the survival of the PRI regime after the 1988 general elections, its hegemony was severely weakened, its credibility shattered, and its place on the moral high ground as the party of nationalism, and the Mexican counterweight toward the overwhelming hemispheric dominance of the USA, and the party of social justice, was lost. This event and the subsequent presidency of Salinas (1988–94) mark the end of the background and the beginning of the years analyzed in detail in this work.

From the perspective of barriers to entry, the year 1988 was very significant, maybe what political scientists call a 'critical juncture'. As seen below, the rise of credible opposition to the PRI from the right and now the left, accompanied by a bankrupt, inward-looking economy, forced fundamental changes in the political and economic spheres. These changes produced a gradual but not linear move from authoritarian to electoral democratic rule in the political sphere, and from a closed to an open economy in the economic sphere.

Notes

1 See for example Jon C. Lohse and Fred Valdez, Jr., eds., *Ancient Maya Commoners*, Austin: University of Texas Press, 2004; Kenneth G. Hirth, *The Aztec Economic World: Merchants and Markets in Ancient Mesoamerica*, Cambridge: Cambridge University Press, 2016; Vernon L. Scarborough and John E. Clark, eds., The Political Economy of Ancient Mesoamerica: *Transformations during the Formative and Classical Periods*, Albuquerque: University of New Mexico Press, 2007.

2 Arte Colonial, "Las castas de la Nueva España", in https://artecolonial.wordpress. com/2011/02/28/las-castas-de-la-nueva-espana/, 28 February 2011, Accessed 19 September2017.

3 Scarborough and Clark, eds., 2007.

4 Positivist analyzes from the nineteenth century highlighted supposed differences in the capacity of the different casta groups to feel emotion and act accordingly. See, Ezequiel A. Chávez, "La sensibilidad del mexicano", in Roger Bartra, ed., *Anatomía del mexicano*, México: Plaza y Jánes, 2002, pp. 25–45.

5 Rafael Barajas Durán, "Retrato de un siglo. ¿Cómo ser mexicano en el XIX?", in Enrique Florescano, ed., *Espejo mexicano*, México: Fondo de Cultura Económica, 2002, pp. 116–177.

6 For a foreigner's views about inequality and racial relations in Mexico toward the end of the first half of the nineteenth century see Frances Calderón de la Barca, *Life in Mexico*, original publication, 1843; New York: Doubleday Dolphin, 1960 paperback edition; another view, from the 1960s which assumes more integration among the races/ethnicities in Mexico than is the case in reality is Rebecca West, *Survivors in Mexico*, New Haven: Yale University Press, 2003.

7 The tension and conflict between the whites and the rest is shown in the classics, Samuel Ramos, "El complejo de inferioridad", Bartra, 2002, 109–120, and Guillermo Bonfil, "México profundo", in Bartra, ed., 2002, pp. 289–294.

8 Academic debates continue about the issue of causation. What caused 'retarded' growth and development in Mexico in the first place, economic destruction or political bickering and fragmentation? I just consider that both of these phenomena fed on one another and created a vicious cycle that lasted more than half a century, leading to Mexico falling behind in relative terms, say, compared with the USA.

9 For Spanish America see John Lynch, *Caudillos in Spanish America, 1800–1850*, Oxford,:Oxford University Press, 1992; for Mexico see David A. Brading, ed., *Caudillo and Peasant in the Mexican Revolution*, Cambridge: Cambridge University Press, 1980; Enrique Krauze, *Siglo de caudillos: biografía política de México, 1810–1910*, Mexico, Tusquets, 1999; Enrique Krauze, *Biografía del poder: caudillos de la Revolución Mexicana, 1910–1940*, Mexico, Tusquets, 1998.

10 In Mexico see Wil G. Pansters, ed., *Violence, Coercion, and State-Making in Twentieth-Century Mexico: the Other Half of the Centaur*, Stanford, Stanford University Press, 2012; in Latin America see Marcus J. Kurtz, *Latin American*

State Building in Comparative Perspective: Social Foundations of Institutional Order, Cambridge: Cambridge University Press, 2013; in general see Francis Fukuyama, *State Building: Governance and World-Order in the Twenty-First Century*, Ithaca: Cornell University Press, 2004.

11 John H. Coatsworth, "Obstacles to Economic Growth in Nineteenth-Century Mexico", in *American Historical Review* (February–December 1978), pp. 80–100.

12 Stephen Haber, Armando Razo and Noel Maurer, *The Politics of Property Rights: Political Instability, Credible Commitments, and Economic Growth in Mexico, 1876–1929*, Cambridge: Cambridge University Press, pp. 29–40.

13 Ibid., p. 41.

14 Ibid., pp. 44–45.

15 A classic liberal interpretation is Jesús Silva Herzog, *Breve historia de la Revolución Mexicana*, 2 volúmenes, Mexico, Fondo de Cultura Económica, 1960; a classic left-wing interpretation is Adolfo Gilly, *La Revolución interrumpida: México, 1910–1920, una guerra campesina por la tierra y el poder*, Mexico, Ediciones El Caballito, 1971; a work that looks at the Revolution in a broader comparative context is Alan Knight, *The Mexican Revolution*, 2 volumes, Cambridge: Cambridge University Press, 1986.

16 Francisco E. González, "Shocks and Social Pressures in the Improvement of the Exercise of Citizenship Rights: Great Britain and Mexico's Different Historical Trajectories", in *Mexican Law Review*, Vol. 8, no. 2, January–July 2015.

3 The Onset and Entrenchment of Misplaced Monopolies in Mexico's Political Economy, 1980s to 2006

Focusing on barriers to entry in the political and economic spheres in Mexico is the most effective way to convey the key themes in this work. Part of the period it covers in detail (1988–2018) is presented in this chapter, by presidential term. The presidential six-year formula in Mexico, known as *sexenios*, of a single term without the possibility of re-election, is and remains a basic unit of analysis for students and scholars of Mexican politics. This is due to the level of power that the head of the executive branch continues to hold over Mexicans, and the interest he (not yet a she) inspires in foreigners who study Mexican politics.

Carlos Salinas de Gortari, 1988–94

President Carlos Salinas de Gortari presided over generational and ideological change in government as well as his party, the Partido Revolucionario Institucional (PRI). His firm hold on the presidency followed his disputed election in 1988. He had become President De la Madrid's (1982–88) closest collaborator, as the Minister of Planning and Budgeting, in the number one problem the country faced: the external debt crisis (mostly contracted by the public sector under the presidencies of Luis Echeverría (1970–76) and José López Portillo (1976–82), and how to rekindle economic growth. Salinas won a head-to-head cabinet conflict over the direction of Mexico's economic policy in 1985–86. The more traditional PRI leaders sided with Minister of Finance, Jesús Silva Herzog. Analysts and scholars called them the nationalists because they wanted to keep the basic framework that prioritized the national market and a degree of state control. A younger group of technocrats, mostly educated in Ivy League universities in the USA, and savvy political operatives, sided with Salinas. Against the nationalists, he and his team favored opening up the economy and, in particular, courting the USA, as the largest US banks were heavily exposed to Mexican debt. The aim was to create an outward-looking solution to the debt crisis, which meant luring back international financial inflows by applying a basket of pro-market policies that later in the 1990s were dubbed the 'Washington consensus.' Salinas, his team and their acolytes started being identified and known as 'the neoliberals.'

The turning point in Mexico's economic liberalization started under De la Madrid's presidency, in 1985–86, was that its main supporter and executor was Salinas and his close circle of technocrats, politicians, and businessmen eager to benefit from a more liberalized economy.

However, it is also important to note that De la Madrid's own convictions (crisis or no crisis) had been conservative and capitalist to start with. An individual who spent four decades at the top of the pyramid of power, starting in the early 1950s, serving in the presidency, as secretary of various ministries, and later on as principal senior counselor for some of the young generation that took over during the De la Madrid presidency, and later consolidated under Salinas, who I will call Cicero, told me in the course of several interviews that the opening up of the Mexican economy was not just a function of the deep crisis in 1985–86. From his perspective, it was important to remember that De la Madrid had originally been a PAN sympathizer and had run for Congress as substitute deputy under the banner of that party.[1]

From this perspective, rather than Mexico being put against the wall due to its financial dire straits in 1985–86, which forced a U-turn in economic policy that translated into the country joining the General Agreement on Tariffs and Trade (GATT) in 1986 and starting pilot cases of privatization, the key to the fundamental change in economic policy orientation also had an ideological component. Therefore, policy decisions were not necessarily dictated only by sheer need. To politicians, interest groups, and citizens who believed in Mexican nationalism and the country's right to relative autonomy to pursue a mixed economy model that was not completely aligned with the USA and its dominant allies both in the political and economic spheres, De la Madrid was the great traitor.

True, the country faced a terrible crisis during De la Madrid's tenure, which he inherited from his predecessor, President López Portillo. Leaving him as his successor in the knowledge that De la Madrid was at heart a conservative, López Portillo was probably even more fundamentally implicated than the chosen candidate himself (at the end of the day, through the '*dedazo*' system of informal rule, López Portillo had a number of alternatives to choose from) in the U-turn enforced on Mexico's economic policy and the role of the state in keeping a measure of cohesion, social peace, and political stability, which came to an end when the electorate voted in De la Madrid.[2]

Likewise, from this perspective it is reasonable to understand one of the reasons why traditional nationalists like Cuauhtémoc Cárdenas and Porfirio Muñoz Ledo launched their opposition inside the PRI in 1986 (the so-called '*Corriente Democrática*'). They were aware about the major reorientation in economic policy carried out by the young neoliberal technocrats, and the high likelihood of an acceleration and deepening of such economic reorientation if Salinas was made De la Madrid's successor. This conviction was at least partly well founded, given De la Madrid's ideological foundations as a conservative who persecuted his own colleagues—the so-called 'Generación de Medio Siglo' (in the PRI); his persecution of strong opposition to his implementation of conservative policies from students, professors and the trade union of the National University (UNAM), the largest public university in Latin America; his preference and advancement of economists over lawyers; and his advancement of individuals who showed strong personal attachment to him. This last point illustrates the role of contingency, the whims of top decision-making, in this case at the top of a traditionally vertical, intolerant, and deferential pyramid of power, and its effects in starting a deep transformation of Mexico's politico-economic trajectory in the medium-to-long term.[3]

Having shown some of the roots that lie behind the ascent of Salinas to the top of the pyramid of power in Mexico, I here disaggregate the four main parameters used in this study (i.e. the state and the regime in the political sphere, and the international and domestic components in the economic sphere) to understand the events that helped to start the creation of the condition I have identified as Mexico drifting toward 'misplaced monopolies' starting in the 1980s. For the purpose of clarity, I repeat the same exposition, based on these four parameters, for all the presidencies, starting with Salinas (1988–94) until the last year in office of Enrique Peña Nieto (2018).

In the political sphere:

i) The state level of analysis: Salinas inherited a weakened state due to more than five years of austerity, a weak presidential figure, distrustful domestic and foreign private business sectors, and disenchanted and rebellious organized labor, and the middle classes, who had seen their quality of life and prospects destroyed after the 1982 economic meltdown. President Salinas possessed the instinct of a political animal. At the start of his term in office he threw in jail corrupt trade union leaders (who had opposed him in the 1988 election) and a banker from a prominent bourgeois family (for financial mismanagement in the crisis that followed the New York Stock Exchange crash in 1987). All relevant actors took note and became deferential to the new president.

President Salinas also reorganized law enforcement and security services. In particular the Mexico-US relationship had been strained since 1985 as a consequence of the kidnapping and brutal torture and murder of the American Drug Enforcement (DEA) agent Enrique 'Kiki' Camarena, and a pilot who had flown him around Chihuahua state to monitor large illegal marijuana crops protected by the Mexican police and military. Salinas dissolved the Dirección Federal de Seguridad (DFS), Mexico's politically controlled police force, which managed anti-narcotics activity, among many other campaigns, and was highly corrupt. In 1989 he replaced the DFS with the Centro de Investigación y Seguridad Nacional. The aim was to create a modern agency for the analysis and execution of national security policy, and anti-narcotics policy was at the top of the agenda. Salinas was very interested to show the US government that he would co-operate in the war on drugs. In retrospect we know that

President Salinas's older brother, Raúl, became the gatekeeper for narcotics activity, brokering and co-ordinating the cartels' activities, in particular avoiding public shows of violence. It worked for a time but this *ad hoc* system was far from effective as, for example, the murder of the Cardinal of Guadalajara Juan Jesús Posadas Ocampo, maybe mistaken for a drug kingpin outside the Guadalajara International airport in May 1993 and gunned down, made headlines around the world.

President Salinas strengthened the state but more in a personal rather than in an institutional way. Aside from his actions against visible members of important pressure groups, the president was a strong centralizing force. He asked for the resignation of 17 of the country's state governors (out of 31 states in Mexico's federal system), and every single one stepped down without any public fuss.

It was not until his last year in power that President Salinas witnessed the sudden weakening if not the collapse of some of his main actions that helped to strengthen the Mexican state in his person. An indigenous rebellion in the southeastern state of Chiapas on 1 January 1994, the same day that the North American Free Trade Agreement (NAFTA) started operating, undermined the President's claim that Mexico was joining the 'developed world' by partnering with the economies of the United States and Canada. Additionally, Salinas's chosen successor, Luis Donaldo Colosio, was murdered on the campaign trail on 23 March 1994 in Tijuana. No designated presidential successor had been assassinated in Mexico since Álvaro Obregón won a non-consecutive re-election in 1928. Likewise, the PRI's Secretary-General, and would-be leader of the *Cámara de Diputados* (Lower Chamber of Congress), José Francisco Ruiz Massieu, former governor of the state of Guerrero and former brother-in-law of the Salinas brothers, was assassinated close to downtown Mexico City on 28 September 1994. According to a person at the center of power at the time, the murders of Colosio and of Ruiz Massieu were connected through the involvement of President Salinas's older brother, Raúl, and an influential but diffuse group of individuals, which included powerful politicians, top advisers, drug cartel kingpins, and businessmen. They were afraid about Colosio's empowerment once he became president, and the likelihood that he would pursue members of this group, given the illegal fortunes they had amassed, the lives they had taken, and the grand corruption they had used with absolute impunity to pursue their goals of amassing power and riches. Ruiz-Massieu was, like many others close to the Salinas clan, also more than aware about these activities, and as the leader of the Lower House (the equivalent of the Speaker in the House of Representatives in the USA) would become one of the most powerful figures in Mexico's political system, and could therefore also cause trouble to the network linked by proximity to Raúl Salinas.[4] The Zapatista rebellion and the two political assassinations led the internationally recognized Mexican writer Carlos Fuentes to describe 1994 as 'the year we lived in danger.'[5]

In summary, having started by raising barriers to entry to the state, recentralizing authority in his person (rather than institutions), and promising a return to strong, effective political rule, Salinas ended up in a weak position after the main political events of 1993–94. Not only did he have to leave the country once he stepped down, in order to avoid potential arrest for illicit enrichment, co-participating or knowing about major political assassinations, and abuse of power, but he also inadvertently contributed to the lowering of barriers which facilitated the entry of non-state actors to exercise force and coercion against ordinary Mexican citizens. In the realm of the state, Mexico became more liable to insecurity, violence, and petty and organized crime after 1994.[6]

ii) The political regime level of analysis: After the highly disputed 1988 presidential election, Salinas himself made a public speech in which he announced "the end of hegemonic party rule." This amounted to more than paying lip service to Mexico's politico-electoral reality at the end of the 1980s. The closely contested 1988 elections deprived the PRI of its two-thirds majority in Congress to amend the Constitution. President Salinas had to forge an informal alliance with the PAN, which enabled him to carry out his revolutionary economic policy program. The program was predicated on the benefits of opening up the Mexican economy and, in particular, getting closer to the USA and locking in his pro-market policies by signing a free trade agreement with the USA and Canada.

In exchange for legislative support, President Salinas allowed the PAN to gain more political representation and thus power. For the first time, PAN contenders to governorships were allowed to win and assume office, starting in 1989 with the state of Baja California. The PRI and the PAN created an informal block in the federal Congress which voted in favor of the repertoire of pro-market policies.

In contrast, Salinas did not acknowledge or worked with the new united left under Cuauhtémoc Cárdenas, which created the largest left-wing party in 1989, the Partido de la Revolución Democrática (PRD). Party members, activists, and journalists who sympathized with the PRD suffered threats and harassment, and hundreds were murdered. Salinas boasted during his final State of the Union address in Congress in 1994, while PRD representatives protested his policies, that he "did not see them or hear them."

Aside from the expedience of strengthening the PAN in exchange for collaboration with neoliberal reforms, President Salinas enacted several politico-electoral reforms that lowered barriers to entry in this realm. In 1990 he created the Instituto Federal Electoral (IFE), which in theory would become a neutral arbiter of Mexican elections. This ended up being the case later but not during Salinas's presidency, due to the Minister of Interior's (Segob) predominant role in this new institution. Likewise, two other electoral reforms gave more resources and media presence to the opposition, as well as allowed foreign observers to monitor the 1994 presidential elections.

In summary, barriers to entry in the political regime fell during Salinas's presidency. However, such lowering of barriers was selective. It helped and supported the conservative PAN, while intimidating and coercing the left-wing PRD. However, laws and institutions, if they continue to operate, outlive their creators and can end up producing consequences unintended by their founders. As seen below, the IFE ended up being a key institutional component of Mexico's democratization. This was not what Salinas had intended.

In the economic sphere:

iii) The international economy level of analysis: This was the area where Salinas carried out what could be dubbed a first wave of structural neoliberal reforms (although opening Mexico up to the international economy started by fits and starts under De la Madrid in 1985). Liberalizing the capital account to allow free financial flows and opening trade through his pursuit of NAFTA were revolutionary moves in a country that had been relatively closed for more than three decades, during which it had tried to pursue inward-looking development via import-substitution industrialization. This level of analysis has been the one that analysts and observers have emphasized since the 1990s, to call Mexico one of the most open economies in the world. Proof of this was that in the 2000s Mexico became the country with the highest number of bilateral and multilateral free trade agreements globally. The consequences of such a U-turn are critical to understand why Mexico joined the countries that embraced (or were forced to embrace) 'globalization.' The advantages were far from negligible. An open economy—in terms of financial and trade flows—was rewarded with seals of approval by international financial institutions and the US government. Both were critical to Mexico's short term macroeconomic recovery and take-off after the 'lost decade.'

iv) The domestic economy level of analysis: In contrast to the international opening to capital and trade flows, the Salinas government concentrated and centralized economic activity in the domestic market. Mexico was highly indebted (in US dollars) to foreign creditors in the 1980s and found it hard to service its debts. None the less, the Echeverría and López Portillo governments had accumulated a significant number of the country's assets during the growth of nationalization of economic activity in 1970–1982. Very attractive opportunities for national capitalists and potential foreign partners were available during the deleveraging (in Spanish *desapalancamiento*—paying off debt to stabilize debt/income ratios) years, which Salinas used as the springboard to relaunch Mexico to become once again an importer rather than an exporter of capital. The story of privatization in the face of acute financial crises is well known and it happened across the world in the 1980s and 1990s (from Mexico to Brazil and Argentina in Latin America, as well as South Korea, Thailand and Indonesia in East Asia). An extreme example was the Union of Soviet Socialist Republics, which after its dissolution in 1991 led to the establishment of 15 newly independent countries, the largest of which was Russia, which rapidly created a new and enduring class of oligarchs: global capitalists with close connections to their nation state's government, and the main captains of industry in other capitalist countries (the Davos annual meeting in Switzerland became the main platform for face-to-face interaction in the course of the 1990s among this power club, before social media such as Facebook, Google, and Twitter could project their soft power in the 2010s). In the case of Mexico, the re-privatization of banking, telecoms, and some broadcast media were blueprints for the new trend of turbo-charged 'super-capitalism' (to use the term coined by Nobel laureate Joseph Stiglitz) which swept many developing and mature capitalist countries, as well as economies that tried and failed with centralized resource allocation—the command economies of so-called communism or 'real socialism.' Mexico's experiment with privatization under Salinas created a small, cohesive block of new capitalists close to the president and his intimate circle. From this work's perspective, the key difference in terms of lowering barriers to entry in Mexico's international economic sector was the opposite in the domestic sector: economic activity dominated by monopolies (both public—like energy—and private, like telecoms), duopolies in broadcast media, or highly concentrated oligopolies with dominant players (like banking). The paradox, at least for Salinas, was that this exercise in tailoring a new, domestically concentrated although internationally open (capital and trade flows) economy acceptable for the 'neoliberal' 21st century met with bankruptcy by the end of his presidency. However, as seen below, in different configurations and partnerships, different concentrated economic sectors continued to be the norm in the Mexican economy: one or two firms or conglomerates creaming off the high profits made in a country that had opened up to capital and trade flows in the international sector, while keeping high barriers to entry and a monopolistic or oligopolistic straitjacket in the main sectors of its domestic economy.

Ernesto Zedillo Ponce de León, 1994–2000

The last president of the PRI period of consecutive rule since 1929, Ernesto Zedillo Ponce de León, doubled down on the belief that a bright economic future for Mexico lay with embracing globalization. His stance was as equally lopsided as Salinas's if not more so. As a consequence of the first of a series of international financial crises in the newly coined world of 'emerging markets'—Mexico's was dubbed the 'tequila crisis', of 1994–95—as well as his close collaborators' belief in the virtue of free markets, Zedillo continued the liberalization and privatization of the Mexican economy. Again, and in the case of banking, much more so due to the 'tequila' crisis, the economy's new private owners were few, thus helping to consolidate the country's mono-polistic/oligopolistic domestic economic structure, despite an international reputation for openness, thanks to capital and trade liberalization. In the political sphere, as described below, the Zedillo presidency was, from this work's perspective, the beginning and accelerated development of the phe-nomenon I have dubbed 'misplaced monopolies': growing economic con-centration of wealth in a few hands, accompanied by state fragmentation and weakening state ruling capacity, which spread to different areas of the federal, state, and municipal levels of government in many parts of Mexico. Orga-nized as well as petty crime strengthened and spread in the wake of the 'tequila' crisis and a federal government that was perceived as significantly weaker than its predecessor.

In the political sphere:

i) The state level of analysis: This area was probably the most negatively affected in terms of the end of the state's capacity to exercise the monopoly over the legitimate use of persuasion/force/coercion against non-state actors in Mexican territory. A different but related and incredibly important issue due to its prevalence and weight in Mexican political culture was the state's inability, incapacity, or unwillingness to use its prerogative against its own members if they broke the law. This is the issue of impunity, which has been and remains dominant in political, economic, and social interaction and transactions in Mexico since colonial times. To illustrate the level of rotten-ness at the core of the state during the Zedillo years, consider the President's appointment of General José de Jesús Gutiérrez Rebollo as his 'drug czar'. Apparently an outstanding and effective member of the military, the General was discovered to be in the pay of the then most-wanted drug kingpin by the DEA, Amado Carrillo Fuentes, known as the *señor de los cielos* (the lord of the skies) thanks to his delivery of hundreds of tons of cocaine to the USA via airplanes.[7] Bringing the military into the narrative during the Zedillo pre-sidency is critical to understanding how the Mexican state was captured by organized criminal groups. Unlike Salinas, Zedillo was not an individual with long and popular militancy in the PRI. While Salinas ruled, his older brother, Raúl, became a low-profile super-minister without portfolio. He was involved as much in agricultural subsidies and the sale of state outlets where agri-cultural produce was sold as in dealing with the main drug kingpins and their cartels around the country. Raúl Salinas de Gortari and his criminal record are common knowledge. The point for the incoming Zedillo administration was that he and his collaborators were highly distrustful of the law-and-order and general security apparatus that President Salinas had used to run the country. Thus, President Zedillo decided to get the military high command involved in running law-and-order and rule of law operations. The thinking was that the military could play a counterweight against the system that the Salinas clan had created, and in particular with anti-narcotics policy. The problem was that the military high command had been involved with the drug-traffickers for decades, and to the extent that they had been kept at arms' length from law-and-order and rule of law matters, once Zedillo brought them into government, they came much more directly into daily contact with kingpins, and this closer interaction contributed to the deepening of corruption, impunity, and lawlessness in Mexico. A counterpoint to this mistake was Zedillo's reform of the federal judiciary arm of the state. Thanks to his reform, this branch of government gained some independence from political whims, but it remained politicized. Perhaps the most important difference between Zedillo and any of his PRI predecessors in the realm of relationships between the Mexican president and the country's 31 state governors (plus the mayor of Mexico City, which became an elected office and was won by Cuauhtémoc Cárdenas in 1997) was the loss of his prerogative to get them to obey his commands blindly. All presidents before Zedillo had asked for the resignation of a number of governors during their terms in office. Up until 1994, this had been one of the unwritten prerogatives of the strong Mexican presidency, backed up by the hegemonic PRI. For example, President Salinas asked for the resignation of 17 governors (all of them having been elected 'democratically' in their states). All left their office when the President asked for their resignation. Not a single one of them made a public fuss. It was part of the country's political culture. However, after Zedillo assumed the presidency, this stopped being the case. In a hotly disputed election in the southeastern state of Tabasco, and in light of ample evidence of fraud by the PRI's candidate, Roberto Madrazo Pintado, against the PRD's Andrés Manuel López Obrador, President Zedillo asked Madrazo not to assume power, only to be rebutted. This was one of several attempts where the presidency tried to retain the centralized system of power run from Mexico City. However, the system broke down. The reasons for it were the great financial, economic crisis of 1994–95 (recovery from which did not start until 1997) and the fact that Zedillo was a weak president because he did not have strong support groups inside the PRI. In summary, the state became seriously weakened, penetrated, and corrupted during the Zedillo years. In other words, barriers to entry fell and non-state actors found it easier to exercise the persuasion/force/coercion in the public sphere, which should be a monopoly of an effective state.

ii) The political regime level of analysis: This was probably the most positively affected area and one for which Zedillo will be remembered in history textbooks. Whereas Salinas had created the IFE after his highly contested election, but the institution remained a tutelary arm of the state, the 1994–95 financial 'tequila' crisis forced Zedillo to negotiate with the opposition. And again, in contrast with his predecessor Salinas, who had established a *de facto* alliance with the PAN to pursue pro-market policies while coercing the PRD, Zedillo opened up to both right and left. Through a 1996 political reform, the IFE became relatively independent from the government (staffed by citizen-councillors and, crucially, without the head of Segob presiding). The *quid pro quo* seems to have been that the PRI regime was willing to open up the political-electoral arena in earnest in exchange for PAN and PRD opposition not to rock the boat or stoke the flames of social discontent and indignation after the 1994–5 economic collapse. The measures worked. As expected, the unpopular PRI (in the light of the economic crises and the stories that circulated throughout the country about Salinas and his circle's illicit enrichment as a consequence of the privatizations and opening of the economy) lost its simple majority for the first time in the mid-term elections of 1997 at the same time that more non-PRI governors started being elected and their victories respected. Prominently, as said above, Cuauhtémoc Cárdenas won the first election for mayor of Mexico City in 1997. Figure 3.1 shows how holding power across Mexico's territory became more plural after the 1996 political reform. The PRI consistently lost governorships despite retaining a majority.

From the perspective of democratization of an authoritarian regime, the pluralization of power in Mexico in the three branches of government and in the territorial politics of federalism after 1996 was a welcome development. The creation of a federal electoral court nested in the judicial branch of government also distanced the federal executive's tentacles from directly deciding electoral contests. The peaceful attainment of electoral democracy in Mexico was Zedillo's high point. In this area there is no question that barriers to entry fell, and this was good for the case of electoral democracy. But democracy has its own problems, which as seen below when discussing subsequent presidencies, helped exacerbate the fragmentation and weakening of central power in a large, diverse, and very economically unequal country like Mexico.

In the economic sphere:

iii) The international economy level of analysis: Zedillo became a visible international figure in the late 1990s, when supporters and opponents of the Anglo-American re-embrace of markets started clashing inside international financial institutions, cabinets, academia, the media, and in the streets. The memorable protests during the World Trade Organization's (WTO) Ministerial Meeting of 1999, which that year took place in Seattle, USA, were followed by many others wherever international bodies representing the 'Washington consensus' (aside from the WTO, the IMF and the WB) met. Dissident academics who had held top positions in some of these institutions like Stiglitz wrote scathing analysis and reportage about what they saw and were asked to do while serving in them.[8] Zedillo was in the opposite camp. He called those who opposed the unfettered opening of markets across the developing world 'globaliphobics', and after leaving the Mexican presidency started running a center for the study of globalization at Yale University, where he did his PhD.[9] With this profile, it is unsurprising that Zedillo followed and deepened Salinas's commitment to opening markets and privatizing state enterprises. In the case of Zedillo, he could use the excuse that the Mexican economy was bankrupt after 1994–95. Mexico had been bailed out by the US government, the IMF and the World Bank to the tune of US $50,000m. Repaying credit lines and using the argument about remaining a creditworthy player in the international capital markets provided the Zedillo administration ammunition to strengthen the impetus for Mexico to keep opening up its economy. During his presidency, Mexico signed a free trade agreement with the European Union (EU), among others. Capital flows remained free while the Mexican government supported and became a leading emerging market that supported the World Trade Organization (WTO), born out of the Uruguay Round of the GATT in 1994. There is no question that barriers to entry in the external sector of Mexico's economy continued to fall during Zedillo's presidency. In terms of a timeline, while the PRI was in power, this fall in barriers to entry focused on the external sector, starting under De la Madrid in 1985–86 has continued ever since. Zedillo remained a strong believer in globalization. But what about the domestic sector of the Mexican economy?

iv) The domestic economy level of analysis: The 1994–95 tequila crisis provided a new opportunity to deepen and extend the first wave of neoliberal policies in Mexico, as I have identified it in this work. Therefore, further privatization of national assets was justified in order that the country could pay its financial obligations in the wake of the crisis to remain creditworthy. Railways and ports were opened up to private bidders. In the energy sector, although oil was not touched (Pemex held too much political as well as financial clout in the Mexican political economy), the government liberalized the power generation market. This was in fact badly needed, due to the accumulated inefficiencies, aging infrastructure, lack of ability to keep supply growing alongside demand, politicization, and corruption at the country's state monopoly provider of electricity, the Comisión Federal de Electricidad (CFE). By far the most important and controversial sale of Mexican assets occurred in the financial and banking sector. As a consequence of the 1994–95 tequila crisis, most Mexican banks had significant liquidity problems (even

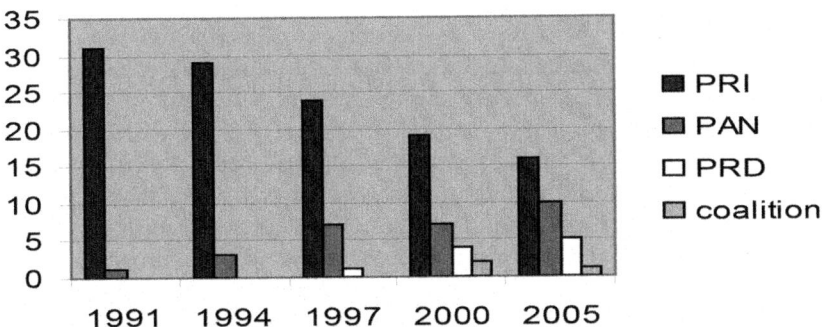

Figure 3.1. Rise of Opposition Governorships in Mexico after 1996
Sources: Data elaborated from the now extinct Instituto Federal Electoral (IFE) and from updates on elections by the Woodrow Wilson Center Mexico Institute, https://www.wilsoncenter.org/program/mexico-institute

if some of the largest were not necessarily insolvent). The Zedillo government decided to open up the banking sector to foreign buyers (something Salinas had not done, although he privatized the banks in many instances to unscrupulous get-rich-quick businessmen who subsequently went bust during the 'tequila' crisis). Allowing foreign ownership of banks was politically charged, and the left (PRD) as well as many in the President's PRI were against it. Nonetheless, a PRI–PAN alliance to pass the laws necessary to make this happen prevailed, and all Mexican banks but one (Banorte) were sold. The main consequence of this sale was a mergers-and-acquisitions process that consolidated the banking and finance industry in Mexico, and strengthened the roots and structure of an oligopolistic market, where five banks accounted for around 85 percent of total banking assets in the country, and the top two—Bancomer, acquired by the Spanish Banco Bilbao Vizcaya (BBVA), and Banamex, acquired by American Citibank—accounted for more than half of all assets and credit in the country. In summary, similar to the Salinas presidency, Zedillo's years in office raised the barriers to entry by concentrating economic activity in the core of any capitalist system: the banking, finance, and credit sector. As of 2018, more than 85 percent of banking assets in Mexico are owned by foreign global banks. This makes Mexico an anomaly as a member of the Organisation for Economic Co-operation and Development. If the main mechanism for the production of future innovation, productivity, and new wealth, (i.e. credit provided by banks), is overwhelmingly owned by foreign entities, it is not unreasonable to suggest that such a country's private and public sectors might not have timely and adequate financing for productive activity when they need it. At the end of the day, the main providers of credit must consider the rules of, and operate within a global marketplace, where an emerging market country, in this case Mexico, is but a pawn in the daily game of global finance.

Vicente Fox Quesada, 2000–06

The accession to the presidency by Vicente Fox in 2000 marked a very important change in Mexican politics, if not in the country's economy. As a member of the conservative PAN, his presidential electoral victory represented the first alternation in power at the apex of the pyramid of political authority (i.e. Mexico's federal executive) in seven decades. The PRI was ousted in a legal, peaceful way through the ballot box rather than agitation, riots, and bullets. Such peaceful alternation in power, while greatly welcome and surprising to a majority when it happened was, according to some views, not surprising at all. Zedillo faced his staunchest opposition not in the PAN or even the PRD but in his own party, the PRI. Many party grandees hated his aloof, technocratic demeanor and his fervent push to keep implementing neoliberal policies. There was concern among many supporters of the Washington consensus about the potential reversal of pro-market reforms if Cárdenas won the election. Having won the first election for mayor in Mexico

City in 1997, Cárdenas had great national visibility in the run-up to 2000. As a consequence, President Zedillo and his close entourage kept some distance from his party's presidential candidate, Francisco Labastida Ochoa. This was probably the right thing to do from the legal perspective. What surprised most PRI members and sympathizers was that such behaviour from a serving president could happen in the first place. It certainly broke with the rigid norm about doing whatever it took to keep the PRI in power. And of course, the factotum of the system's continuity had always been the outgoing president and his overt and covert support for the successor he had chosen. Zedillo probably felt more secure about the permanence of pro-market reforms with the victory of the conservative PAN candidate, Fox. Nationalists in the PRI started referring to Presidents Zedillo and Fox as the first Mexican 'gringo' presidents, meaning that the US government's favored vision of friendly countries adopting pro-market policies was secured through party alternation in Mexico.[10]

Against general expectations that democratic change after Fox's clean victory in the 2000 presidential election would bring about all-round improvements for most Mexicans, the political sphere continued to deteriorate. In turn, the economy underperformed at the same time that concentration of activity was reinforced in the main sectors of productive activity. From the perspective of this work, the condition of misplaced monopolies in the political and economic spheres accelerated and reached a low point during Fox's presidency.

In the political sphere:

i) The state level of analysis: Fragmentation and weakening of federal rule, inherited from the Zedillo government, accelerated and created a power vacuum at the heart of Mexico's traditional political system. This vacuum was filled by both legal and illegal actors: governors, *caciques*, and organized criminal cartels. The federal state lost credibility in its ability to keep basic order and stability. In January 2001, just one month after Fox took office, Joaquín 'el Chapo' Guzmán, one of the leaders of the most powerful narcotics cartels in Mexico—the Sinaloa cartel—escaped from a top-security prison. This event grabbed domestic and foreign headlines. The story retained high domestic and international visibility and the reason for this, in retrospect, was not just the apparently film-like jailbreak of 'el Chapo', according to which he had escaped by jumping in a laundry cart and hiding before being wheeled out from prison[11], but its dreadful consequences for the type of violence that would be unleashed in Mexico. Within a couple of years of Guzmán's escape, the Sinaloa cartel started challenging the other largest narcotics cartel, the *cartel del Golfo*, over coveted transit routes into the USA in the Gulf cartel's own home turf in the Mexico-US border state of Tamaulipas. Sinaloa targeted in particular the city of Nuevo Laredo, the most lucrative point of access into the USA in terms of volume of goods, services, and people who cross from Mexico into the USA, alongside Tijuana (at the western tip of the Mexico-US border) and Ciudad Juárez (roughly midway along the more-than-2,000-mile border shared by the two countries). From around 2003 onward, turf wars between the two cartels and other, smaller ones that felt encroached on by these two (the Tijuana and Juárez cartels, as well as *La familia michoacana*) proliferated and grew in territorial extension, as well as intensity of violence carried out by the contenders. Like Zedillo, Fox kept and reinforced military participation in law-and-order and rule-of-law functions around the country. He reformed the police forces to try to make them less corrupt. However, both measures did not show positive results. More military as well as police officers and personnel were corrupted by organized crime. In effect, the state became penetrated by these criminal organizations at the three levels of government. If the federal government lost its capacity to exercise a monopoly over the use of persuasion/force/coercion throughout Mexican territory, the state and municipal (local) levels fared even worse. This was an issue related not just to scarcer material and human resources at the subnational level, but also about more points of entry below the federal level of government, in which criminals could capture state authorities due to the presidency's relative weakness in its oversight and command-and-control capacity.

ii) The regime level of analysis: Political power became more decentralized and plural during the Fox years. On the plus side, the central state set the bases for more accountability of public authority by passing a freedom of information act; allowing full freedom of expression (visual and printed media censorship or control was and continues to be more associated with PRI governments, although it was also used by Fox and Calderón to intimidate or stop supporting publications or broadcasts, for which revenue depended significantly on government advertising); and getting the federal executive to play politics by accepting the checks and balances prescribed in the constitution vis-à-vis the legislative and judicial branches of government. The three main parties (PRI, PAN, and PRD) had fair and effective room to operate in the three branches of the three levels of government in a majority of Mexico's 31 states, plus Mexico City. The PRI remained dominant in around half of the states, but the tide toward the pluralization of power in the light of relatively free and fair elections strengthened during the Fox presidency. On the negative side, some of the democratic virtues on paper, such as effective checks and balances, or a robust federalism respectful of states' rights, led to several problems. First, the national government was unable to implement its main policy program because by accepting checks and balances in earnest, Fox and his allies became prisoners of the PRI, whose representation at the federal and subnational levels remained large enough to give it veto power to shoot down any initiatives coming from the president or his party (the PAN).

While Fox continued to be regarded as honest and trustworthy as a person (not so his wife Marta Sahagún and her sons by her first marriage), public opinion also showed that a significant majority of Mexicans believed that he was a weak, ineffective politician, who had been good as a campaigner but not as a leader after he assumed the presidency. In the eyes of the political class and the public at large, Fox became a lame duck president after the mid-term elections of 2003, as shown in Figure 3.2, which weakened the PAN's representation in Congress. Worst of all, Fox did intervene in the politico-electoral arena in a crucial issue that created a substantial and lingering political conflict. Concerned about the general popularity of the PRD's then mayor of Mexico City, Andrés Manuel López Obrador, President Fox tried to get him impeached. The evidence for such a procedure was shaky—it involved the use of land that was supposedly ill-gotten, on which to build a hospital. Politicians and analysts interpreted the attack, which did not prosper, as Fox's attempt to sabotage López Obrador's chances to become a presidential candidate in 2006. Fox's move backfired. It gave López Obrador ample media coverage; portrayed him as the injured party of a political vendetta; and strengthened his politico-electoral appeal. Fox continued to voice his personal antipathy toward López Obrador. And once the left-wing politician ran for the presidency in 2006, Fox continued to disqualify him from participating in public forums. Mexican presidents are prohibited by law to engage in partisan debate, promoting or disqualifying candidates. Mexico's federal electoral court admonished Fox after the elections for his continuous public interventions against López Obrador. However, the court fell short of considering the charge as enough evidence to annul the 2006 election. The end result was the sowing of doubt among the electorate about the fairness of electoral institutions. Around one-third of voters became López Obrador supporters who believed that the election was rigged against him, and the result, which gave victory to the PAN's Felipe Calderón, was illegitimate in their eyes. From this perspective, President Fox contributed significantly to the rise in popular appeal of López Obrador. It also created a partisan cleavage that has remained alive in Mexico since then: on one hand, a public perception according to which the PAN and the PRI work in tandem (detractors of this supposed partnership call it the 'PRIAN') to alternate in power, maintain the neoliberal *status quo* and, on the other, López Obrador is cast as the populist outsider who, if triumphant in presidential elections, which he finally achieved in July 2018 could become a radical head of executive similar to Hugo Chávez in Venezuela, and Mexico could become a more unstable, conflictive polity if it embraced leftist policies. The jury is out there.

In the economic sphere:

iii) The international economy level of analysis: Fox's main plan was to relaunch NAFTA. He wanted Mexico's trade partnership with the USA and Canada to resemble more the EU's arrangements. He and his team of close collaborators wanted particularly to get labor mobility across the three

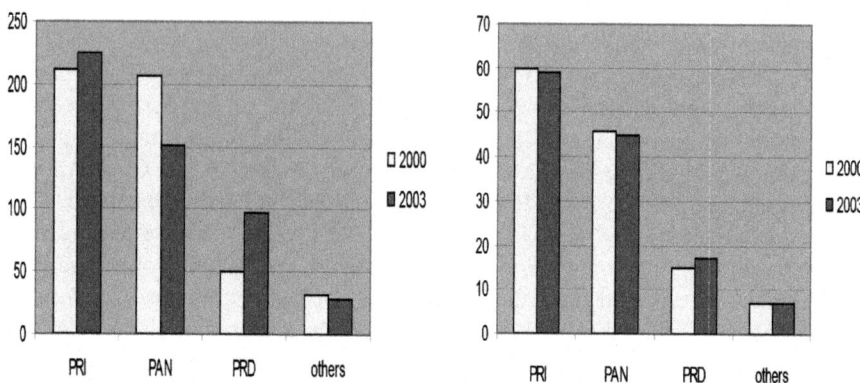

Figure 3.2. The PRI Retained Veto Power to Enact or Thwart Legislation after
        Democratization
Source: Data elaborated from Instituto Nacional Electoral, http://www.ine.mx/, 2017.

NAFTA member states regulated, and also desired the creation of institutional mechanisms to redistribute wealth from Canada and the USA to
Mexico, similar to the structural funds that the EU has used to mitigate
inequality between core and peripheral member countries. Even though
there seemed to be goodwill and good chemistry between President Fox
and President George W. Bush, the attacks of 11 September 2001 on the
World Trade Center in New York City and the Pentagon in Washington,
DC (9/11) changed dramatically US perceptions about the outside world.
Security along border areas was beefed up and the USA subsequently
invaded Afghanistan (2001) and then Iraq (2003). Any possibility of
working to improve NAFTA was drowned out by 9/11 and the US reaction against the world beyond its borders. Instead, Fox and his government continued to pursue bilateral free trade agreements, like his
predecessors Salinas and Zedillo had done. Against the spirit of openness,
Mexico was the last country to accept China's accession to the WTO in
2001–02, on the grounds that the rising manufacturing giant would eat
into Mexico's share of the US market for basic consumer goods. This
assessment was correct, as Mexico lost ground against China in the US
import market during the subsequent decade.

iv) The domestic economy level of analysis: Continued and growing
concentration of economic activity remained the norm during Fox's presidency. Any attempt to promote structural reforms along free market lines
was opposed by the PRI in Congress. Thus, telecoms continued to be dominated by Carlos Slim's Telmex monopoly and its growing international

arm, América Móvil. Due to his political weakness, Fox was also unable to touch the state energy monopolies in oil (Pemex) and electricity (CFE). The three or four largest banks in the country, owned since the Zedillo years by foreign banks including Citibank, BBVA, Santander, and HSBC, colluded to charge high fees for services while limiting very significantly access to credit for productive activity. Only the largest corporations and the government could access bank credit. Small and medium-sized enterprises were left desperate for funding, outside institutional credit channels. Lastly, visual media remained a duopoly dominated by Televisa, and to a lesser extent by TV Azteca. The broadcasters became political power brokers through their intervention, whether promotion or criticism, of parties or specific politicians in the run-up to elections. It became a truism that the 'televisoras' (the main television networks) could make or break reputations and political careers. A game of cat-and-mouse ensued: in the run-up to elections all parties—left, right, and center—doubled down to court the main media outlets by promising them campaign money through advertising to promote their parties in general and candidates in particular; advantageous legislation once they were in power; and growing government advertising business if they triumphed. In turn, after elections, all parties united to repel such promises and to try to keep the media under control. Barriers to entry in the main sectors of the domestic economy remained high and well protected by the few dominant insiders.

Conclusion

The onset and entrenchment of misplaced monopolies in Mexico was a complex process that involved political and economic factors, as well as domestic and international, intentional and unintended. The hegemony of the PRI was undermined in 1982 when the country's public finances were bankrupted by President López Portillo and his corrupt administration. His successor, President De la Madrid, was a conservative by conviction and the pitiful state of the Mexican economy enabled him to prioritize paying the country's external debt to US banks, over the basic welfare of the Mexican population. De la Madrid's main operators—young, ambitious, US-trained economists, led by Carlos Salinas de Gortari—were successful in implementing the necessary austerity policies that kept Mexico paying its foreign obligations in timely fashion and forging important links that gave them credibility with the US government and the leaders of the IMF and the World Bank. However, following this path incurred a significant political cost of losing support among the middle and working classes (and a significant number of Mexican voters passed the invoice, so to speak, to Salinas by voting for Cárdenas in the 1988 presidential election). For their part, the upper classes had stopped supporting the PRI after President López Portillo's nationalization of the banking system in 1982.

President Salinas's capacity to strengthen both himself, and the political system crafted around the hegemony of the PRI, should not be underestimated. During his first five years in power, barriers to entry were raised at the state level, while they were lowered selectively at the level of the political regime, to create an informal alliance with the PAN to enact the first wave of neoliberal restructuring. The main problem about strengthening the Mexican state the way it was done, was that it was implemented in a personalist way (everything was built with Salinas's shadow and demeanor of authority underlying it) rather than in a non-partisan, institutional way. And, of course, to that has to be added Salinas's sixth and last year in power, 1994. The Minister of Foreign Affairs under Fox, as well as activist, scholar and ubiquitous sharp commentator, Jorge G. Castañeda, titled a book about 1994 *Sorpresas te da la vida* ('Life throws surprises at you').[12] The title comes from lyrics by the Panamanian Afro-Latin musician and actor Rubén Blades, and it was directed straight at President Salinas, who considered that he had strengthened the Mexican state; engineered an economic restructuring from which he, his clan and other close associates benefited enormously, and would go on to be the first director of the WTO, US President Bill Clinton having pledged his support for him. However, after the Zapatista rebellion, the high-level political assassinations, the economic deterioration that culminated in the 'tequila crisis', and the arrest of the ex-president's elder brother, Raúl, who was charged with the murder of Ruiz Massieu and illicit enrichment, Carlos Salinas disappeared for a while and went to live in Ireland, a country with which Mexico did not have an extradition treaty.

The 'tequila' crisis empowered the continuation of privatization of state assets and, crucially, led to a mergers and acquisitions process that sold and consolidated ownership of all Mexican banks in the hands of international giants including BBVA, Citibank, Santander, and HSBC. While barriers to entry in the domestic economy remained high and all major sectors in the economy remained dominated by monopolistic or oligopolistic structures, the government under Presidents Zedillo and Fox continued opening up the international side of the country's economy, signing more free trade agreements and trying hard to 'sell Mexico' to foreign investors. In the political sphere, power was pluralized and the PRI hegemony became a subject for history books. Electoral democracy lowered barriers for non-PRI aspiring politicians and technocrats to enter and serve in the public sphere. This was a good thing, at least in the sense that prolonged concentration of power naturally corrupts those who exercise it. It was less clear if a multiparty democracy could be effective at keeping Mexico's relative social peace and political stability (enforced beforehand through authoritarian one-party rule) in place. By far the most pernicious result of the long onset and deep-rootedness of misplaced monopolies in Mexico was the fall in barriers to entry in the state sphere. During both the Zedillo and Fox presidencies, non-state actors (drug-trafficking cartels and other organized criminal groups, as well as common criminals) successfully challenged the supposed monopoly on the legitimate use of persuasion/force/coercion that an effective state should enjoy. In addition, state actors (corrupt governors, rogue police and military forces, and corrupt *caciques*) strengthened their capacity to follow their ways, against the law, and without the federal executive being able to do anything about it. This new system of fragmented authority was very different from the one under a strong center via one-party hegemonic rule. Fragmentation of authority created myriad entry points for criminals and their associates to capture or work with state authorities. Nowhere was this more clear than in the realms of drug-trafficking, kidnappings, and, incipiently, extortion. By 2004–05 the Mexican population lived in fear, as barbaric violence became commonplace, including human heads displayed in public places; bodies hung from pedestrian bridges; *narcomantas* or protest-style cloth banners hung in public spaces usually "containing threats or explanations of criminal activity"[13]; the streaming of interrogations, torture, and execution of members of some cartels by members of others on YouTube; radio stations playing *narcocorrido* songs, which glorify the deeds of kingpins and issue taunts between contending drug cartels, with increasing frequency; and television series and films obsessed with the world of 'Los Narcos' taking over public and private life. Daily life in the second half of President Fox's government became a Hobbesian state of affairs in many Mexican communities. The rest of the world started taking note too.

Notes

1 Author's interview with Cicero, 16 August 2011.
2 Ibid.
3 Author's interview with Cicero, 22 August 2011.
4 Author's interview with Cicero, 22 August 2011.
5 Carlos Fuentes, Nuevo tiempo mexicano, Mexico, Aguilar (Nuevo Siglo), 1995.
6 Arturo Alvarado, "Violence and Criminality in Mexico: an Analysis of Recent Trends," presentation at the conference "Mexico at the Crossroads: Learning from History, Facing the Future,"17–18 November,2011, Tulane University, New Orleans.
7 Gabriela Cortés, "El zar antidrogas que protegió a un capo," in *Milenio*, http://www.milenio.com/policia/zar-gutierrez-rebollo-antidroga-muere-senor-cielos-carrillo-fuentes-narcotrafico_0_211179372.html, 12 December 2013, Accessed 8 November 2017.
8 Joseph E. Stiglitz, *Globalization and its Discontents*, W.W. Norton, New York, 2002.
9 Yale Center for the Study of Globalization, https://ycsg.yale.edu/about-center-1, Accessed 8 November 2017.
10 Author's interview with Cicero, 16 August 2011.
11 Anabel Hernández, *Los señores del narco*, Mexico, Grijalbo Mondadori, 2010. According to this versión 'el Chapo' had bought off support from most authorities that ran the prison and the day that the country's Under-Secretary of Segob in charge of prisons, Jorge Tello Peón, visited the prison, 'el Chapo' went to the infirmary, was given a federal police uniform and left the place which that day was full of federal police officers.
12 Jorge G. Castañeda, *Sorpresas te da la vida: México 1994*, Mexico, Aguilar (Nuevo Siglo), 1995.
13 Wiktionary, "Narcomanta," https://en.wiktionary.org/wiki/narcomanta, Accessed 4 February 2018.

4 Looking in Vain for Exits from Misplaced Monopolies Since 2006

The levels of wealth concentration and growing inequality, barbaric violence running amok, and the problems arising from a very diminished and ineffective state, were at the forefront of a majority of Mexicans' minds, when they voted in the 2006 presidential election. From the perspective of this work, misplaced monopolies had grown and reached levels that Mexican public opinion found unacceptable, and people started protesting against them in a co-ordinated, effective way during the second half of Vicente Fox's presidency (2000–06).

The rationale for breaking the historical sequence in 2006 and starting a new chapter follows the logic of the condition of living under misplaced monopolies, in a society that can vote parties in or out of office. Since 2005–06, most public opinion surveys in Mexico have shown remarkable consistency in the ranking of citizens' main concerns: insecurity/violence, and lack of economic opportunity/dynamism have been the top two. These concerns can change places in the top ranking, but they remain by far the two most consistently identified by a significant majority of Mexicans polled.

Politicians, their advisors, and their image marketing teams heard the message and started talking about these issues and telling the citizenry that they would prioritize improvements in these areas if they were voted into public office. All political actors, including the three largest parties as well as the smaller ones that regularly participate in elections, adopted this discourse. That is why this chapter is entitled 'looking...for exits from misplaced monopolies.' The main addition, 'looking in vain...' is a judgement passed by an analyst like I am, who is observing politico-economic conditions in Mexico in 2018. Thus far, the condition of misplaced monopolies might have been altered, particularly in the area of pro-competition policies in the domestic economic sphere. But the fundamental circumstances of concentrated wealth and growing violence have continued to dominate in Mexico. Still, both Presidents Felipe Calderón and Enrique Peña Nieto were elected on platforms that promised to address these two priorities for a majority of Mexicans. The shortcomings of their management and the results they produced are the subject of this chapter.

Felipe Calderón Hinojosa (2006–12)

The Partido Acción Nacional (PAN) managed to keep the presidency after Fox's disappointing government. However, retention of the top public office did not come without costs. The PAN's candidate, Felipe Calderón, was not Vicente Fox's anointed candidate (he preferred Santiago Creel). In addition, Calderón faced an increasingly popular left-wing candidate, the former mayor of Mexico City, Andrés Manuel López Obrador, proposed by the Partido de la Revolución Democrática (PRD). The 2 July 2006 general election was the closest in recorded Mexican history. More than 41 million votes were cast. The difference between the winner (Calderón) and runner-up (López Obrador) was less than 250,000 votes (0.56 percent of the total votes cast). Such a close race opened up a Pandora's box of resistance, recrimination, measures, and countermeasures by the opposing political camps. On the night of the election Elba Esther Gordillo, the head of the Partido Revolucionario Institucional (PRI)-affiliated schoolteachers' union (the SNTE), who had distanced herself from her party and become very close to President Fox's wife, Marta Sahagún, and engineered the change in support by the Fox marriage from Creel to Calderón, appeared at Calderón's headquarters, raised his arm, and declared him the election winner in front of all the assembled national television cameras.[1]

In turn, the Federal Electoral Court did not allow a total vote recount, but an official representative random sample of around 10 percent of the ballots was tallied and the statistical calculation did not change the original result. Calderón assumed power with around one-third of the electorate believing that the election had been rigged. López Obrador mounted a resistance campaign which included taking over Mexico City's downtown with more than half a million of his followers over a period of five months (until a few days before the swearing-in of Calderón on 1 December 2006). López Obrador enacted his own parallel swearing-in ceremony, and named a cabinet.

Theatrical politics can come across as ridiculous but still be symbolically powerful. The PAN and PRI leaderships and new congressional deputies were concerned about a head-on collision. The PRD blocked access to the Congress and created a human shield around the central podium, where Calderón, according to the Constitution, had to be sworn in. Calderón had to enter Congress through the back door, and after a scuffle between his supporters and opponents, managed to make his official pledge, left Congress, and went straight to the country's principal military base (Campo Militar número 1), where he received a pledge of allegiance as Commander-in-Chief from the top brass in the armed forces.

Such a polarized beginning to a presidential term had important effects on the political and economic spheres, and how President Calderón managed them. In the political sphere, he tried to raise barriers to entry in the state (see below). An all-out 'war on drugs' was predicated in part to consolidate the president's authority; as an answer to heightened public opinion concern resulting from the growth of barbaric and visually traumatizing violence (i.e. human body parts, particularly heads displayed in public places; and You-Tube videos of torture, including decapitation) among the main organized criminal groups—the main drug cartels—vying for influence and territory; and also as an attempt to try to recentralize the weakened, fragmented power of the federal executive, which grew during the Ernesto Zedillo (1994–2000) and Vicente Fox (2000–06) presidencies. At the level of the political regime, Mexico remained a plural democracy, and parties across the political spectrum continued to win public office.

However, an ominous by-product of lower barriers to entry became the financing and backing by organized criminal groups of candidates, particularly at the local (municipal) and state levels of government. By 2010, analysts considered that more than one-third of the almost 2,500 municipalities in the country were under the control of organized criminal groups, whose main business was the narcotics trade but, increasingly, included kidnapping, extortion, and human and weapons-trafficking. In turn, the economic sphere was characterized by more continuity: at the international level, Mexico continued to support bilateral and multilateral free trade agreements; it aligned itself with the USA in supporting pro-market as opposed to state-led policies; and it tried to gain some of the lost ground against rapidly expanding Chinese exports to the USA to the detriment of Mexican products. President Calderón was more successful than his predecessor, Fox, in the implementation of modest structural reforms. Such reforms, meant to inject competition into Mexico's monopolistic/oligopolistic domestic economic structure, were symbolic rather than truly transformational. However, after more than one decade of stasis and deadlock in this area, Calderón's reforms in the energy sector of Pemex, and of the labor market to make it more flexible, paved the way for more radical pro-competition reforms (i.e. a lowering of barriers to entry) under his successor (see section below on President Peña Nieto).

In the political sphere:

i) The state level of analysis: This is the area where change was enacted most decisively during Calderón's presidency. Having come to power in a highly contested election, the new President tried to strengthen the state by recentralizing power. Calderón tried to strengthen the federal executive, first and foremost, by declaring a 'war on drugs' only 10 days after he took office. To enact this plan, Calderón used the Mexican military to a degree not seen since the 1920s. Aside from the military, the President also purged and tried to beef up the federal police. Halfway through his six years in office, more than 50,000 soldiers and police were deployed in many parts of Mexican territory pursuing organized criminal groups. However, federalism had strengthened since the Zedillo presidency, and it was not possible to rein in the power and relative autonomy of state governors. As a consequence, the country had become more complex and diverse, and much more difficult to manage and control from a single center. The general view about geographical distribution of crime and violence, and its political connections during the Calderón years, suggested that out of the 31 governors, around one-third were clean and cooperated with the federal government in fighting drug-traffickers; another third stood on the fence, and while not committed wholeheartedly to fight the drug cartels, at least tried to strike a balance between law enforcement and the proliferation of crime and violence in their states; while the remaining third of governors cooperated little with federal authorities and in several cases were corrupted by the cartels. These governors facilitated criminal operations, and amassed vast personal fortunes from the dirty money they accepted from the cartels.

Within the armed elements of the state, the rule of thumb has been that municipal police forces are the weakest and also the most likely to be in collusion with organized crime. State police forces are less weak but they have been likewise penetrated to a high degree by the criminal cartels. Likewise, the federal police has been penetrated by organized crime up to the top level, although not to the extent of the other two levels of government. In turn, in the armed forces it is reckoned that the army (Ejército Mexicano) is significantly more corrupt and has been penetrated by organized crime to a much larger degree than the navy (Armada de México).

A key element of Calderón's strategy to combat organized crime was to reach out to the US government under President George W. Bush. In 2007 both governments established cooperation through the Mérida Initiative, which within five years of its operation, starting in 2008, disbursed more than US $1,400m. in hardware, communications, logistics, training, and joint covert operations. Mexican administrations before Calderón had always been cautious and reticent in cooperating with the USA. Therefore, such close cooperation can be considered a radical change in Mexican foreign policymaking. The extent to which it helped to restore the falling barriers to entry to non-state actors who exercised growing violence and extortion against Mexican citizens with great impunity, is not as clear.

Lastly, another radical change at the state level during Calderón's presidency was the transformation of Mexico's criminal justice system. Mexico's justice system was (and on the whole remains) very different from that of the USA. The Mexican system is inquisitorial rather than adversarial; it does not contemplate the presumption of innocence (rather, a suspect has to prove his/her innocence because they are presumed guilty if they were arrested); suspects are not tried by peers in a public court of justice, but rather by prosecutors and a judge who emits a sentence in writing; all evidence and testimony are presented in writing rather than verbally. The end result has been in practice an incredibly dysfunctional system that rewards the powerful, the rich, and the influential, while disadvantaging the rest of society. Calderón and his collaborators were right in targeting this system for radical change. All parties including the PRI and the PRD supported this change, which was enacted in law in 2008. But they did not do this as a consequence of careful analysis or enlightened criticism of such a rotten system. Instead, they were pushed to address the systematic abuse of authority and prevalence of injustice that surfaced and made international headlines as a consequence of the 'war on drugs', and tarnished Mexico's reputation in the eyes of the world. As the death toll grew exponentially between 2007 and 2011, the dysfunctional ways in which individuals who were presumed guilty were mistreated or the way in which state officials (including the police, but particularly the military), got off the leash after gross violations of the basic human rights of Mexican citizens, many of whom were innocent but got caught in the extermination logic of the war on drugs, gained domestic as well as international visibility. In summary, the state might have been somewhat recentralized under President Calderón, but the means used to carry out this objective were blunt, violent, indiscriminate and, once in operation, difficult to stop.

ii) The regime level of analysis: Mexico remained an electoral democracy during the Calderón years. Power was divided and the federal executive had to negotiate with a plural opposition which was still dominated by the PRI, but with important representation also for the president's party, the PAN, the left-wing PRD and smaller parties. Calderón shown himself a more effective power broker and negotiator with the opposition than Fox had been. During his term in office, mild structural reforms (of the fiscal regime, Pemex, and labor laws) were enacted thanks to cooperation between the government and segments of the opposition. The media remained freer under Calderón, as had been the case under Fox, compared with PRI administrations. However, Calderón was less tolerant of criticism and picked public fights with media outlets that criticized his inflexibility regarding the need to introduce changes to the 'war on drugs.' The state continued to use its clout in media advertising and threats about cutting such advertising, as an effective tool to moderate or silence criticism of its actions. However, by the mid-2000s myriad new online outlets were streaming daily news on the ground; blogging; writing commentary, as well as publishing reportage. The mass communications realm was definitively transformed and any government, left, center, or right, had to deal with this new phenomenon.

In terms of parties and the party system Mexico City remained under the politico-electoral control of the PRD, but the PRI's fortunes improved after the mid-term elections of 2009, by which time a growing proportion of the electorate felt great fear and insecurity related to the war on drugs and the mounting toll of killed, wounded, kidnapped, and disappeared individuals, many of whom got caught in the crossfire of turf wars, or were mistakenly arrested by authorities, or were targeted by criminal groups or authorities because they threatened to expose collusion, corruption, impunity, and abuse.

The PRI started regrouping and planning a comeback through the power and resource capacity of its governors. In contrast, the left split, and its most visible leader, López Obrador, left the PRD and formed his own movement, the Movimiento de Regeneración Nacional (MORENA). By the end of Calderón's administration, the PAN had lost significant support after two terms in office and the PRD had split, paving the way for a return of the PRI.

iii) The international economy level of analysis: Mexico remained an exemplary emerging market during the Calderón administration. 'Exemplary' in this case means what international financial institutions (i.e. the International Monetary Fund—IMF—and the World Bank) have considered to be good policies since the 1980s: open economies to trade and capital movements, conservative fiscal and monetary policy, light regulation, secure property rights, and other such policies identified with the so-called 'Washington consensus.' This qualification is not shared by detractors of US-style globalization and other opponents of unbridled crony capitalism. The Calderón administration's toughest challenges were the Great Recession (2008–09), the SARS pandemic, which kept millions of tourists away in 2009 (tourism accounts for around 10 percent of Mexico's annual GDP), and China's market share growth in exports to the USA, which competed directly with Mexico. On the positive side, as a consequence of the runs on banks and government debt after Lehman Brothers' bankruptcy in 2008 triggered a global sell-off of risky assets, the IMF instituted a new lending instrument, which rather than helping countries with liquidity or solvency problems, was meant to be a preventive mechanism to avoid crises by extending credit lines to allow countries whose macroeconomic fundamentals were healthy to fend off attacks against their currencies. Mexico's 'exemplary,' prudent, macroeconomic management since the Zedillo government allowed the country to be the first one in the queue to receive such help. In addition, the US Treasury considered some countries as key nodes in the global financial system which had to be protected through the extension of similar preventive credit lines to avoid a major meltdown: Mexico, together with Brazil, South Korea, and Singapore, were thus given up to US $30,000m. each to defend their currencies. In all, barriers to entry remained low for Mexico in its international economic sector. This gave the country flexibility to confront external shocks, because its macroeconomic record was in tune with the international financial institutions and the US government. The shocks should not be underestimated. During the Great Recession the Mexican economy contracted by more than 6.5%. This contraction was higher than the one Mexico experienced during the 'tequila crisis' of 1994–95. None the less, low barriers to entry and orthodox economic management gave Mexico financial lifelines in the course of the 2000s which were absent in the 1980s and the 1990s.

iv) The domestic economy level of analysis: The continuation of monopolistic and oligopolistic domestic economic structures became a subject of growing public debate during the Calderón administration. Visual, print, and audio media honed in to the extraordinary fortunes amassed by the heads of these entities, both private and public, and their close associates. Public debate and criticism about an economy led by 'rentiers' grew, and spilled over from specialist to popular discourse. Carlos Slim, the wealthiest individual in the world according to *Forbes* magazine for a number of years (alternating with Bill Gates, founder of Microsoft), became the face of rentier capitalism in the internationally open Mexican economy. Good political brinksmanship by Calderón and his operatives helped him to do what Fox had been unable to do. Riding the popular wave of opposition to the great concentration of economic gains, the President managed to pass mild structural reforms (which had stalled since the second half of the Zedillo presidency) which opened up to a small degree Pemex and the labor market. None the less, pillars of Mexico's political economy such as the banks, telecoms, and the media/entertainment networks (Televisa and Azteca), remained untouched.

Enrique Peña Nieto (2012–18)

As the war on drugs took its toll and tens of thousands of Mexicans suffered violent deaths, and the economy stalled due to domestic concentration (high prices, low-quality goods) and external shocks (2000–02, 2008–10), the PRI's star regained some of its shine. Such popular reassessment of the PRI's capacity to govern had a negative rather than a positive tint. A popular phrase that spread around the country in 2010–12 was 'to fight the mafia you need the mafia.' The meaning of this phrase was straightforward to Mexicans, if not many foreigners. Early on, during the Fox presidency, the PAN had been well meaning in trying to govern according to the law, but had been ineffective. In turn, Calderón had tried to reinstall order and stability by calling the military and the police to the streets in a large offensive move, which tried to strengthen the central state. However, politico-economic dynamics were already decentralized and fragmented enough that it was not possible to restore the *status quo ante* (i.e. the years of social peace and political stability at the cost of authoritarian rule under the hegemonic PRI). With the war on drugs claiming more lives and igniting new hot spots of crime and violence during the Calderón administration, the average citizen thought that bringing back the PRI could put a lid on the Pandora's box of chaos and suffering which, in theory, the PAN had opened up through its ignorance and lack of experience in managing the dirty side of Mexican politics.

 i) The state level of analysis: Peña Nieto won the 2012 presidential election by a margin of more than 5 percent. This result meant that he was able to avoid the type of post-electoral conflict that ended up being so politically polarizing among Mexican society after the previous election in 2006. Peña Nieto and his team tried to change the general perception about the war on drugs without changing the general strategy or main tactics. This required a new mass communication strategy. The media, in particular Televisa, by far the biggest network with penetration in excess of 70 percent among Mexico's population and a key ally and source of support for Peña Nieto, helped by downgrading organized criminal stories compared to their permanently top headline status during Calderón's administration. On the one hand and beyond media manipulation, violent deaths per 100,000 inhabitants fell during the first half of Peña Nieto's term in office (although they had started falling from a high point in 2010, during Calderón's administration). On the other hand, crime and violence picked up again from 2015. During the month of October 2017, violent deaths totalled 2,371 or around 76 each day, surpassing the most lethal monthly previous high, which was back in 2010. Thus, the war on organized crime continued. Also, like Calderón and unlike Fox, Peña Nieto tried to force a recentralization of authority in what was by now a well-entrenched federalist, fragmented system of power and authority. Like Calderón, Peña Nieto did not succeed in trying to put back the lid on pluralism; multiple points of entry for influencing authority and power; and, crucially, corruption and impunity. Organized crime continued to operate with great impunity, despite the supposed 'mafia' (i.e. the PRI) coming back to power. The crucially important change in criminal justice from an inquisitorial to an adversarial system continued at a slow pace. Due to Mexico's federal framework, in 2008 states were allocated a period of time, during which they were expected to have adopted the new system by 2016. This turned out to be mere wishful thinking. Vested interests in many states blocked or slowed down the implementation of the criminal justice change so much so that toward the end of Peña Nieto's government in early 2018, less than a one-third of the 31 states (plus Mexico City) had started implementing this fundamental change in the governance of Mexican territory. In summary, barriers to entry at the state level of the political sphere during Peña Nieto's administration remained relatively low, compared with the years of hegemonic PRI rule.

ii) The regime level of analysis: Likewise, barriers to entry remained low at this level. Easier entry to contest power and become involved in institutional politics was part of a pact, the so-called 'Pacto por México,' which the Peña Nieto government enacted in order that the opposition, on both right (PAN) and left (PRD), supported his revolutionary program. Revolutionary in this sense means the formulation and implementation of wide-ranging pro-market, pro-competition structural reforms. As mentioned above, such reforms had been minimized or thwarted completely since the Zedillo administration. This was the case due to the PRI's loss of hegemony at the three levels of government, but particularly at the federal level, where nationwide legislation is passed. Peña Nieto's close operators helped to co-ordinate this broad, multiparty pact after he assumed the presidency. This pact was meant to unlock the said structural reforms which had gained broad support among a wide section of the Mexican population during the Calderón years. Even uneducated, low-skilled citizens had become aware through media and peer interaction that the Mexican economy was highly concentrated and that there were a few tycoons who dominated the main sectors of the country's economy, reaping the lion's share of wealth-generation in the country. The 'Pacto por México' brought together a broad multiparty coalition to redress this highly salient popular issue. Barriers to entry in fact continued to fall at the regime level due to the introduction of 'independent candidacies' (before that, any individual who wanted to seek public office had to do so through one of the registered national political parties). Pulling in the other direction, the Federal Electoral Institute (IFE) was transformed into the National Electoral Institute (INE). Whereas the IFE had been in charge of federal elections and each of the country's 31 states had their equivalent state electoral institutes, the reform that created the INE was intended to re-centralize the organization, execution, and assessment of elections throughout the territory in one consolidated institution. The move toward centralization was criticized as an attempt by the presidency to reassert control over elections. An even thornier issue remained the unquantified but apparently significant contribution of 'dirty money' (funds derived from the proceeds from organized crime) to elections. This issue gained public attention during the Calderón presidency but it continued to grow under Peña Nieto. In many cases, powerful criminals intimidated candidates not to run for office unless they wanted their families and themselves dead. Such intrusion of criminal elements, added to the recentralization of electoral organization, dented popular trust about the freedom and fairness of elections at the three levels of government among Mexican public opinion.

iii) The international economy level of analysis: Mexico under Peña Nieto continued to champion the open, pro-market international framework represented by Washington consensus policies. The president made sure to appoint US-educated technocrats (a PhD in economics from MIT, Chicago, Harvard, Yale or Stanford became the gold standard) to run the economy. This move simply followed what at least had come to be seen as best practice since the Salinas administration.

In fact, many of the economists who were freshly minted US Ivy League graduates in the late 1980s and early 1990s continued ascending the public service ladder, irrespective of changes in the governing party. Thus, two or three generations of such economists served, some since the years of Miguel De la Madrid (1982–88), in both PRI and then PAN administrations. This core of neoliberal technocrats, who populated the powerful Ministry of Finance in particular, the Central Bank (Banxico, which has been independent of the government since 1994), and the Office of the Presidency, ensured that Mexico's image in international capital markets remained very positive, even during downturns after the tequila crisis (1994–95) in 2000–02 and 2008–10. Likewise, on the trade front, Mexico continued being an outspoken leader of free trade integration (bilateral or multilateral), and joined both the Alianza del Pacífico group and the Trans-Pacific Partnership. Leading Mexican businessmen and technocrats continued to be part of the neoliberal global circle, attending the annual Davos conference and gatherings of the multilateral financial institutions, and thus the country continued to be seen by emerging markets analysts and investors as a relatively safe bet, thanks to its low barriers to entry and exit in its external economic sector, coupled with conservative macro-economic management. In any case, shocks to the global system created uncertainty not only for Mexico but also for many other developing as well as mature capitalist economies.

A strengthening storm globally evolved into a wave of populism that gained momentum in Europe when the electorate in the United Kingdom voted in a referendum to leave the European Union (Brexit), while several other populist movements were performing well in France, Germany, the Netherlands, Austria, the Czech Republic, Hungary, and Poland, exploiting many voters' doubts about the benefits of a global economy open to the movement of capital, goods, and people. For Mexico, the toughest test became the triumph of Donald Trump in the US presidential election of 2016. Trump promised to build a wall across the Mexico–US border; singled out Mexicans as criminals and rapists, instilling great fear among white Americans about immigration, not just of Mexicans but in general of non-whites (in what observers called a revival of white nativism); and, crucially, Trump targeted the North American Free Trade Agreement (NAFTA) for renegotiation or cancellation. Although by early 2018 none of these threats had been carried out in the radical fashion that Trump and his supporters had hoped during his election campaign, NAFTA renegotiation was underway; the Department of Homeland Security had accelerated operations through Immigration and Customs Enforcement to arrest and deport undocumented individuals; and Trump continued to energize his electoral base by orchestrating chants of "build the wall" at quintessentially populist rallies and gatherings. Such a backlash against US-style globalization that had been the norm since the Ronald Reagan presidency in the 1980s reverberated in Mexico. The most salient issue in the short term was the strengthening of populist voices who countered Trump and his supporters' racism and 'America first' rhetoric through the defense of Mexican nationalism and its supposed popular, anti-plutocratic roots (coda for opposition to policies favoured by big business and the Washington consensus). As a consequence, López Obrador and MORENA became the most influential political voice and source of collective action from below, in the run-up to the presidential election held on July 1, 2018, and which AMLO won by a landslide.

iv) The domestic economy level of analysis: NAFTA entered into force in 1994, and Mexico increasingly became, in the words of a widely quoted study by McKinsey management consultants "a two-speed economy." Big business and corporations that managed to integrate themselves into global production chains in electronics, automobiles, trucks, and aviation, for example, benefited greatly; their productivity grew like that of firms in developed capitalist countries; and their skilled employees reaped significant benefits. The result was that the Mexican rich became much richer (the so-called 'one percent,' which appears to be a transnational phenomenon, and which is more pronounced in developing, emerging market countries than in mature capitalist ones), while a middle class made up of professionals, managers and merchants also grew. In great contrast, a majority of medium and small-sized enterprises, usually run by families, as well as the 40–50 percent of Mexico's total economically active population, who work and survive in the informal economy (as well as in a shrinking subsistence, rural economy) saw their incomes, opportunities, and prospects for themselves and their descendants deteriorate from an already meagre base.

Such bifurcation of fates was not solely the responsibility of NAFTA. The middle, lower middle, and working classes, as well as the rural poor, had experienced a dramatic collapse in living standards and economic prospects since the 1982 external debt crisis, and the prolonged stabilization, austerity, and restructuring that ensued. However, a key enabling element for the bifurcation of the Mexican economy was the first wave of privatization of state-owned enterprises carried out by Presidents De la Madrid, Salinas and Zedillo. The most important elements of such reforms were formulated and implemented by Salinas. And, as seen above, such reforms led to the creation or consolidation of private monopolies or oligopolies in the major sectors of Mexico's economy. Fast forward two decades and some of the leading captains of industry in Mexico had become emblematic symbols of the growing inequality, unfair advantage, and rigged system that produced and continued to feed Mexico's two-speed economy. Thus, names such as Carlos Slim (telecoms), the richest man in the world; Emilio Azcárraga and Ricardo Salinas Pliego (media/entertainment), who manage a duopoly that can make or break reputations through advertising, news and television shows; Eugenio Garza Lagüera and Roberto Hernández, owners of the two largest Mexican banks until they were acquired by Banco Bilbao Vizcaya (BBVA) and Citibank as a consequence of the general financial bankruptcy produced by the 'tequila crisis' of 1994–95; and, of course, also public sector billionaires—bureaucrats or trade union leaders who were in charge of state monopolies such as Pemex (oil and gas), CFE (electricity), and SNTE (the national teaching union) and reaped great fortunes from grand corruption, cronyism, intimidation, and even murder. The popular impetus against the few great winners of neoliberal restructuring in the 1980s–1990s gathered steam and media exposure during the Fox presidency, but took a more political and confrontational stance only during Calderón's administration.

Such popular revulsion against the post-1982 system of growth and capital accumulation, which was built on the back of domestic monopolies and oligopolies, combined with international openness to capital and goods, created a ripe climate for a second wave of pro-market restructuring by the time Peña Nieto was campaigning to become president in 2011–12. This second wave of pro-market/competition reforms was, allegedly, more radical even than the package brought in by Salinas. However, the similarities were not just a coincidence. On the contrary, Salinas and several of his closest collaborators became the senior *consiglieri* to Peña Nieto and his team. In many cases Peña Nieto's close collaborators had worked directly under Salinas or one or other of his closest ministers. The cases of Pedro Aspe, Salinas's finance minister, and Luis Videgaray, Aspe's *protégé* and Peña Nieto's closest collaborator and financial *éminence grise* since the time Peña Nieto was governor of México state in 2005–11, and who served as Minister of Finance in 2012–16; or of Emilio Lozoya Thalmann (son of the governor of Chihuahua state, Jesús

Lozoya, in the 1950s), a close friend and collaborator of Salinas as director of ISSSTE and also Minister of Energy during his administration, and his son Emilio Lozoya Austin, head of Peña Nieto's international policy team since Peña Nieto was presidential candidate and, once elected, appointed director of Pemex in the run-up and early implementation of the energy reform which opened up the oil-and-gas market in 2013–14 to private investment in Mexico, became emblematic symbols of an older PRI leadership generation passing the baton to a younger one, albeit their policies, thinking and *modus operandi* were the same: command-and-control, public contracts to cronies. Firms like Higa, led by PRI front-men or foreign firms such as the Spanish-owned OHL, which were led in Mexico by technocrat-politicians also linked to the PRI, became the public face of cronyism, and directly stained the reputation of, at least, President Peña Nieto, his family, and Videgaray, in late 2014 due to the scandals surrounding the so-called 'Casa Blanca' (a mansion built for the First Lady by the CEO of Grupo Higa and one of Peña Nieto's favorite contractors) and the 'Casa de Malinalco' (another mansion built by the same firm for Minister of Finance Videgaray).

Since then a justified seed of distrust was sown regarding all the assets to be privatized or monopolies/oligopolies opened up during this second wave of economic liberalization in Mexico. How could society and its political representatives control the adjudication of contracts or the sale of assets without the predominance of politically connected businesses? Peña Nieto had promised to create an anti-corruption agency during his presidential campaign. He sent a bill to the Senate to reform several constitutional articles in 2013. Then, as the crony scandals hit the President and his closest collaborator, journalists and analysts started digging deeper into Peña Nieto's record as Governor of México state. The results were a great embarrassment for the administration, as it transpired that a small number of companies, led by Higa and OHL, systematically got the lion's share of public contracts in the state during Peña Nieto's tenure. Public calls for the President to accelerate the creation of the agency became more widespread and intense. The laws that finally created the Comisión Nacional Anticorrupción were enacted in 2015. However, there was no triumph to celebrate. The government dithered in passing secondary legislation to regulate how the agency would operate; it also delayed naming key personnel to staff the agency; moreover, as with the criminal justice system reform of 2008, each of the 31 states was given autonomy as to how and when to create their own anti-corruption agency.

President Peña Nieto's attitude toward criticism about his and his close colleagues' voracious appetite for enrichment led him into troubled waters. For example, there was a reassertion of control over the media, particularly general intimidation toward voices that exposed government corruption. A highly embarrassing event happened in a closed-door meeting between the President and senior Mexican captains of industry, which symbolised the close connections between political and business élites. During the meeting, Peña Nieto admonished one of the emblematic leaders of the group, Claudio

González, about his son's non-governmental organization, Mexicanos contra la Corrupción y la Impunidad, and its incessant criticism of the rampant cronyism, corruption, and impunity under the government led by Peña González[2] told the President that he was proud about the work his son and his collaborators were doing. Touché! The aftertaste of this and other episodes in which the government had tried to elbow its way through intimidation to restore an authoritarian political culture are ominous. I expect Mexican society, fully socialized in the complex and pervasive world of mainstream and social media, to push back. An easy restoration of authoritarian practices just because a sitting president wills it is not easy to achieve in Mexico. Even pro-market, conservative institutions like the US Council on Foreign Relations have come out against the voraciousness of Peña Nieto and his closest associates. An article recounts how Gerardo de Nicolás, brother of one of Peña Nieto's college roommates, manipulated the accounts of a real estate company, Desarrolladora Homex, which attracted investment from such well-known groups such as Pimpco, Bank of America, and the World Bank. The company sold around 100,000 'phantom' homes which were never built, and by 2018 faced a fraud investigation by the US Department of Justice and the Securities and Exchange Commission to the tune of US $3,000m. for fraud and criminal activity.[3] So much for Wall Street's naïve belief in Peña Nieto and the 'new PRI.'

Conclusion

Those who served in the presidencies of Felipe Calderón and Enrique Peña Nieto were keenly aware of the destructive dynamics that misplaced monopolies create. However, they did not know about this concept, which was formulated by an academic far removed from action on the ground. None the less, they are keenly aware of the main symptoms of this phenomenon—political fragmentation and the weakening of the state (and therefore Calderón's attempt to strengthen it by greatly increasing the deployment of military and police officials, by more than 50,000, to try to retake control of the public sphere, which has become overwhelmed by extreme violence) and the great and growing concentration of wealth by rentier tycoons (which led to Peña Nieto attempting to enact pro-competition policies by staging a second wave of economic liberalization).

The great paradox is that the attempts to reverse misplaced monopolies in Mexico not only did not succeed, but in important ways they actually backfired. The case of President Calderón's war on organized crime led to a fragmentation of criminal groups, which increased their number, and made the restoration of relative peace and order in the public sphere of many villages, towns and cities in Mexico much more difficult to achieve. Furthermore, the attempt, through President Peña Nieto's structural reforms, to inject competition into the Mexican domestic economic sphere has already been tainted with the favoritism, cronyism, and corruption associated with him and his associates.

In fact, calling this chapter 'looking in vain for exits' from misplaced economies probably missed the more fundamental point that looking for such exits was tainted even before these governments started actions to try to reverse the condition.

Each of these governments had *ex ante* ulterior motives which were not about reversing the main symptoms of misplaced monopolies. In the case of Calderón, his declaration of a war against organized crime was at least partly a function of the early need to legitimize and strengthen his authority in the face of severe post-electoral disorder in 2006, when around one-third of the Mexican electorate believed that the election result was fraudulent, and the winner was actually López Obrador. In turn, the case of Peña Nieto and his crusade to break up monopolies and oligopolies to inject competition into the Mexican economy was tainted by the ultimate aim he and his group—advised by the elder statesmen of the Salinas era—pursued: creating a power bloc that would enrich them; establishing a network of mutual politico-economic loyalties thanks to the monetary, influence, and power bestowed on the beneficiaries; and, if successful, making it a trans-sexenal project (i.e. ensuring that the leading players at the commanding heights of political and economic decision-making remained in post, irrespective of the six-yearly change in administration). It was the same project that Carlos Salinas and his group attempted, but failed to achieve in 1994. Could this time be different and the PRI and its allies manage to create the bridge that would allow the current generation to continue ruling, and amassing wealth, power, and influence beyond 2018? It looks unlikely in the face of AMLO's landslide presidential victory.

Notes

1 According to Cicero, President Fox disliked Felipe Calderón, and this was no secret. However, the power behind the throne was Fox's wife, Marta Sahagún. Elba Esther Gordillo convinced Sahagún that it was in her interest and Fox's to support Calderón (who had more grassroots support inside the PAN than Creel to win the presidential candidacy) because it was better to have a powerful enemy in the open who knew, and knew that other powerful figures knew, that he owed them both a big favor (the party's presidential nomination). Among other things, once Calderón became President he had to pay back the favor and, among other things, made Gordillo's son-in-law Under-Secretary of Education while allowing her to continue running the SNTE as her private fiefdom. Author's interview with Cicero, 22 August 2011.

2 Azam Ahmed, "A Scion of Mexico Fights Corruption, and Becomes a Target," in *The New York Times*, 30 August 2017, https://www.nytimes.com/2017/08/30/worl d/americas/mexico-claudio-gonzalez-laporte.html, Accessed 4 February 2018.

3 Shannon O'Neil, "Mexico's Voters Have Bigger Problems than Trump," in *Bloomberg View*, 31 January 2018, https://www.bloomberg.com/view/articles/2018-01-31/m exico-s-voters-have-bigger-problems-than-trump, Accessed 4 February 2018.

5 Why Does Mexico Experience Low Growth which is Distributed Unfairly?

The main problem that Mexico has faced since the 1990s, according to economists, has been its low relative growth, particularly compared with many large, high-growth emerging economies, at least during the 2000s (the so-called BRICS countries—Brazil, Russia, India, China, and South Africa) and other countries in South East Asia, and Central and Eastern Europe). To understand what is meant by low or mediocre growth in the Mexican context, it is possible to contrast average expansion/contraction in different periods. Such comparison is very telling, particularly when the 1950–1982 period is contrasted with the years between 1982 and 2010: between 1950 and 1982 it expanded by 3 percent on average annually; the years 1982 to 1988 saw an average annual fall of 2 percent (indeed, economists refer to the 1980s as a 'lost decade'); between 1988 and 1994 it saw average annual growth of 2 percent, while 1994 to 2000 saw lower annual average expansion of 1.6 percent. The years 2000 to 2006 saw annual average growth of 2.3 percent, while the years 2006 to 2012 saw lower annual average expansion of 1.8 percent. In total, the years of the Partido Acción Nacional (PAN) in power, between December 2000 and December 2012 saw an average expansion of GDP per capita of 2.3 percent.[1] This last figure was by no means a disaster, but it is one-third short of what was considered high growth before 1982 (albeit such high growth was bought at the price of high or very high inflation in the 1970s, 1980s, and after the 1994–95 'tequila crisis').

Scholars have offered several explanations about Mexico's sluggish growth and external vulnerabilities. Three broad perspectives can be identified. The first one can be summarized in Gordon Hanson's influential paper 'Why is Mexico not Rich?'[2] Accordingly, despite three decades of more or less following the 'Washington consensus' policies in order to achieve free markets rather than state control of production and allocation of resources, the country has had a disappointing economic growth trajectory. Hanson included both domestic and international factors to explain Mexican economic underperformance. In his words:

> Some combination of poorly functioning credit markets, distortions in the supply of non-traded inputs, and perverse incentives for informality creates a drag on productivity growth. These are factors internal to

Mexico. One possible external factor is that the country has the bad luck of exporting goods that China sells, rather than goods that China buys.[3]

Second, other scholars and analysts have concurred with all or some of the factors that Hanson proposes for the paradox of Mexico's persistently low-growth economy. However, they pay closer attention to issues related to monopolies, politico-economic collusion, and a classic political economy conflict among different groups in any society fighting for a share of the economic pie. For example, a group of scholars brought together by Santiago Levy and Michael Walton analyzed issues of equity, competition (or the lack thereof), and many of the 'perverse incentives' that have created a major drag on productivity growth for decades in Mexico. The volume that came out of that collaboration established an intellectually rigorous, credible series of yardsticks and arguments for Mexico's lackluster performance in the 1990s, 2000s, and 2010s.[4]

Three broad political economy issues and their interactions were singled out as culprits:

i unequal influence by politico-economic élites who are self-serving; the way they use their money, influence, and power is self-reinforcing, increasing inequality or at least not allowing for a more productive use of resources (capital, land, labor, knowledge);

ii the way élites have kept benefiting from high rates of return to their investments is by erecting high barriers to entry, particularly in production markets, which includes both capitalists and white collar professionals as much as blue collar workers and their trade union leaders;

iii in turn, low competition coupled with institutions designed to reward labor informality, tax avoidance, and informal protection by being close to politico-economic leaders who act as patrons and protectors of networks of extended families, communities, territorial sub-regions, and states (31 plus the capital city) given the absence of the rule of law and concomitant high rates of impunity, violence, and corruption have created a self-reinforcing logic where dominant, powerful, sectional, short-term interests and benefits trump middle-to-long-term investment that might help to spark high productivity, a wide distribution of newly created wealth, and sustained high-growth activities.

The corollary of this analysis is that this dynamic, closely associated with 'rent seeking', has created since the 1990s a system of self-reinforcing power, influence, money, and use of legal, illegal, and political institutions for self-serving purposes among Mexico's élite. The outlook for this politico-economic élite and how it has used its dominance to keep and grow its resources, power, and influence is well captured in Alberto Díaz

Cayeros's characterization of Mexico's type of 'access order' as one of 'entrenched insiders.'

Third, another school of economic thought, which is closer to classic Keynesian economics, observes Mexico's low growth and relative stagnation in several sectors as, first and foremost, a macroeconomic problem. Economists like Jaime Ros have suggested that the very conservative fiscal and monetary management of Mexico's economy since the Ernesto Zedillo government (1994–2000), with its emphasis on targeting inflation and weak stimuli, in order to raise aggregate demand, have created permanent slack and under-utilization of factors of production, constricting the possibility of sustained demand expansion and higher growth.[5] Other scholars and economists with a long trajectory in high-level public management both in the federal executive and legislative branches in Mexico who are closer to the old Partido Revolucionario Institucional (PRI) formula of a mixed economy with robust private business participation, but also leadership and resources from the state for the provision of public goods and more employment-generation capacity, echo the critique of a macroeconomic management under a Washington consensus straitjacket, which in their view has kept growth at low rates and reduced economic opportunities.[6]

I take note of the three perspectives. Each one is rigorously argued and set against systematic observation and analysis of macro- and microeconomic data. I take two elements from these different explanations for my analysis. First, focusing on the international economy dimension, the Keynesian critique pays attention to the opening of Mexico's economy since the mid-1980s (culminating in the integration of Mexico with its northern neighbors through the North American Free Trade Agreement—NAFTA); the highly orthodox fiscal and monetary policies adopted by the neoliberal economic policy making establishment, and implemented in synchronicity with economic liberalization since the mid-1980s; and the fact that this policymaking approach became the undisputed, dominant way to formulate and implement economic policy after the 'tequila crisis' of 1994–95, irrespective of which party has been in power.

Second, focusing on the domestic economy dimension, this work's emphasis on 'barriers to entry' in the political and economic spheres means that issues highlighted by Hanson and also by Levy, Walton and their collaborators such as monopolies, collusion, restrained competition, under-production, overpricing, and legal impunity for the powerful and well-connected, helps to partly validate my analysis based on the idea of misplaced monopolies (i.e. in this case a weak state in an internationally open economy to capital flows, coupled with strong, influential, and highly concentrated domestic economic sectors).

In the next subsections I observe each of the two components (international and domestic) of the economy to determine the extent to which misplaced monopolies have contributed to low growth and worsening wealth and income distribution in Mexico.

Mexico's International Economy: Neoliberal Technocrats and the NAFTA

A Neoliberal Technocracy

Many variables intervene to shape the basic characteristics of an economy (i.e. more oriented to private or public activity; more or less concentrated sectors; relatively open or closed to international markets; its neighbors; its natural as well as human-made comparative advantages, among others). A fundamental variable that is at the interface of the international and domestic sectors of any economy is the people who are in charge of the formulation and implementation of economic policy. Therefore, the question 'who runs the economy?' is crucial to understand some if not all of the fundamental characteristics of economic activity in a given country. In particular, if technocrats of a similar school of economic thought manage to stay in power for several decades, their particular way of steering the economy can end up shaping long-term growth and development that carries with it the imprint of the school of thought that they have followed. Cases of this phenomenon span the entire ideological spectrum, from the centrally planned, command economies of the Union of Soviet Socialist Republics (USSR) or China under Mao Tse Tung, to the radical free market economics implemented by the 'Chicago boys' in Chile under Gen. Augusto Pinochet or the attempts, equally radical in intention but less so in terms of actual policy, of Margaret Thatcher in the United Kingdom or Ronald Reagan in the USA in the 1980s.

For the case of Mexico, this issue is of fundamental importance to understand the radical changes the country's economy underwent before and after the mid-1980s. Between the 1940s and 1970s the commanding heights of the economy were dominated by relatively orthodox economists who nonetheless embraced the post-war Keynesian consensus of macroeconomic steering, through state intervention, as well as the ideas of development economists who believed that poor, rural, agrarian countries could modernize and become richer, urban, and industrial through strategic state protection and incentives (import substitution industrialization). As seen at the end of Chapter 2, between 1970 and 1982 Mexico experienced episodes of economic populist rule under Presidents Luis Echeverría (1970–76) and José López Portillo (1976–80), of which the major results were the growth of state bureaucracies, of state instruments to intervene in the economy, and of nationalization of firms and entire economic sectors. In 1982 the experiment of state-fuelled and -guided economic growth and development fumbled and eventually crashed. The transition from so-called nationalist to neoliberal economists in charge of steering the commanding heights of the economy took place during President Miguel De la Madrid's term in 1982–88. It was consolidated under Presidents Carlos Salinas (1988–94) and Zedillo (1994–2000), and it has cemented itself since then, irrespective of which party has been in power, at least until 2018. Continuity or change in macroeconomic policy management will remain one of the most important dividing lines in the politics of Mexico. After more than 20 years of conservative monetary and fiscal management, neoliberal technocrats, well-to-do Mexicans, the international business community, international financial institutions, and the US government support its continuity, despite its mediocre results in producing growth and formal employment. In contrast, nationalists, the progressive intelligentsia in universities, the media, and left-wing parties and movements who have joined the former leader of the Partido de la Revolución Democrática (PRD) Andrés Manuel López Obrador's call to get rid of "la mafia en el poder" (the mafia in power—the politico-economic élite that has supported and benefited exorbitantly from the continued implementation of neoliberal policies since the Salinas presidency), propose 'change.' What this change might entail is more difficult to specify than voicing the idea of change itself, which gathered growing politico-electoral support in the run-up to the 2018 presidential elections and translated into victory for AMLO and his MORENA.

Returning to the creation of the neoliberal technocratic coalition back in the 1980s, most of their members were in their late thirties and forties. They conquered power in 1988 after Carlos Salinas won the hotly contested and to many fraudulent presidential elections that year. This group of technocrats and their young acolytes, educated and socialized like them, continued serving under Presidents Zedillo, Vicente Fox (2000–06), and Felipe Calderón (2006–12). Of particular importance is that Fox and Calderón were members of the conservative PAN, but they continued to hire neoliberal technocrats, who ended up moving smoothly between the PRI and the PAN. This has tended to be the case since alternation between the two parties started in 2000. They have remained a relatively tight network who consider themselves above party loyalties. Their loyalty has been and will remain to strictly orthodox monetary and fiscal management; to keep the Mexican economy open and subject to the forces of international markets; and keep 'selling' Mexico to the international business community, international financial institutions and particularly to the US government and US private sector.

Their takeover was not indiscriminate in the sense that their presence was not widespread throughout the Mexican public bureaucracies. It mainly concentrated at the federal level of government, and in particular in the Ministry of Finance, the Central Bank (Banxico), the Ministry of the Economy, the Office of the Presidency of the Republic, and the main regulatory agencies of economic activity.

This predominance at the federal level did not rule out their prominent presence at the state level of executive power. The most notable case to date is that of Luis Videgaray, highlighted in chapter 4. A member of the PRI's Juvenile Front since his late teens in 1987, he was close to Pedro Aspe, Secretary of Finance under Salinas, earned his undergraduate degree in Economics from the prestigious Instituto Tecnológico Autónomo de México (ITAM) in Mexico City and his PhD in Economics from MIT. Having worked for Aspe in private banking, he was made state Minister of Finance by the young, incoming governor of the México state, Enrique Peña Nieto, in 2005. The rest is history. Videgaray, a prototypical member of the ITAM network, became Peña's point man, manager of his presidential campaign, powerful Minister of Finance from 2012 until 2016 and, thereafter, Minister of Foreign Affairs. His image became tarnished with corruption after news was published of the construction of a large holiday home for him and his family in Malinalco by Juan Armando Hinojosa Cantú, owner of construction firm Higa, among others, and noted for his very close links to Peña Nieto's group in power. Furthermore, Videgaray is a friend and supporter of Peña Nieto's chosen PRI presidential candidate for 2018, José Antonio Meade Kuribreña who ended in third place in those elections..

By the time President Peña Nieto assumed power in December 2012, many of the original neoliberal technocrats of the 1980s had become elder statesmen or *consiglieri* of a younger generation of technocrats who had worked under them. Some of the younger generation can trace their lineage directly to their own fathers, who were friends and close collaborators of President Salinas—such as Emilio Lozoya Austin, son of Emilio Lozoya Thalmann. The latter directed the Social Security Institute for Public Workers and was later appointed Minister of Energy under Salinas, a friend since college, and both members of the PRI family (both men's fathers were prominent PRI members). In the case of Lozoya Austin, he served as the co-ordinator for international affairs of Peña Nieto's presidential campaign, and after Peña's victory was appointed CEO of Pemex. He helped to formulate and implement the energy reform that opened up the Mexican oil sector in 2013–14, but was removed from office in 2016, and since then has faced allegations of corruption in respect of Brazilian construction giant Odebrecht which sought access to public contracts throughout Latin America.

Of great importance is the fact that the older generation has a foot in both the public and private sectors of the Mexican economy. Classic cases have been, for example, Guillermo Ortiz Martínez, the Under-Secretary at the Ministry of Finance in charge of bank privatization during the Salinas government; Minister of Finance under Zedillo; Governor of the Central Bank in 1998–2009, covering the latter Zedillo years, all of Fox's presidency, and the early part of Calderón's administration, and since then was Chairman of the largest Mexican-owned private bank, Banorte, and a director at several large Mexican firms and conglomerates. Another case is Francisco Gil Díaz, also Under-Secretary at the Ministry of Finance under Salinas; Vice-Governor of the Central Bank; CEO of Avantel telecoms; Minister of Finance under Fox, and Chairman of Spanish telecoms giant Telefónica for México and Central America.

Likewise, the younger generations have also combined working experience, power, and influence in both public and private sectors. The cases of Videgaray and of Lozoya Austin, as well as those of many other children of the original neoliberal technocracy, is telling. Many of them served under surrogate political fathers both in public service as well as private banking. They became part of a revolving door that was clearly and closely acquainted with, spoke the same language as, and shared a similar outlook for future international developments with neoliberal technocrats from many other countries. Like them, they or their predecessors had managed to conquer control of the commanding heights of their national economies, and met regularly in free market, pro-business oriented forums such as the World Economic Forum at Davos or International Monetary Fund (IMF) meetings.

In the case of Mexico, the generational change regarding steering economic policy in the public sector was handled relatively smoothly, from older to younger neoliberal technocrats. Hence, the younger technocrats came of age and took up the reins of economic policymaking gradually between the Fox and the Peña Nieto administrations. Although smooth and gradual, this generational change among top economic policymakers and their close circle was executed without a centralized master plan, but rather through a network of socialization and contacts.

The main channel that created the conditions for such a network to develop and grow was an undergraduate education at the Universidad Nacional Autónoma de México (UNAM) and later on this path was overtaken and dominated by an undergraduate at ITAM, particularly in Economics, although by no means exclusively; Applied Maths, Law, Politics, Public Accountancy, and International Relations' graduates also participated. The key has been socialization and education at this private-tuition establishment, with a strong pro-private business ethos which caters to the sons and daughters of well-to-do families, and also to bright scholarship students from deprived backgrounds. Going to ITAM did not guarantee belonging to this network. Students from other top universities such as UNAM, El Colegio de México, and the Instituto Tecnológico y de Estudios Superiores de Monterrey, known as Tec de Monterrey, could also be part of the network.

The likelihood of success to become part of the network and help to colonize the commanding heights of economic policymaking and management increased significantly if an individual went on to pursue postgraduate studies, first and foremost, at an Ivy League university in the USA. MIT, Chicago, Harvard, Stanford, Yale and Princeton dominated, although other major universities in the USA and the United Kingdom were also respected. The gold standard was rather convoluted: a BA in Economics from ITAM, coupled with a BA in Law from UNAM, and followed by a PhD in Economics from MIT or Chicago University. Such a gold standard was derived from the trajectory followed by notable technocratic leaders such as Jesús Reyes Heroles González Garza, who aside from being the son of one of the most respected intellectual leaders of the PRI during its years of hegemony, followed this educational path and ended up serving as Minster of Energy, Mexican Ambassador to the USA, CEO of Pemex and *éminence grise* of the PRI. Jesús Reyes Heroles, Jr, is also a perfect example of the bridging role that neoliberal technocrats played when the PRI was thrown out of office and the PAN took over in December 2000. Hence, Reyes Heroles opposed the

PRI's presidential candidate for 2006, Roberto Madrazo Pintado, and supported the PAN's Calderón, who won that fiercely and controversial election. As a consequence, Reyes Heroles was made CEO of Pemex in late 2006 until 2009. Younger technocrats who followed in the footsteps of Reyes Heroles are, for example, Lozoya Austin, who studied Economics at ITAM and Law at UNAM (although he did not do a PhD) and José Antonio Meade Kuribreña, 2018 presidential candidate for the PRI, who studied the same two undergraduate degrees at the same universities, and then went on to do a PhD in Economics at Yale University.

The case of Meade Kuribreña illustrates clearly the continuity of neoliberal technocratic economic policy management between both PRI and PAN governments. Meade, whose father was a PRI member, and whose maternal great-uncle was one of the founders of the PAN, worked in financial regulatory agencies under PRI administrations in the 1990s and then went to the Ministry of Finance and was director of the state bank Banrural under President Fox of the PAN. Under President Calderón, also of the PAN, he served at the Ministry of Finance and became Minister of Energy, then Minister of Finance and later Minister of Foreign Affairs. When the PRI returned to power under President Peña Nieto in December 2012, Meade was asked to stay as Minister of Foreign Affairs. In 2015 he became Minister of Social Development and in 2016 Minister of Finance. In November, 2017 he resigned the ministry and became the PRI's presidential candidate for the election in July 2018. Having had no party affiliation until then, he joined the PRI in December 2017 in order to contend the 2018 elections.

Whether the PRI or the PAN is in power, the technocrats who belong to the ITAM network (known deprecatingly as 'the ITAM mafia' in Mexico) consolidated their hegemony of the commanding heights of the country's economy. However, the Mexican political class that has been in power since the alternation that brought the PAN to power and then swung back in 2012 to the PRI is not necessarily just affiliated by schooling and service under De la Madrid or Salinas presidencies. Many politicians and top public servants are second-, third-, or fourth-generation members of prominent local, state-level, or national families who have dominated politics and business throughout Mexico since the end of the Mexican Revolution.[7]

Perhaps the only real challenge to their dominance will be the victory by the left led by López Obrador, although his Movimiento de Regeneración Nacional (MORENA) is very broad and inclusive, and has gained the adherence of members of the three main parties, including technocrats. Otherwise, what Mexicans also call 'the PRI-PANato' or 'PRIAN' (i.e. the years since the top leadership of both parties started collaborating to implement economic liberalization in Mexico during Salinas's presidency since the end of 1988) gathers credence, at least in the broad area of economic policy orientation, not necessarily in areas devoted to law and order, security or broader social issues, where, nonetheless, younger members of influential, powerful families close to the summit of politics for generations continue to dominate the public sector.

Of course, ideas, however strongly held by widely dispersed or concentrated networks of individuals or groups, cannot guarantee on their own that an economic policy trajectory (or policy in other spheres of public affairs) will automatically be followed. The neoliberals' triumph in Mexico was part of a much larger change in material interests and ideas around the world as a consequence of the end of the Cold War, the defeat of 'real socialism,' in eastern Europe and the triumph of 'free market' American capitalism. This global change produced a systematic realignment of international institutions, regimes, and the world order in general. In economic policy all developing capitalist countries plus the new countries that had been ruled by centralized planning were told to adopt liberal democratic regimes in the political sphere and relatively free markets in the economic one. International financial institutions like the IMF and the World Bank, led by Washington, DC, rewarded those countries that followed this route while they dithered or penalized those that did not.

Therefore, political and economic decision-makers from Latin America to Central and Eastern Europe or from Africa to the Far East (after the 1997–98 Asian financial crisis) were influenced and limited in the scope of policies that could be implemented, not just by their preconceptions, training, and regular interactions with like-minded colleagues. The operation of the international economy itself followed the 'Washington consensus' ideas. International bureaucracies, overseen by successive US governments, nudged or in some cases forced (through extension or withholding of credit lines) the 'emerging' capitalist countries to follow the neoliberal model of capitalist growth.

Hence, specific policies that were part of the neoliberal model such as open capital accounts allowed 'hot money' (i.e. short-term financial inflows/outflows) to reward 'emerging' economies that followed conservative macroeconomic management while punishing, by exiting, those that defied the tenets of the Washington consensus. As a consequence, leading public economic policy technocrats in Mexico, as well as Russia, Turkey, Brazil, Thailand, and South Korea, faced similar constraints and opportunities. There was a general bias against pro-active fiscal and monetary policy management, which meant that even when countries were suffering a slowdown or a downright crisis, they were advised against, for example, running fiscal deficits or cutting interest rates to spur domestic demand.

Free market ideas had been circulating in universities, academic conferences, and policy circles since the 1960s and early 1970s as critiques to the Keynesian post-Second World War consensus that consolidated welfare states in most of the advanced capitalist economies. New generations of social scientists, many of them nationals from developing or poor countries doing postgraduate education at top American universities, were educated and socialized under this broad critique of state-oriented growth and protection. And once 'middle road' approaches that still relied significantly on the state (like Latin American or Asian countries) suffered severe financial-economic crisis, in addition to the fall of centralized planning and command economies (in the USSR, Central and Eastern Europe, Central Asia and South East Asia), a new global alignment was reinforced that combined ideas, institutions, decision-making power and allocation of resources with a pro-Washington consensus bias. From this perspective, Mexico was part of this broader, global phenomenon, rather than an outlier trying to forge a new economic policy trajectory.

Mexico's Economic Integration with North America through NAFTA

At the beginning of the 1990s, economists expected sustained high growth and development in Mexico for a variety of reasons. One of the most important reasons highlighted was the coming integration of the Mexican economy with those of the USA and Canada through NAFTA.

It was sensible to assume that Mexico's integration with bigger, more modern and dynamic economies would spur its own growth. The main proponents of NAFTA used the basic idea of comparative advantage to sell the project to their citizens. Accordingly, whereby the more advanced countries (the USA and Canada) would provide knowledge and capital, and the poorer (Mexico) would provide labor, the end result would be mutual gains. This is not the place to do a detailed study about NAFTA and its impacts. The main conclusions are, first, that NAFTA helped to integrate the three countries by raising significantly trade among them. Second, that there were winners and losers in the three countries— for example, workers in the automobile industry in Canada and the USA lost ground, while those in Mexico won and continued growing; or farmers in the USA won and small farmers and peasants in Mexico lost ground. Third, and very important, for long-term prospects of growth in Mexico, NAFTA led to a closer synchronization of the business cycles of the member countries, led by the largest economy, that of the USA.

GDP growth data since the early 1980s suggests that such synchronization predates NAFTA and is probably the result of the economic pull—with or without a free trade agreement—that the USA exercises on its smaller neighbors. In fact, the Canadian economy tracks the USA more closely than Mexico. However, the synchronization of the three countries' growth trajectories became stronger in the course of the late 1990s, and has been like this ever since. A fall in growth for the USA since then has meant a fall in growth in both Mexico and Canada. Two observations are important to understand some of the main political economy consequences of NAFTA integration for Mexico, at least in terms of general economic growth.

First, close synchronization was not always the case. For example, Mexico's economy took a nosedive in 1985–87, while the USA remained stable until 1988–89. Likewise, Mexico's economy grew and did well during the US slowdown and recession of the early 1990s. Second, growth variation is much more apparent in Mexico compared with the USA and Canada. The crux of the matter is that Mexico's trajectory continues to resemble more the boom-and-bust trajectories associated with many developing rather than mature, capitalist economies. Such greater variation has been associated with developing countries' states weaker capacity to implement countercyclical economic policies than the states of mature capitalist countries. The end result is that Mexico's good and bad economic times are tightly linked to US economic performance, and also that Mexico's economic results (during both upswings and downswings) are clearly more pronounced than those of the USA or Canada.

During both upswings and downswings, Mexican élites have done better, while the bulk of the country's population, i.e. middle classes, organized working classes, informal workers, have done worse. This is due to the élites' more diversified wealth portfolio, which includes not just cash, as with a majority of the uneducated and poor, but also securities, land, luxury durable goods, and foreign investments. Mexican élites usually have bank accounts in the USA and in European countries such as Switzerland. Therefore, the proportion of wealth they keep abroad is not affected by Mexican crises. In fact, inasmuch as the Mexican currency devalues as a consequence of a crisis, they make net gains through all their foreign-denominated currency investments. Likewise, the price of assets such as land, real estate, and some luxury durable goods like jewels, paintings, or vintage wines tend to depreciate significantly less than paper currency during a devaluation. Because the Mexican rich possess much more of these effective means for the storage of value than the non-rich, they have tended to be better cushioned than the great majority of households, where cash and maybe a real estate investment, which is also used to live in, predominate.

Since the 1980s Mexico has suffered four dramatic economic crises: 1982–83; 1986–87; 1994–95; and 2008–09. In addition, Mexico also suffered a recession in 2001–02, which followed the so-called 'dot.com' bubble on US stock markets after irrational gains for internet-based start-ups in the second half of the 1990s, and which burst in the course of 1999 and 2000. Since 2012, the Mexican economy has grown at lower rates year on year. A particularly negative factor for the economy's growth prospects was the weakening experienced after 2015 as a consequence of the collapse of international oil prices (starting in the second half of 2014) which remain of crucial importance for the Mexican government and its capacity to stimulate the economy, because oil foreign earnings have represented between 30–40 percent of annual federal budget revenue.

In total, tying the Mexican economic wagon to its northern neighbors did not ameliorate its business cycles. It might in fact have exacerbated both the good and the bad times. This is illustrated by the US recessions of 2001–02 and 2008–09. In both episodes, the rate of growth contraction was far higher in Mexico than in the USA. Such tight economic integration with the USA also helps to explain Mexico's continued vulnerability to external shocks, even in the absence of domestic macroeconomic imbalances (like the recessions of 2001–02 and 2008–09) or the entry of China to the World Trade Organization (WTO) in 2001, and the loss of market share for Mexican goods in the US consumer market to Chinese competitors. For Mexico, the US consumer market is not only the largest in the world, but also the final destination of 70–80 percent of its total annual exports. It is no mere figure of speech to say that when the US economy catches a bad cold, Mexico succumbs to pneumonia.

On the positive side, economic liberalization through integration with the USA and Canada in the 1990s changed conditions on the ground, helped to restructure the country's economy, and provided new opportunities to modernize and grow in some sectors of the Mexican economy. Thus, while in the early and mid-1980s around 80 percent of the country's exports were oil, by the 2010s, although crucially important for public finances and therefore state spending capacity, oil represented less than 20 percent of total exports. Mexico thus avoided the curse of becoming a petro-state like Venezuela or Ecuador. Likewise, Mexico started from a meagre base of manufacturing exports, whereby all the components of a manufactured good came from abroad (and were therefore imports), and Mexico just added value by having its workers assemble or put together the finished goods for overseas sale (these accounted as exports). These so-called *maquiladoras*, which started operating along the Mexico-US border in the 1960s and then experienced a massive boom as a consequence of NAFTA, increased and became more sophisticated. Starting in sectors of cheap re-exports such as basic apparel and textiles, they grew to include sophisticated goods such as autos and auto parts, microelectronics, durables (from refrigerators and plasma televisions to cellular phones), medical and industrial equipment, and aviation.

Of particular importance was that at the beginning of the NAFTA years, all the inputs and components except for the final assembly of a good for re-export came from abroad (usually the USA). Therefore, whereas in the 1990s Mexico added only around 1–10 percent of value (equivalent to the manual labor of assembling a final good), by the 2010s, Mexico was adding around 30–40 percent of value to final goods for re-export. This change suggested that Mexican producers of intermediate goods (suppliers of raw materials; transformation into usable components of a given good; design of the good itself) had managed to start operating, and had inserted themselves in the long supply chains of sophisticated manufacturing, and as a result were creating formal, well-paid employment, particularly for highly educated Mexicans.

For example, the world started taking notice of Mexico becoming a major player in the global auto industry in the course of the 2000s. Of course, all the brands of automobiles, pickup trucks, SUVs, and other types of auto-transportation that Mexico exported were foreign (i.e. mainly US, Japanese and German brands). The point highlighted in Mexico's favor was that a growing percentage of inputs or components of such automobiles were sourced from Mexico itself, not from abroad as had previously been the case. It is no coincidence that high-growth states in Mexico in the last two or three decades like Querétaro, Aguascalientes, Guanajuato, Nuevo León, and

Coahuila are tightly connected to the global auto supply chain. Some of these states have experienced growth spurs of 8–10 percent average annual expansion during two or three consecutive years since the 1990s. The explanation for such high growth, which matches or surpasses that of many star developing countries like the BRICS during the 2000s, is that it is closely connected with the process of foreign auto brands setting up assembly plants in these states and the parallel growth in time, in such states, of input and component suppliers located close to them, usually in the same state. The end result: growth in highly paid formal, skilled employment which contributes economically to growth, politically to relative stability, and socially to the growth of the middle classes.

On the negative side, a Mexican sector that was badly hit through integration via NAFTA was subsistence agriculture. In particular, corn and bean subsistence producers were squashed by stronger, more efficient US producers. More than three million Mexicans were displaced by this process. US farmers had on their side a capital-intensive system of large holding agriculture lubricated by generous annual federal government subsidies. The Mexican subsistence farmers had nothing to resist with. In a majority of cases, resistance took the form of emigration from the countryside to cities in Mexico, but more likely, to the USA, in search of employment and a livelihood for these rural families.

Emigration to the USA by Mexicans has been a constant since the latter part of the 19th century. This is a huge issue, with myriad implications. As of 2018, more than 10 percent of Mexico's 120 million-plus population live in the USA. The second largest city inhabited by Mexicans is not in the country's territory but in the USA: Los Angeles. When taking into account second-, third- and fourth-generation US citizens of Mexican descent, their number is more than 20 million. Their presence, although scattered throughout the USA, is concentrated in the two largest states (by size of economy and population) of the Union: California and Texas. Of all individuals without migratory documents in the USA, between half and two-thirds are Mexican.

For the purposes of this work, the point that has to be highlighted is that spikes in mass migration to the USA from Mexico has been driven, by and large, by national crises (the Mexican Revolution; the lost decade of the 1980s; the 'tequila crisis' of 1994–95; the opening of basic staple agriculture to US farmers in the 2000s) or by the relatively constant pull of labor demand in the USA (agricultural workers during the Second World War and until the 1960s through the Bracero program and, since then, informally and more or less constantly in agriculture and accompanied by high growth in construction and general services). Poorer, low-growth states in Mexico have traditionally seen more inhabitants migrate to the USA. However, these are not just mainly rural, agriculture-based states. Among these, states like Oaxaca and Michoacán have traditionally had a large subsistence agriculture population, and also high rates of migration to the USA. But, Zacatecas, whose economy is based on mining in otherwise poor agricultural soils, has likewise experienced high migration to the USA.

Protection for basic staples like corn and beans remained after the implementation of NAFTA, and was gradually reduced. Therefore, there was not a sudden exodus of small subsistence farmers from the Mexican countryside to the cities or to the USA. Or at least not directly linked to the beginning of NAFTA implementation on 1 January 1994. As seen in Chapter 3, that year was atypical inasmuch as Mexico suffered political and economic stress that led to the 'tequila crisis' at the end of that year. The systemic crisis of that year was responsible for the growth in flow of Mexican migrants, from the countryside as well as the cities, to the USA. Subsistence farmers exited the Mexican countryside for the USA at higher rates in the course of the 2000s, as protection for their production faded and subsidized US grains flooded the Mexican market.

As mentioned above, the most significant factor for Mexican migration to the USA has been the more or less constant pull of American demand for cheap labor. Therefore, the 2007–09 financial crisis, which started in the US real estate sector and then spread and grew into the global Great Recession, weakened the pull and as a consequence migration rates dropped very significantly. This is not a linear process. The return of dynamism and sustained growth in the USA could very well strengthen the pull factor again. The push factor, of course, is the sluggish Mexican economy (and those of most Central American and Caribbean countries, as well as some South American ones) or even if these economies are not sluggish, the distribution of income and wealth that they produce is highly unequal, leaving a majority of able-bodied individuals of working age without a chance to get jobs that allow them to provide for themselves and their families.

Regarding the way that the Great Recession hit Mexican and more broadly Latin American workers in the USA, remittances from these workers to their families back in their countries of origin started falling in the second half of 2007. This was more than a year before the collapse of Lehman Brothers bank and the subsequent global credit freeze that engulfed the world in mid-September 2008. Mexicans and individuals from other countries who are undocumented and work in the USA are overrepresented in sectors such as construction, landscaping, and other related activities in that sector. Therefore, as the US housing market imploded, workers and investors in that sector were like the canary in the coal mine, anticipating the deeper, longer financial explosion that spread around the world a year later. To all intents and purposes, immigration officers, analysts and advocates saw a very significant fall in people trying to cross the Mexico-US border without documents in 2009–10.

The global economy's slow and erratic recuperation from such a shock, while not as bad in the USA as in, say, Europe, meant that the pull factor for demand for cheap labor in the USA deaccelerated across the board. As a consequence, since around 2010, immigration policy and law enforcement experts noticed significantly lower numbers of Mexicans trying to cross into the USA without papers in search of work. For several years, the net number of Mexican migrants returning to Mexico has been slightly higher than those trying to go to the USA in search of work.[8]

Mexico's Domestic Economy: Concentrated Wealth, a Weak State, and the Prevalence of Poverty and Inequality

Archaeological and historical records show, as pointed out in Chapter 2, that the territory that today is Mexico has been characterized by great socio-economic and political inequality for millennia. Such high levels of inequality and material deprivation (poverty) for the majority have been the norm across space and time, according to long-run historical studies. Therefore Mexico is not necessarily distinctive. Changes from more to less inequality among human groups and societies have, accordingly, been exceptions rather than the norm—and usually as a result of violent change such as global wars, revolutions, state collapse, and health pandemics.[9]

Mexico was not a significant participant in either of the two World Wars of the 20th century. But the country did experience a prolonged revolution (1910–20) that led to state collapse which, in turn, was compounded by the 'Spanish flu' pandemic of 1918. Therefore, it might not have been just a coincidence that barriers to entry into the political and economic spheres fell as a consequence of such major disruptions. The best evidence for the formal establishment of such lower barriers to entry was, as mentioned in Chapter 2, the 1917 Constitution and its progressive aspirations regarding education, land tenure, and working conditions and remuneration for organized workers. However, this state of affairs changed once peace was re-established and a new regime and state built in the course of the 1920s and 1930s. As recounted in Chapter 2, access to political and economic opportunities were reduced or, in other words, barriers to entry were raised again as the PNR-PRM-PRI matured, its grasp on power was consolidated, and it ended up creating a political regime based on the rule of a hegemonic party.

The main implication for the domestic economy was that barriers to entry fell for those who were connected to the regime through the PRI's main sectors: organized workers, organized peasants, and organized public sector employees (including doctors and teachers). Likewise, capitalists (domestic and foreign) who had an informal working relationship with PRI leaders had access to state support—from trade barriers that protected domestic producers to licenses to operate; from subsidized credit to guaranteed prices for their goods. In contrast, those who were not connected to the PRI or defied its monopoly on the exercise of power faced not only higher barriers to entry in both the economic and political sphere, but also, potentially, baiting, harassment, incarceration or, in extremis, disappearance.

From this perspective, violence or the threat of its use, even if applied selectively and with relative restraint (compared to, say, many military dictatorships in South American countries) was the ultimate tool used to arbitrate the barriers to entry for participation in politics and the economy. And because the establishment of these barriers was decided in respect of individuals and groups' relationship with the PRI, Mexico was carved into a society characterized by insiders (relatively few individuals and groups, from very poor peasants to major captains of industry and bankers, who were close to or were members of the PRI) and outsiders (the majority of Mexicans who were not, but whose livelihood improved on average at least between the 1940s and the 1970s, during which period the country's economy posted sustained high growth rates and monetary stability—although the latter was lost in the course of the 1970s).

Concentrated Wealth in the Very Few

By 2015 Mexico was home to the richest individual in the world—the telecoms tycoon Carlos Slim— while more than 53 million individuals (45 percent of the total population) lived in poverty. The four richest Mexican billionaires[10] controlled the same amount of wealth as the 20 million poorest Mexicans. Mexico had 16 billionaires at the time. Their average wealth in 2015 grew by around 5.5 percent, while the country's gross domestic product (GDP) expanded by less than 2 percent. The richest 10 percent of Mexicans owned 64 percent of the country's wealth.[11]

These statistics put Mexico among the top quartile of the most unequal societies in the world. Widespread poverty continues to pass down from generation to generation, just as extreme wealth continues to concentrate among the same few families, with only a few new more millionaires joining their ranks. The high rate of relative wealth accumulation among the few, and the weakness of 'trickle down' mechanisms are the main factors why Mexico is so unequal, and almost half of the population lives in poverty despite the country being around the 15th largest economy in the world in terms of GDP.

The weakness of 'trickle down' mechanisms is the product of many factors, but the most important can be summarized: i) the taxation system (where taxes on consumption rather than income and/or wealth predominate); ii) the inordinate influence that the very rich have over politics to get favorable policies that in turn secure and strengthen their wealth and influence (a phenomenon known as 'political' or 'state capture'); and iii) the systematic exclusion of certain population groups, first and foremost the Amerindian or indigenous nations, from channels of wealth and income generation (poverty incidence among indigenous groups is four times as high as among the non-indigenous population).[12]

How unique is the great concentration of wealth in very few individuals in Mexico compared to the rest of the world? Sadly it is not unique at all, which in any case should not be a source of great consolation. Several issues can help to place Mexico in comparative perspective. First, Mexico is a country in the most unequal region of the world, namely, Latin America.[13]Historical factors associated with colonial history and institutions, racial inequality, state capture by élites, low investment in public goods such as education, sanitation, health and infrastructure, corruption, lack of public transparency and accountability, among others, have been proposed to explain the persistence of great inequality in this region.

Second, a variety of so-called conditional cash transfers (CCTs), created in Latin America in the first place in the course of the 1990s, and shown to have helped to reduce inequality in different regions of the world, including in Latin America, have helped to reduce the extreme inequality seen during the 1980s 'lost decade' and the 1990s 'neoliberal restructuring.' Such reduction in inequality, which is not seen as a silver bullet that could solve the problem of poverty and inequality once and for all, but at least has shown statistically significant effects in reducing the transmission of poverty from one generation to the next by, for example, making babies and young children healthier through basic universal vaccination and later keeping them as children and teenagers longer in school (rather than dropping out and being forced to work), has given hope to international financial institutions such as the World Bank, about the potential to stop the semi-automatic transmission and reproduction of poverty and inequality in developing countries.[14]

Third, high growth *per se* can simply lead to more inequality, particularly in contexts where élites have managed to capture politics and the state in a way that they manage to keep getting an exorbitant slice of the growing economic pie at the expense of the middle, the working, and the underclasses. Numerous studies have shown that high growth in several countries in Latin America that are dependent on exports of raw materials, led to some reduction in poverty and inequality in the 2000s. In particular, the attention of scholars and international policy analysts at international financial institutions became focused on the growth of the middle classes. According to some reports, the middle class doubled in size in the course of the 2000s. Thus, of the roughly 600 million individuals who inhabit this region, around 90 million were considered middle class in 2000, while 186 million had achieved that status by 2008.[15]

Still, the perspective of international financial institutions was cautious. The World Bank and the Inter-American Development Bank included in the new middle classes households that earned between US $4–5 and $10–12 a day. They considered this emergent middle class as 'precarious.' This judgement had to do with the fact that the amounts that defined the threshold were quite low and therefore easily subject to being wiped out if the sustained spur of high growth was reversed, in which case many of these households could fall back into poverty.[16] This is exactly what happened after the global financial meltdown in 2008–09 and then, in a more sustained fashion, set in as the so-called super-cycle of high commodity prices led to lower prices for raw materials from 2012–13, due to global factors such as China's economic slowdown; the prolonged debt crisis in the European Union, particularly Eurozone countries' since 2010–11; erratic and only mild recovery in the USA and other English-speaking countries; continuation of stasis in Japan since the 1990s; and lower growth and demand for goods from oil-producing countries in the Middle East and North Africa.

Fourth and last, Mexico is in no way the only country that has experienced high inequality and poverty. Recent analyses of data for most of the world have shown that, on average, inequality fell, particularly in advanced capitalist and communist countries between the end of the Second World War and the 1970s. However, since around 1980, inequality has grown throughout the world. For example, the work of Thomas Piketty, *Capital in the Twenty-first Century*, helped to popularize and in a way politicize this type of highly technical research.[17] According to this research, which has grown in importance and output across the world[18], the type of inequality associated with the years since the 1980s seems to be characterized by its accelerated growth among the top earners and richest people in the world. This means that as an analyst observes different income distributions in many countries around the world, the higher in the socio-economic pyramid one observes, the higher the shares of income the people closest to the apex of the pyramid manage to capture. Thus, among the richest 1 percent in countries like the USA and the UK, economists who study inequality have observed that income accumulation grows exponentially toward the top of the pyramid distribution. In contrast, income has remained relatively constant or has grown at low annual rates for everybody below the top decile (the richest 10 percent). Something similar has happened in Mexico where billionaires' wealth since the 2000s has multiplied by around 5 percent annually (and from a very high base as the fortunes of the wealthiest Mexicans amount to billions of dollars) whereas general GDP has grown less than 2 percent annually (and off a low base as the average annual Mexican income is less than $10,000).

Wealth Concentration Intimately Linked to Politics and the State

Most of the great fortunes created in Mexico since the mid-20th century are intimately tied to politics and the state in terms of their genesis, growth, and consolidation. During the years of hegemonic PRI rule, leaders from such diverse groups such as peasants, industrial workers, bankers, and captains of industry were able to amass fortunes through patronage bestowed on them by party leaders and successive PRI governments. The process entailed a *quid pro quo* whereby the leaders of these different socioeconomic groups controlled the rank-and-file in their areas of production, and pledged support to the continuation of the PRI in power. In exchange, successive PRI governments raised barriers to entry into the political and economic spheres in order that such leaders of the different sectors of the Mexican economy enjoyed monopolistic or oligopolistic power and monetary profits: they and their close associates got favorable treatment through legislation, representation through the PRI in public office, government licenses, permits and procurement, as well as an array of policies meant to keep them as the party's loyal clientele.

The law was used as an instrument of domination rather than the means to dispense justice. Authorities followed the execution of the law in a discretionary fashion, and the closer a person or group was to the PRI and its widespread networks, the higher the likelihood that they would not have to face penalties or just punishment if and when they violated the law. The opposite happened to those who questioned or opposed openly the rule of the PRI. Those who championed PRI domination through their factions inside the party could in some cases literally get away with murder (from the Tlatelolco and Corpus Christi student massacres of 1968-71, to the murder of hundreds of PRD members and sympathizers during the Salinas years, to the assassination of presidential candidate Luis Donaldo Colosio in March 1994). A case where justice caught up with one PRI grandee was the arrest of Raúl Salinas de Gortari, older brother of the then former President Carlos, for the murder of his former brother-in-law, Secretary-General of the PRI and would-be majority leader in the Chamber of Deputies, Francisco Ruiz Massieu. However, in that case justice 'catching up' and dispensing punishment was not impersonal, but rather a political move by President Zedillo to assert his authority soon after he assumed office and had to shake off the shadow of former President Salinas, the figure who, in the words of a historian close to Salinas's open markets philosophy, was called "the man who wanted to be King."[19]

The symbiotic relationship between the hegemonic party regime and its clients created a culture of everyday practices characterized by corruption, miscarriage of justice, impunity for the powerful and well-connected, and crony capitalism. The top echelons of each government, starting with the President himself and his close associates, used these practices to keep political stability, social control, and to amass personal fortunes. Many at the top of public affairs used frontmen to hide their ill-gotten gains, and many of these frontmen in turn became members of the club of the richest individuals and families in Mexico.

For the purpose of this analysis, it is therefore important to acknowledge that the practices of a corrupt state and crony capitalism predated the period of the lost decade (1980s) and neoliberal restructuring (1990s). There were, nonetheless, important differences between the type of collusion, cronyism, and selective benefits that operated during the high years of PRI hegemony (between the 1940s and the 1987–88 economic bust) and the subsequent neoliberal era.

The creation of new millionaires and billionaires during the years of neoliberal policy orientation happened more quickly, and more deeply, and has resulted in a process of incredible capital accumulation in the hands of very few individuals and families, which is perhaps unmatched since the *Porfiriato* (1876–1911). The two major waves of privatization identified in Chapter 3 (in particular the Salinas government) and Chapter 4 (the Peña Nieto government) lie at the heart of such outcomes. The Salinas years (1988–94) were unique because, among other factors, significant amounts of productive activity had been nationalized during the Echeverría (1970–76) and López Portillo (1976–82) governments, therefore leaving such significant amounts of national economic production open to the possibility of privatization.

The Banking Sector

Of paramount importance was the privatization of the banking industry (18 banks) which López Portillo nationalized in 1982 and Salinas privatized between mid-1991 and mid-1992. New banks were also allowed to form and operate (19 were created). The importance of this privatization process lies in the fact that the system of savings and credit creation and allocation is central to the functioning of modern economies. There is also a symbolic element, inasmuch as investment confidence is tied to a variety of elements, but one of the main ones is the quality and capacity of a country's financial sector.

In Mexico, the Salinas government sought to maximize the selling price of these assets. The rationale was that the Mexican state had to be recapitalized to pay off its crippling foreign debt, as well as to provide resources for public investment to kick-start economic growth after seven years of crisis and austerity. The rationale for selling all the banks in such a short period of time was that the authorities did not want to give economic and commercial advantages to the banks that were privatized first, while others remained in the hands of the state.[20]

While understandable, such rationales created perverse incentives and led to unintended consequences. Prioritizing and choosing the highest bids when the banks were auctioned meant that the businessmen who won these bids ended up facing large liabilities. In fact, the state lent them money through public banks like Nacional Financiera (NAFIN) in order that they could make large bids. Most of the businessmen who bought the banks already owned other businesses. The sale of the banks allowed them to create conglomerates made up by a variety of firms such as construction firms, hotels, mining, retail and other services. The newly privatized banks became the providers of credit for these other businesses. In effect, many of the new bankers started loaning themselves big amounts of credit to capitalize these other businesses, in order to force them to pay back, among other things, the high cost of acquiring a bank in the first place. A majority of the individuals and business group who acquired banks had close connections to President Salinas, his family, and many of his close collaborators.[21]

Aside from being a notorious example of cronyism banking privatization contributed to the collapse of the Mexican economy in 1994–95. A lax, ineffective regulatory system, deregulated in 1991 (for example, the new system included unlimited liability guarantees by the state—a recipe for moral hazard), was unable to identify the large amounts in soft loans that the government lent to the bankers, and that the bankers lent to themselves and their close business associates, and by 1996, after the disorderly currency devaluation of December 1994, ended up in more than 52 percent of all outstanding loans in the economy as non-performing loans—which meant that there were more unpayable than payable loans in the Mexican economy.[22]

The government of President Zedillo (1994–2000), with the support of the US government and the international financial institutions, bailed out the banks in particular and the Mexican economy in general. Bailing out the bankers was very unpopular. Their liabilities were subsumed under a fund, FOBAPROA, later renamed IPAB, which became the political target of all left-wing forces, many groups inside the PRI itself, and some members of the PAN. The bailout of the entire economy amounted to close to 20 percent of Mexico's GDP. The economy contracted more in 1995 than in either 1982 or 1983. The main difference was that thanks to the hefty injection of credit and money provided by the US government and international financial institutions in 1995, the economy managed to hit rock bottom in that same year and then experienced a sustained recuperation between 1996 and 2000.

One final issue that is very important to understand why Mexico's banking structure is a salient example of the country's domestic economic concentration, despite opening up to the international economy in capital and trade flows, is the sale of most banking assets after the 1995 crisis to foreign banks. President Zedillo, with help from the conservative PAN and his own reluctant party, the PRI, changed the Constitution between 1995 and 1997 to allow foreign ownership of banks. A wave of mergers and acquisitions ensued after the banking system collapse, and the changes in the Constitution enabled giant, multinational banks to buy most Mexican banking assets. Thus, the three biggest Mexican banks, Bancomer, Banamex, and Serfin were bought, respectively, by Banco Bilbao Vizcaya (BBVA), Citigroup, and Santander. Other banks such as HSBC and Scotia Bank also entered the Mexican credit market. The end result was that whereas just before the big opening-up of the banking sector started in 1997, in December 1996 only 7 percent of total banking assets in Mexico were owned by foreign capital. In contrast, by December 2003, a staggering 83 percent were owned mainly by large multinational banks.[23] The three largest banks control more than 50 percent of credit in the country, making it an oligopolistic system. As a consequence, collusion has allowed them to set prices and banking conditions in the whole country. The result has been low credit provision, particularly for small and medium-sized enterprises, high fees for services, and credit extension for consumption rather than investment and production.

Mexico remains near the bottom of credit provision among high- and medium-income countries. The Peña Nieto government was unable to change this situation despite making financial reform one of its aims. In the 2000s, total credit provision as a percentage of GDP hovered at around 20 percent. Toward the end of Peña Nieto's term in office this situation did not change. In 2017 total credit provision as a percentage of GDP in Mexico was 21.7 percent. In contrast, the percentages for the other six largest economies in Latin America were: Peru (31.7 percent), Colombia (40.5 percent), Brazil (66.4 percent) and Chile (75.5 percent). The only country with lower credit provision to GDP was Argentina (11.7 percent). The contrast with advanced capitalist economies was also very significant: USA (49.5 percent), Germany (79.7 percent), and Japan (103.9 percent).[24]

In summary, the Mexican banking sector's oligopolistic structure contributes significantly to the curse of misplaced monopolies in Mexico. If credit provision drives innovation and entrepreneurship, Mexico is weak on these fronts. Large Mexican multinational firms can obtain credit in international capital markets. In contrast the vast majority of small and medium-sized firms cannot. This case illustrates accurately the image of a 'two speed economy' (or more) that McKinsey management consultants identified in Mexico. The very few largest actors dominate and set conditions that allow them to reap high profits through rentier activities (fees for services), rather than through loans that can spur productive activity. In this regard, their job is relatively straightforward. Their best clients in credit provision are the Mexican government and large multinational Mexican firms. Everybody else is underserved and underrepresented. They just pay to use banks' services or are encouraged to take consumer credit rather than capital for investment. This is not the road to a broadly fair and prosperous society anywhere in the world.

Telecoms

If banking provides a glaring example of lack of competition, oligopoly power, and cronyism, then the telecoms sector is a basket case that has allowed a developing country to create the wealthiest individual in the world, according to some editions of the *Forbes* annual list of billionaires. The name Carlos Slim is ubiquitous in business circles. Similar to the case of Mexican banks, the giant state telecoms monopoly, Telmex, was privatized. President Salinas made this the first big-scale privatization of his time in office (announced in 1989 and finished in 1992) for a variety of reasons: Telmex shares already traded on Mexican and New York City stock exchanges, so pricing was easier than other assets; the government required the proceeds of the sale of big assets to repay external debt, and to use as patronage with its allies; privatization of a mammoth firm (in 1988 Telmex was the fourth largest firm by sales in Mexico, after Pemex, Chrysler, and General Motors) sent a strong signal about the start of a major economic liberalization process under Salinas.[25]

The privatization was tailored to transform a public sector monopoly into a private sector one. The law established that: whoever controlled 21.4 percent of 'AA stock' presided over voting rights on the company's board; it had to be owned by Mexicans; the owners would have a monopoly over long-distance calls for six years (the Mexico-US telephone connection was the second in the world in terms of daily calls); whoever owned Telmex would also get a cellular telephone license to operate throughout Mexico (no other companies could); and the President also announced that communication and transportation services would be indexed to inflation (to ensure profitability).[26]

The business group Carso, owned by Slim, and close to President Salinas and some of his close associates, won the bid (against two others) by buying 51 percent of AA shares (around 10 percent of the firm's total stock) by partnering with Southwestern Bell and France Telecom.[27] Popular lore in Mexico has it that Slim was a frontman for President Salinas and that he would have not been able to secure the winning bid for such a big profit-making asset without his proximity to power and soft loans from state banks like NAFIN. Be that as it may, there is no question that Slim is an incredibly shrewd businessman, and his fortune predated the Salinas privatizations. His empire continued to grow as he went into domestic and later international mobile telephony, as well as continuing to grow his existing assets in finance and construction.

By the mid-2000s Slim and his empire had come to symbolize very graphically the malaise of misplaced monopolies in Mexico. Thus, in the economic sphere he represented one individual whose businesses or business ties created an estimated one in every four or five formal sector jobs in the country; someone who used his money and influence to deploy the judicial branch of government to attack would-be competitors or stall legislation against his monopolistic practices through injunctions; an insatiable tycoon trying to get into the visual media sector (which he did through the streaming online of Uno TV); and to some, the creation of a state within a state, at least in terms of the influence and resources that he could deploy to pursue any aim within Mexico's jurisdiction, and fulfil it.[28]

In contrast, the political sphere since party alternation in Mexico's presidency in 2000 was characterized by a weaker federal authority incapable of enforcing regulations to check the power of tycoons like Slim; the rise of regional centers of power focused in the governorships of the country's 31 states (plus the capital city), through which captains of industry had many points of entry to safeguard and continue pursuing their self-interest; and, most worryingly, the penetration of resources from organized criminal activity, most prominently drug-trafficking, into some of the newly privatized firms in Mexico, as a way to launder money. We know this through a Swiss court report (the Roschacher Report) which details how part of the capitalization of some of the newly privatized firms during the Salinas government was achieved through proceeds from drug-trafficking cartels. The report is the product of Swiss judicial investigations into the unexplained fortune that Raúl Salinas amassed during his brother's presidency, and it was commissioned as part of a judicial process after Raúl's wife was arrested in Geneva, Switzerland in November 1995, while trying to retrieve large amounts of money from accounts held with several Swiss banks.[29]

However, unlike the banking sector, where the second wave of liberalization under President Peña Nieto does not seem to have had a significant impact, the telecoms sector has undergone large changes through the introduction in 2014 of anti-trust legislation and regulation 'with teeth' that can sanction and punish positions of dominance in the market. According to some observers, the reform had short-term positive results, at least in terms of increasing competition and reducing prices in fixed-line and mobile telephony services.[30] For example, American AT&T and Spanish Telefónica grew their market share in Mexico. However, Slim continued to protect his dominant position in the market. The Mexican Supreme Court ruled in favor of Slim's America Mobil in August 2017. Whereas the 2014 pro-competition reform tried to force Slim's telecoms empire to stop charging so-called interconnection charges (i.e. charging other telecom carriers to pay a fee for calls made to customers on the networks Slim owns—by far the largest in Mexico), the Supreme Court upheld them and said that the regulatory agency Instituto Federal de Telecomunicaciones should be in charge of setting those charges.[31] If the situation stabilizes, but Slim and later on his heirs manage to hold the dominant position in Mexico's telecoms sector, the principal victims will be Mexicans themselves, who will continue to face higher communication costs than consumers in many other countries. Such costs to the vast majority, which benefit only one family or, better put, one clan, are the opposite of how a modern, competitive economy should operate. They are a national embarrassment for anybody around the world who cares about Mexico's prospects for equitable growth and development.

Media

Unlike banking and telecoms, the general media (visual, audio, and print) was never in the hands of the state in its entirety. This is a basic distinction between the type of authoritarian rule that existed in Mexico and many other countries, and totalitarian rule as it existed in the USSR, or China under Mao. In the case of Mexico, the state had its own communication channels—newspapers, radio, television channels—alongside other public broadcasters such as the largest public universities in the country like UNAM and the Instituto Politécnico Nacional, as well as a variety of privately owned media outlets. Observed in a disaggregated way, it would seem as if Mexico is a country with a plural and vibrant media. There were and continue to be many private media outlets at the local, state, and federal levels, with different social and political perspectives and persuasions.

However, when the media sector is observed as a function of mass penetration and influence, it has been, and remains, highly concentrated. Print media, despite its variety, has a relatively small audience. Radio's is larger. However, by far the largest source for news, information, and entertainment that Mexicans consume comes from television, which is dominated by Televisa (with 70 percent of market share), Azteca (25 percent), and others, including public channels (5 percent). Since the advent of the internet and social media, the same corporations and their offspring have populated this space, although the many platforms and myriad blogs and sources of information on the internet make it, so far, a plural space, at least when it comes to news and information (or for that matter 'fake news' and disinformation) for the public at large.

Just as banking provides the credit and telecoms the human communication necessary for the investment and the human interaction and co-ordination that can lead to productive activity and growth, the media help to shape the perceptions of all those individuals who in turn communicate with one another in pursuit of common or divergent goals. In republics, the modern media has rightly been called the fourth branch of government. Inasmuch as the media has a strong influence in the type and quality of oversight and accountability over a given ruling government, this characterization is not just rhetorical. In Mexico the state, at least since the rise of the PRI, has constantly tried to diffuse and weaken the functions of oversight and accountability of its activities by the media. A traditional way the state and the authorities emanating from it have used to distort and manipulate information in the media, is by paying journalists and radio and television broadcasters to deliberately give prominence to stories or provide perspectives or points of view that are advantageous to them and detrimental to their enemies. This payment (or bribe) has been known for decades in popular lore as *chayote* (i.e. originally a fruit of the same family as squash and cucumber) and those who receive it *chayoteros*. Sadly, it is a widespread practice and different political cliques from the different political parties have their preferred journalists and broadcasters whom they tap constantly in order to distort and manipulate information in their favor. Even more important in terms of the amounts of money involved, media censorship and manipulation is carried out by different governments (particularly the federal and state levels and all their different agencies) which threaten media outlets with bankruptcy or a serious cut in earnings, by withdrawing government advertising from media outlets. Governments are the largest clients of print, radio, and visual media. Federal and state authorities spend millions of US dollars every year. An investigative analysis in the *New York Times* was memorably titled "With Strings Attached: No Negative Coverage."[32]

Televisa owns around 70 percent of the visual media market and Azteca around 25 percent, so the Mexican media sector suffers great concentration, in this respect. This is a phenomenon that started since the appearance of radio stations in the 1920s and 1930s, which then became the base for television broadcasters. By far the most dominant player has been Televisa which is a third-generation, family-owned multimedia mass media conglomerate (owned by the Azcárraga family). It is the largest in the Spanish-speaking world, and has important presence in the USA through its partnership with the largest Hispanic-speaking network, Univisión, as well as in parts of Europe, Africa, and Asia through its sale of trademark *telenovelas* or soap operas as well as transmission of Mexican top division football games. The group also owns the América and Necaxa teams, both with a long historical trajectory and strong, popular following.

Thanks to its dominance over the shaping of public perceptions and opinion, Televisa, created as such in 1973, but started since 1955 as Telesistema Mexicano, which included the first three television channels that broadcast in the country, has been a fundamental political player behind the scenes. The second-generation family owner, Emilio Azcárraga Milmo famously (or infamously) declared in public during the campaign trail of 1982, "I am a *priísta* by conviction … if more air time is given to the official party and the government it is because they have more need for communication, and we are evidently soldiers of the President of the Republic, and not of the others."[33] After the demise of hegemonic PRI rule, the emergence of democracy was not at all bad for Televisa, either. The third-generation family owner, Emilio Azcárraga Jean, declared that "democracy is a good client"[34] at a US-Mexican chamber of commerce meeting in 2004. He was right that the main determinant of profit was not the presence or absence of a hegemonic party, but a market for political mass communication and political media marketing for would-be public officeholders, irrespective of the number of parties involved. Just as Slim has been criticized for monopolizing the telecoms sector, the Azcárragas and Televisa have been criticized for doing the same in the media, particularly but not exclusively in visual media.

Televisa did not remain the only private provider of mass media services and entertainment. The first wave of big privatizations, under President Salinas, included auctioning the main state television network, Imevisión. Ricardo Salinas Pliego (no family relation of the Salinas de Gortari clan) was, nonetheless, close to President Carlos Salinas and his brother, Raúl. In 1993 he won the bid and created T.V. Azteca. This became the second nationwide, privately owned television network, after Televisa. As with the handing over of Telmex to Slim, similar suspicions and allegations were made about Salinas Pliego as a frontman for Carlos Salinas and his close associates. The Swiss judicial investigation that traced Raúl Salinas's financial transactions during his brother's presidency obtained testimony from a scion of the Monterrey captains of industry élite, Adrián Garza González, about how the Salinas brothers approached him in the run-up to the privatization of the state's television channel in which they would invest, but wanted to remain anonymous, and how he accepted under pressure but ended up transferring the money he received in Switzerland to an account whose power of attorney and signature was under Ricardo Salinas Pliego.[35]

This case is another illustration of the crony capitalism that gained impetus during the first wave of privatization under President Salinas, and continued unabated during the second wave of pro-competition or further market liberalization under President Peña Nieto: the scandals surrounding the privileged access and exchange of favors between Peña Nieto, some of his closest collaborators and construction firms Higa (Mexican) and OHL (Spanish) hit the President's popularity irreversibly from 2014.

Salinas Pliego, an unabashedly controversial tycoon who relishes in that image as much as he does in his business empire (which includes consumer-credit banking, telecoms, television, and retailing throughout Latin America), which continues to grow and offers high rates of return to his investors, has defended his position in the visual media sector by saying that thanks to him the *Televisa* monopoly in television broadcasting was broken up in Mexico. Bittersweet consolation to a majority of Mexican consumers who have enjoyed two networks instead of one since 1993—but both have kowtowed to whoever is in power during their tenure, and have not provided the checks and balances critical to properly informed public opinion, whose role is to participate in keeping representative government under effective parameters of transparency and accountability.

The *televisoras'* duopoly has striven to keep its monopolistic power, and the two networks have fought the potential entry of competitors just like Slim has in the telecoms sector. Due to their power to shape public opinion and in this way their capacity to make or break reputations, the television networks are politically more powerful, particularly in the run-up to elections, at which times all parties, whether right, left, or center, court them to get preferential coverage. This dynamic gathered strength as the PRI's hegemony was diluted in the second half of the 1990s and became a dominant characteristic of the sector in the 2000s. In the run-up to elections the *televisoras* would get advantageous legislation and regulation, and after the elections the newly constituted representatives would rollback such advantages and return to the *status quo ante*. In 2008 several legislators, including the prominent Santiago Creel of the PAN, proposed legislation to guarantee air time for all parties by the *televisoras* during election campaigns, free of charge. The legislation was enacted despite the strong lobbying the *televisoras* mounted against the measures. Their tactics ended up sometimes resembling those of the Politburo's Central Committee in the USSR under Stalin, when individuals were airbrushed from official portraits, photographs of gatherings, and documents of the Soviet Communist Party. In the Mexican case, coverage of any activity by Creel and other senators who voted in favor of the bill was dropped. They simply disappeared from public view. Unlike the purges in the USSR it was not because they had been literally eliminated. Rather, inasmuch as television coverage is the main way in Mexico for politicians and any other individuals who rely on the public sphere to make a living, their disappearance from the screens weakened and isolated them.

Likewise, the *televisoras* also put up a good fight during the second wave of economic liberalization under President Peña Nieto. The pro-competition reforms for both the telecoms and media sectors were part of the same bill. Among other things, the great tycoons in both sectors had been trying to penetrate one another's coveted fiefdoms since the mid-2000s. By 2011, Slim and Azcárraga disliked one another openly and lobbied the government, the former to gain entrance into content and data transmission (media) and the latter to gain entrance into telecoms (mobile telephony). The case became one of large-scale monopolistic capitalism trying to be forced open not by popular pressures or state action (although these had gathered momentum as evidence accumulated and was circulated about the high prices and low quality that the average Mexican got for their telecoms and media services), but by the clash of tycoons themselves.

The PAN government under President Calderón had tried to get Slim to give in to stronger regulatory measures while cultivating Televisa and Azteca for favorable coverage, as his controversial 'war on drugs' started taking a heavy toll in terms of brutal, random violence and a mounting death toll in many of the country's main cities.[36] By the time the 2012 presidential elections were held, there was a strong popular preference to force the largest corporations to open up to competition.

The PRI reaped rewards from this popular mandate, and President Peña Nieto created a multiparty coalition in Congress (the so-called 'Pacto por México') to force pro-competition reforms in the key areas that had resisted such measures since the 1990s. The result was legislation that forced some opening of both the telecoms and media sectors. Slim, however, declared that the legislation was not fair and that his sector would become more heavily regulated and easier to break up than the media sector. For example, the reform in telecoms allowed foreign investment to own 100 percent in specific ventures (although no single participant, including Slim, should control more than 50 percent of market share without becoming liable to penalties and potentially forced trust-busting). In contrast, in the media sector a ceiling allowing no more than 49 percent foreign ownership of specific participants in this area was created.[37]

Probably the most powerful contemporary example of Televisa's both hard and soft political power is the extent to which it managed to create, nurture, and project the career of Peña Nieto—the young, telegenic would-be governor of México state and contributed to his success in becoming Mexican president in 2012. The issue gained traction in the run-up to those elections after the British newspaper, *The Guardian*, published a cache of documents showing contracts that the government of México state had signed with companies associated with *Televisa* to promote a positive image of the governor, Enrique Peña Nieto, through various means to parachute him into the Mexican presidency: positive news coverage; appearances in political debate programs, as well as popular entertainment; and positive coverage and the permanent presence of Peña's image in magazines, and on Facebook and YouTube, as well as other means of mass communication and advertisement.

Did all this amount to fake news? Partly of course, inasmuch as Peña Nieto's state government's achievements were exaggerated, while its mistakes, abuses, and corruption were covered up. However, this integral strategy to promote (and discredit) specific politicians depending on money paid to Televisa by proxy to do so, was more than just the crafting of fake news. It was more akin to the packaging, branding, and commercialization of consumer products. The difference was that the products were politicians rather than tissues or toothpaste. But the aim was the same one: to sell them for mass consumption.

Although this information only came to international public attention in 2012 as a consequence of *The Guardian*'s revelations, the nexus between Televisa and Peña Nieto was known about in Mexico as early as 2005. Back then, investigative journalism magazine *Proceso* published similar contracts to those that *The Guardian* published in 2012. In 2005, however, those contracts were meant to create a positive image of then candidate Peña Nieto to the governorship of México state. Not least among the reasons why the young candidate needed to polish his image was that he had been designated as successor by then-governor Arturo Montiel. His inexplicable personal fortune had been made public when he competed to become the PRI's candidate to the presidency in 2006. He got to the final two, along with Roberto Madrazo. The way the two candidates went after one another was savage. Both were shown to have benefited from long careers tied to the PRI and public office. Corruption was the word on everybody's lips. The end result was that by the time Madrazo was chosen as presidential candidate, both men had been effectively disqualified in the eyes of Mexican public opinion. The PRI went on to record its worst ever showing in the presidential, legislative, and gubernatorial elections of 2006 (the PRI did even worse in the 2018 elections).

The problem for Peña Nieto was not just that he had worked for a very corrupt politician. Montiel also happened to be Peña Nieto's uncle. First, it is illegal for an elected politician to appoint relatives to office, which Montiel did with Peña Nieto. Second, the latter denied on several occasions the relationship with his uncle until it became a public embarrassment and he had to acknowledge it. Third, the governor did not just appoint his nephew as a secretary in his administration, but also chose him as his successor. Fourth, as a consequence Peña Nieto, once he became a gubernatorial candidate, faced two big problems. First, he had to create a public perception of distance between himself and his uncle. Second, he had to create the right conditions in order that the electoral result in México state was strong enough not only for himself to be elected governor, but also to have strong enough PRI representation in the state's legislature for him to throw out a case that the special prosecutor had brought against his uncle for embezzlement and grand corruption. This is where Televisa comes into the picture, and the media conglomerate managed to help Peña Nieto to achieve both aims. This saga is retold in a book by an investigative journalist and a family relation of Montiel.[38]

Moreover, the same integral strategy to sell would-be governors or presidents like mass consumption goods applied in reverse to criticize, disqualify, or even demonize others. Most prominently this happened also under the auspices of both Televisa and Azteca in the run-up to the 2006 elections. The target back then was the leftist candidate López Obrador. According to the same information obtained by *The Guardian,* this strategy involved then President Fox of the conservative PAN, who asked and paid both Televisa and Azteca to mount smear campaigns against López Obrador, particularly in the light of the latter's high approval rates in most public opinion polls at the time. The company behind the smear campaign was run by a then Vice-President of Televisa, who was the same person who promoted the image of Peña Nieto that enabled him to become governor of México state first, then President of Mexico later.[39]

Similar to the analysis of previous areas earlier in this work, the great concentration in ownership and operations in the media sector has shortchanged most Mexicans. If bankers live off fat fees thanks to collusion, while small and medium-sized firms are starved of credit; and if a telecom mogul can become one of the wealthiest individuals on earth in a country where half its population lives in poverty, then it is because the dominant media moguls accumulate wealth, power, and influence through their symbiotic relationship with public authority by manipulating public perceptions and selling pre-packaged dreams (and nightmares about the opposition) to the citizenry.

This is far from being just a Mexican phenomenon. On the contrary, it applies conspicuously to the political influence, wealth, and influence of Silvio Berlusconi in Italy or Rupert Murdoch in the UK, Australia, or the USA. But this is no consolation. If anything, the selective lies that these individuals' media outlets have spread, while covering up the truth, has demeaned and impoverished the public culture of those countries, the quality of governance in some cases, and the overall prospects for the majority of people who live where such tycoons control broadcasting.

Energy

The Mexican energy sector has been left until last to be analyzed in this work, because it is the most important in terms of its intimate relationship with the state. In fact, in many ways the state's material dependence on the proceeds of the sale of oil by giant state monopoly Pemex in particular (the company's taxed revenue has provided between 30–40 percent of the annual federal government budget ever since the early 1980s) have contributed significantly to the Mexican state becoming sluggish rather than nimble; dependent rather than empowered; rentier rather than productive; and crooked and corrupt rather than straight.

The story of the sector has been recounted in many studies and from different perspectives.[40] In 1938 President Lázaro Cárdenas (1934–40) nationalized the industry with compensation for the assets of the 17 private oil companies that operated on Mexican territory. Mexico, abundantly endowed with hydrocarbon resources, was the second largest world producer of oil after the USA in the 1920s. The nationalization was a result of a conflict over pay and labor conditions between the foreign company managers (mainly from US, British and Dutch oil firms) and Mexican oil workers and their labor unions. After the companies lost their case in the Supreme Court and ignored the ruling to compensate workers for working time lost during their strike, the companies refused to pay. Cárdenas called their bluff, tried to get the companies to pay, but after they refused to do so again, the President used the fact that the companies had committed contempt of court (before the highest court in the land) to enable the process of nationalization. The event galvanized Mexican society across social classes. Film footage and many newsreels of the time show Mexican citizens, (poor, middle class, and rich alike) queueing to pawn their valuables to enable the government to pay fair compensation to the private oil companies, for the nationalization. The process was therefore not a confiscation of assets. Cárdenas merged the 17 nationalized companies and created Petróleos Mexicanos (Pemex). It became a state firm that was given a monopoly, in Article 27 of the Constitution, over exploration and production of hydrocarbons throughout Mexican territory. The nationalization of foreign oil firms galvanized Mexicans' patriotism and became one of the proxies that defined some of the achievements of the Mexican Revolution, almost 20 years after the main military battles had been fought.

The widely held view that Mexico shunned foreign participation in its energy sector in general, and its hydrocarbons sector in particular, is not true. The electricity sector, which I will touch upon briefly, was fully nationalized in 1960, and the Comisión Federal de Electricidad (CFE), also created in the 1930s, became a state monopoly for the generation, distribution, and transmission of electricity.

The point that has to be made against the conventional wisdom, according to which no private participation (domestic or private) was allowed in the Mexican energy sector, is false. What was not allowed was private investment and ownership of any assets in the field. However, this left ample room for Pemex and the CFE to contract services with private domestic and foreign businesses. Therefore, Pemex was a good client of, say, Texan, oil services companies like Haliburton or Schlumberger, particularly when Mexico's industrial development policy prioritized Mexican oil production with the aim of making the country a leading world producer and exporter of oil in the course of the 1970s and 1980s. Services were also provided by international majors like Shell. Therefore, international firms, particularly the eco-system of rich Texan firms' based in Houston have had a long acquaintance with, knowledge of, and co-operation with PEMEX. Many Mexicans who work for the oil sector have lived at least part-time in Houston since the dramatic growth of Mexican public investment in the 1970s, to make the country a major global oil player. In electricity, likewise, private US companies like EBASCO Services, Inc. provided many of the services and know-how about Mexico's entry to nuclear-generated power in the country's only nuclear power station with two reactors, Laguna Verde, in the 1980s and 1990s.

The Mexican presidency's discretionary powers over the energy sector, enabled by the robust legislation that protected the state's monopolies in this sphere, ended up going too far in the direction of maximum exploitation and short-term revenue-making, at the expense of long-term perspectives and social development tied to the rents obtained from finite resources such as oil or natural gas. Analysts who want to make the case about the growth, sustainability, and development tied to the hydrocarbon sector (which incidentally tends to condemn most of the countries reliant on the production of oil and natural gas in the so-called 'resource curse'[41]) discuss the case of Norway as a relative success. They usually highlight that Norway had a well-entrenched democratic system that held effective checks and balances, transparency, and accountability before the major exploitation and windfalls from oil happened from the 1970s.[42] Therefore, the revenue streams that flowed from such new-found wealth were planned for, regulated, and consideration was given to social utility, rather than a few insiders dominating the sector, and the benefits accruing to a small number of investors, rather than society as a whole. Norway also has to cater to fewer than five and a half million citizens, while many big oil producers like the Middle East autocracies, Russia, Mexico, Nigeria, and Venezuela have to cater to anything between 25 and up to 150 million inhabitants. Likewise, none of these countries managed to create well-entrenched liberal democratic mechanisms enabling the state and society to regulate windfalls, in order for social rather than private utility to be prioritized.

Be that as it may, in Mexico the creation and growth of Pemex and the CFE, closely tied to the hegemonic party (the PRI), became some of the jewels in the crown of patronage and clientelism that ensured that the interests of the major party and oil sector interests became hard to distinguish. Just as the so-called *chayote* was a tool of information control (i.e. the bribe paid to journalists and broadcasters to publish and broadcast views positive to the PRI and its system, while smearing the opposition), in the realm of heavy industry, including oil and electricity, as well as railroads and mining, the PRI appointed union leaders who were loyal to the regime first and only second to their members. They were known as '*charro*' leaders (i.e. the name derived from one of the early regime loyalist union leaders, JesúsDíaz de León, who wore, *charro*, or Mexican cowboy dress, to official meetings of the union). The *chayote* bribe and the *charro* leaders were some of the effective means in the toolkit of political domination used by the PRI. The power of these union leaders that was co-opted by the regime was a function of the wealth and power of the sectors they controlled. Therefore, soon after the nationalization of the oil industry, this sector's union emerged as one of the strongest in Mexico. As a consequence, it enjoyed great perks in the PRI regime. Some of its leaders traditionally won governorships, seats in Congress, and its workers had among the best social security provisions in the country, including good salaries, paid vacations, social housing, good retirement packages, and even their own state-of-the art hospital.

The lifestyle of the oil workers' trade union (STPRM) leaders became part of popular gossip, particularly their rapaciousness, their extravagant, lavish and tasteless lifestyles, and those of their clans. The same applied to other wealthy trade unions like the teachers' union (SNTE). However, it would be a big mistake to ascribe such extensive extraction of wealth for ostentatious luxury consumption to just blue collar workers and, in particular, their leaders. A majority of white collar workers, executives, and the managerial Pemex and CFE corps (all of them political appointees of the government-in-turn), had access to the substantial perks that their sector granted them, and many of them made illegal fortunes through the granting of procurement, the choice of suppliers for projects, and their financing and execution.

In short, the energy sector might have played a crucial political role as the glue of loyalty and self-interest that kept the PRI and its main supporters together, to show up in public marches that supported the regime, and to vote *en masse* for the continuation of the party in government. The dark side was the coercion and elimination of countless individuals who were against corruption, the squandering of wealth produced from the sale of finite resources into lavish consumption, and political patronage and clientelism. Such culture was the opposite of what major and successful hydrocarbons firms around the world did: reinvesting in the business of exploration and production, while facing competition and therefore having to try to retain an edge through research and technological innovation; investing in human resources; and the maintenance of a strict distance between the business of oil exploration, production and sale, and political commitments or obligations to the political, economic, and regulatory regime in which they operated.

In Mexico this was impossible to do during the years of PRI hegemony when party, state, government, and the main publicly owned corporations were one and the same, or at least were manned by individuals all of whose present and future material and political prospects were connected through a vast political network to the sitting President of the Republic. It proved to be impossible even after the PRI lost its hegemony and even more so after the PRI lost the presidency. For all the promises made by the conservative (PAN) and left-wing (PRD) opposition to the PRI about breaking the stranglehold of political patronage and clientelism over the largest, richest state-owned companies if the PRI was kicked out of office and they were elected, the two governments under presidents that emanated from the PAN (Fox and Calderón, 2000–12), this did not happen.[43] Pemex and the CFE continued to be used to provide employment and perks to supporters of the incumbents, current expenditure continued to grow, and productivity per-worker continued to be very low.

Still, a few caveats are necessary to portray this sector of the economy. This is in contrast to the other sectors analyzed above. On the one hand, this was a sector that President Salinas did not dare to open up, as he did with the other three mentioned above. Thus, the big absentee sector from reform during the first wave of liberalization and privatization was energy—it was not opened up either to private domestic investment and was left out of the NAFTA negotiations. Aside from its powerful symbolic value as a conquest of Mexican nationalism over foreign dominance, oil and its monetary proceeds provided a strong and effective glue to cement political loyalties.

In the run-up to the 1988 elections, several traditional PRI allies, among them oil workers, teachers, and their *charro* leaders, disliked the neoliberal orientation of then-candidate Carlos Salinas. The head of the oil workers' union, Joaquín Hernández Galicia (also know as 'La Quina'), was particularly open about favoring Cuauhtémoc Cárdenas's candidacy, which promised to protect the *status quo* characterized by state-led development and protection against foreign competition. Having made threats about getting the union's rank-and-file to vote for Cárdenas, and ultimately, given how close the presidential election appears to have been (so close that the Minister of Interior stopped counting, alleging a 'crash' of the computing system tallying votes), Salinas's reaction was expressed through a major military operation in January 1989, less than two months after assuming power. The President had La Quina and his close associates arrested. La Quina was condemned to 35 years behind bars (although he received an amnesty from Salinas's successor, President Zedillo in 1997, and died in 2013).[44] Salinas went on to appoint a loyal leader (Sebastián Guzmán Cabrera) but replaced him in 1993 and appointed an even more pliant leader, Jorge Romero Deschamps. This super-*charro* was still 'leading' the STPRM in 2018, and is a great embarrassment to the PRI in particular and to Mexico in general. Despite multiple arrest orders against him while he and his family were exposed multiple times showing off an incredibly lavish lifestyle, Romero Deschamps has retained immunity from prosecution by serving continuously as a deputy or senator in Congress (public officeholders in Mexico enjoying legal immunity while they serve in office).[45]

On the other hand, the energy sector did experience reforms after Salinas and before the second wave of economic liberalization under Peña Nieto. Thus, during President Zedillo's administration, legislation was enacted in 1995 to allow some small private actors, named Productor Independiente de Energía, to produce and sell electricity. Likewise, in 1998 legislation was passed to allow the supply of natural gas to the local governments (delegaciones) of Mexico City by a private company connected with Spanish energy firm Gas Natural SDG. Similarly, in the same year Zedillo gave a concession to US energy firm Enron (which later went bankrupt) to import natural gas to Mexico. Zedillo's ultimate intention was to break up the bulk of the state-owned electricity monopoly and open it up to private investment and competition. However, after the PRI lost its majority in the Chamber of Deputies in the 1997 mid-term elections, the intended reform floundered in Congress in 1999.[46] During President Fox's term from 2000, natural gas imports grew at a high rate, but he was unable to enact any reforms.

In turn, during President Felipe Calderón's administration from 2006, two important changes took place in the energy sphere. Mexico reached peak-oil production in 2004, producing around 3 million barrels per day (b/d). After that, production started falling increasingly fast. Aside from the long-term disinvestment that Pemex had suffered cumulatively, given its use as a cash cow for political purposes and to keep the federal government's financial solvency year in, year out, Pemex's high production stemmed mainly from oil in one super-field, named Cantarell, in the shallow waters off the coast of Campeche in Mexico's southeast. Between the late 1970s and the early 2000s, Cantarell supplied around two-thirds of daily oil output in Mexico.

The depletion and steep decline of output from Cantarell after 2006 hit not only Mexico's oil revenues but also Mexicans' complacency. Used to relying on a cheap, abundant source of oil for domestic consumption and exports to the USA, projections in the mid-2000s showed that if no new oil discoveries were made, Mexico could end up being a crude oil importer by the early 2020s. To demonstrate the gravity of the situation, Mexico was the country that suffered the highest depletion rate of oil reserves anywhere in the world in the 2000s (see Figure 5.1).

It is difficult to overstate the shock that this information created in Mexican public opinion. President Calderón and his close advisers thought that the time was ripe to mention the unmentionable: reforming Pemex and opening up the oil sector to competition. The process that led to the implementation of the 2008 reform was out of the ordinary. The Senate invited, aside from the main authorities in charge of energy issues, a broader spectrum of specialists and general citizens to voice their positions about opening the Mexican sector. These forums lasted more than two months, and the end result was only mild reform. Of crucial importance, the board of directors was asked to bring in technical experts devoid of any political party affiliation. It limited the workers' representatives on the board, by not allowing them, for example, to vote on issues regarding budgeting. It cut taxation on Pemex, so that the company could start investing in exploration and production rather than just paying taxes and accumulating debt (around US $50,000m. in 2012[47]).

In addition to accelerating rates of lower crude production, Pemex also had to face the growing problem of becoming the subject of the theft of significant oil and refined products. Such crime has been perpetrated by organized criminal syndicates like the Zetas, a transnational organized criminal organization that control most of the geography where Mexico's oil and natural gas reserves, infrastructure, and operations are located, namely, the Gulf of Mexico rim, from Campeche in the southeast to Tamaulipas, which shares a border with Texas, USA, in the northeast. Some of the investigative journalism that uncovered the ruthless way that organized criminals were fleecing Pemex, and continue to do so to this day, including the theft of oil and its derivatives from pipelines or lorries; the intimidation and kidnapping of Pemex personnel, and the extortion demanded by criminals from the company to operate in remote areas of exploration or production (effectively buying security in typical mafia fashion) astounded ordinary Mexicans.[48]

Jesús Reyes Heroles, who was appointed as CEO of Pemex by President Calderón at the start of his term in office in December 2006, until September 2009, pointed out that the reform had not transformed Pemex, but it had at least made a difference. While in the 1990s the average annual investment in exploration was around US $500m., after the 2008 reform this amount grew to between $4,000m.–$5,000m., which allowed the company to make new finds. However, compared with the large international oil companies, which in good times (when the oil price is above $70 per barrel) invest $15,000m.–$20,000m. Pemex has a long way to go. The main point for Mexico's public finance viability, in his view, was decoupling fiscal policy from energy policy: the abundance of oil and its proceeds made Mexican policymakers lazy when it came to tax collection. Something had to give if the country was not to end up becoming a net importer of crude oil, and if the Mexican federal government was to gain relative autonomy from its long-term dependence on Pemex resources.[49]

Another important decision that President Calderón took during his term in office was shutting down in 2009 the firm Luz y Fuerza del Centro, which supplied electricity in densely populated central Mexico. The company had a

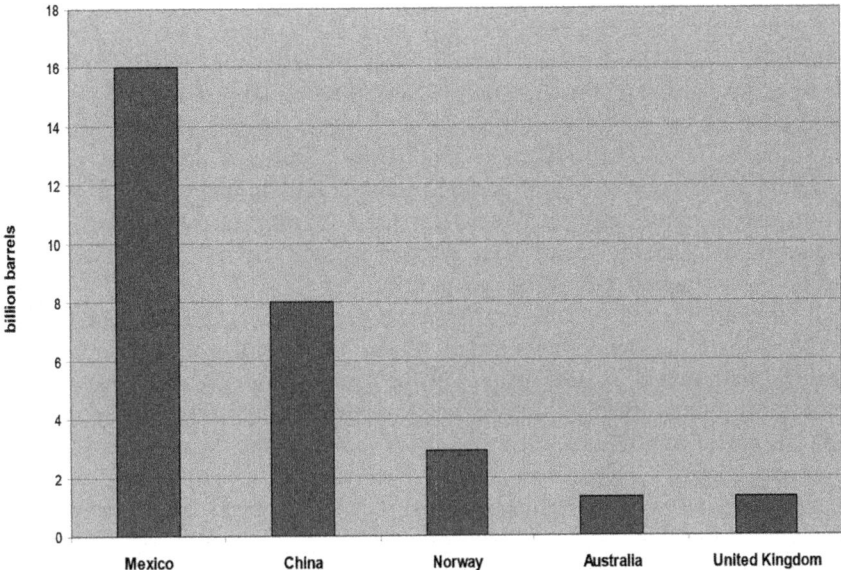

Figure 5.1. Big Rise in Loss of Oil Reserves that were not Replaced
Source: Data elaborated from British Petroleum, *BP Energy Outlook*, 2008.

reputation for unreliability, but there were also political motivations behind the decision to close its operations. The firm was home to one of the most combative semi-independent unions, the Sindicato Mexicano de Electricistas, which had clashed with both PRI and PAN administrations. Many analysts compared Calderón's takeover of Luz y Fuerza with the arrest by federal police and military personnel, on behalf of President Salinas, of La Quina and his associates in the oil sector. These shows of force were successful and therefore strengthened the image of the presidents who decreed them. They also show how intertwined the energy sphere, the Mexican state, and politics are in Mexico. This action was controversial and drew a lot of applause, as well as criticism.[50]

There is no doubt that the most important recent change in the energy sphere was the opening up of the sector to private investment introduced by President Peña Nieto in 2013–14. This was the signature policy of the second wave of economic liberalization (if we consider Salinas and Zedillo's privatizations as the first wave). It can be considered the jewel in the crown of economic openings mentioned above in banking, telecoms, the media, and also (even if not covered in detail here) education and labor (the mild liberalization of labor law happened during the last days of President Calderón, but it was enabled by the PRI as a token of goodwill before Peña Nieto took over as President in December 2012).

The energy reform under Peña Nieto allowed domestic and foreign private investment in oil exploration and production. The prohibition of these activities had been the red line that kept the symbol and the reality of Mexican nationalism triumphant in the hydrocarbon sector for many decades up to that point. But this red line had weakened after the country reached peak-oil production in 2004, and thereafter experienced accelerating rates of depletion and lower production. Within a decade of peak-oil production, Mexico was producing around one-third less crude oil per day (from more than 3 million b/d to less than 2.5 million b/d). This reform, arguably the most difficult that politicians had to sell to the Mexican public, was enacted relatively successfully.

It turned out to be bad luck that international oil prices tumbled significantly in 2014–17. Thus, the first two rounds to auction oil blocks located onshore, in shallow waters, and in deep waters of the Gulf of Mexico, did not fetch the expected amounts when oil was trading in international markets at around US $90 per barrel in 2012–13, rather than $30–$60, as was the case between late 2014 and late 2017. Of great importance to changing the rent-seeking culture in Pemex and CFE was their constitutional redefinition from state enterprises to 'productive state enterprises.' This change means that the Mexican public energy behemoths will participate in market activities alongside private operators, and that their performance will be measured through similar profitability criteria as private firms. The state retains the prerogative to sanction Pemex and CFE if they lag behind or their performance is deemed unsatisfactory. The law contemplates transferring projects and activities where such underperformance is identified and properly documented, with the result that they could be taken away from the state-owned firms and given to private firms to manage, in theory, more efficiently.

Moreover, there are still plenty of untapped proven reserves that will go under the hammer in an environment where it is hoped that oil will remain at or above US $70 per barrel (at which level it traded in early 2018)—a threshold that attracts major as well as medium-sized firms, private and public, from around the world to produce oil. Another potential advantage for the future is that Mexico is very well endowed with shale resources (both natural gas and oil). According to the US Energy Information Administration, Mexico is among the top ten countries in terms of proven reserves of shale resources.[51] Because the shale production revolution happened in the USA, thanks to know-how, industry structure, and financing capability present there but hard to replicate elsewhere, it is highly probable that many of the Texas-based companies that championed shale production could expand operations into Mexico. Several issues still have to be sorted out before this happens, however. Paramount among them is security on the ground for workers in this industry (as mentioned above, oil workers and Pemex officials have suffered violence and extortion by organized criminals). Until the security situation improves in Mexico, and for the case of oil and natural gas production, assets and infrastructure in the eastern part of the country and the Gulf of Mexico rim are crucial, investments in shale production are unlikely to materialize on a commercial level.

The power generation sector has received less attention so far, although it was also part of the 2013–14 energy reform. Intimately linked to hydrocarbons due to the continued growth of gas-fired plants that supply Mexico's different energy consumer sectors (industrial, commercial, residential, transportation, and hydrocarbon extraction and processing), the reform aimed for some unbundling, in order for private firms to participate in the intricate chain from generation to retail delivery of electricity. This is an area that is also tied to national security for a variety of reasons: from keeping the lights on, to power-intensive manufacturing activity, to the availability and protection of water resources, which are necessary for power generation. Regarding this last point, Mexico, unlike most Latin American countries, where water resources are relatively abundant, is not blessed with large reserves of water. In fact, issues linked to water security and food security are intimately tied to the country's growing deficit in water capacity.

In summary, there is no other Mexican economic sector that has suffered such a great degree of change as the energy policy sphere has since 2013. Oil and its role in Mexico's modern history, economy and popular psyche is highly salient. The opening-up of the sector was badly needed in the light of chronic disinvestment in exploration and production, which led to the country experiencing accelerating rates of depletion since the mid-2000s.

Facing the possibility of becoming a net crude importer in the 2020s while the country is rich in conventional and unconventional hydrocarbon resources, is a folly to be avoided at all costs. Before opening its doors to private investment, the government held a 'round zero' bid in 2014. Its purpose was to allow Pemex, unopposed by other firms, to choose what it would keep. Pemex kept 237 fields, which is equivalent to 83 percent of the country's current 2P reserves (that is, proven and probable) amounting to about 20,500m. barrels of oil equivalent. The company was also given around 31 percent of total current estimated prospective reserves (close to 32,000m. barrels of oil equivalent) during round zero.[52]

By the end of 2017, the Mexican authorities, through the regulator *Comisión Nacional de Hidrocarburos*, which was established as part of the 2013 reform, had held two bidding rounds. More than 70 contracts had been adjudicated, involving dozens of companies, private and public, from around the world. It was estimated that if the projects that have been allocated come to fruition, they could generate more than US $60,000m.[53] Or potentially more, if the price of oil stays above $70 per barrel. Likewise, and following the introduction in late 2017 of new rules for requiring Pemex to meet a certain level of productivity as a public sector company, the company's management threatened the rank-and-file that they would sell blocks and projects where prospective targets were not being met.

Of the sectors analyzed so far, energy, in particular oil and natural gas exploration and production, is the one that will probably change the most, and in which monopoly power and its contribution to private and sectional rather than public and general gains will be most affected, given the *status quo ante* in which a state-owned behemoth, and its intimate relationship to the state and the politics of Mexico, gave it great political weight and influence, while suffering accelerated rates of depletion of its output, as well as politicized administration, which turned it into a cash cow for government incumbents and a war chest for money in the run-up to elections.

Still, there is no absolute guarantee that introducing competition, some transparency and a measure of effective regulatory capacity will create the conditions for the sector to grow and be exploited rationally and efficiently. The ideal situation would translate into, on the one hand, significant reinvestment of the proceeds from the sale of hydrocarbons into exploration and production, to avoid another crisis of resource depletion, as happened in the 2000s. On the other, proceeds from the royalties and taxation obtained in this sector should be invested in the provision and nurturing of public goods, above all human capital (health, education, housing, and security).

Conditions on the ground militate against such ideal outcomes. A first concern for many investors and believers in the opening of the sector is that the liberalization reforms will be reversed in the future. Their reasoning is based on seeing many openings of the energy sector in countries around the world, followed in subsequent years by a downturn in the sector and the return of so-called resource nationalism—the nationalization of assets or outright confiscation. In Mexico the main opponent of pro-opening, pro-private investors is the hard left, which is represented by López Obrador and his MORENA movement. People with knowledge of Mexico's political institutions point out that nationalization is unlikely, even under López Obrador's coming presidency, which might revise awarded contracts. The supermajorities needed in both federal chambers of Congress plus a simple majority of state legislatures (at least 17) also voting for reversal of the energy reform is very low probability. The possibility, however, still exists.

A second concern is that due to the cronyism and corruption that have been exposed and well documented about President Peña Nieto and his close associates, favoured contracting firms such as Higa, OXL, and others, will have preferential access to join the major consortiums that will develop future projects. The concern, aside from the illicit enrichment and the special access for politicians and their favored businessmen, is that they will not win licenses to operate, thanks to the high quality of their work but rather to their political connections. The end result could be, as has happened in many cases of major infrastructure development, poor performance for consumers, yet high profit margins for the favored contractors.

The culture that has dominated large energy projects in Pemex and CFE for generations sadly resembles much more the cronyism and special access to favored contractors than a level playing field that adjudicates results based on technical competence, a track record of high-quality delivery, secure working conditions for workers, and cost effectiveness. In this area the Peña Nieto government followed what has been standard practice since the Mexican state started investing billions in the course of the 1970s to make Mexico a big player in international oil production. Reversing that culture requires more than updated regulation and a modicum of rules that force some transparency in the handling of transactions from bidding blocks and fields to suppliers of the huge and complex chain of inputs that makes hydrocarbons exploitation possible. And beyond accounting, of course, a major concern remains upholding the rights of indigenous communities where such projects are developed—in Mexico this is a big issue in states such as Veracruz, Tabasco, Campeche, and Chiapas—as well as enforcing regulation meant to protect the environment and ecosystems where such extractive activity takes places.

In summary, opening up the energy sector represented a major step in helping to mitigate some of the problems created by misplaced monopolies (i.e. lack of competition due to entrenched insiders, misallocation of resources, lavish consumption rather than social investment of proceeds from the exploitation of finite natural resources, and strengthening of the politics-business connection whereby state capture is achieved by public and private interests—from bureaucrats, trade union leaders, and politicians, to private sector investors, banks, and major oil services firms). However, in and of itself, the opening-up is only a first step to good outcomes, which will ultimately be judged by how the proceeds of oil and potentially natural gas production are invested in Mexico.

State Weakness

After observing the international and the domestic sectors of Mexico's economy, a third issue that has to be examined to understand why inequality and poverty have persisted, and why Mexico has become a more polarized, conflictive society since the 1980s, is the Mexican state. During the decades of PRI hegemony, the state loomed as a very strong presence in the Mexican psyche. The President and the pyramid of power over which he presided commanded a mixture of respect, fear, and awe. Of course, these perceptions were the result of an authoritarian, disciplined political regime that was quite effective at command-and-control, and managed to achieve its objectives, even if some or many of them were unfair and unjust, such as persecuting vocal critics, lining the pockets of supporters, and tampering with electoral results.

The so-called Mexican 'imperial presidency' ran its course and, as seen in Chapter 3, weakened in a gradual way in the 1970s and 1980s as a consequence of a variety of factors, but mainly due to the country's deep financial, economic crises in 1976 and 1982. None the less, the state had not been as strong as it portrayed itself. A proxy for the Mexican state's strength or lack thereof is its extractive and redistribution capacity. Jesús Reyes Heroles pointed out in 2012 that the last major fiscal reform the country experienced was in 1977 with the introduction of the value-added tax (VAT). The Mexican state faced fiscal precariousness due to its incapacity to tax income (apart from formal wages, which can be easily taxed) and wealth. While Organisation for Economic Co-operation and Development (OECD) member state governments collected around 35 percent of revenue as a proportion of GDP annually on average, Mexico collected less than 20 percent. In addition, thanks to productive activity and investments that translate into future revenue streams, the OECD countries spent an average of close to 45 percent of annual GDP on the public sector, while Mexico spent less than 25 percent. The end result was a widening gap between the rich and the middle classes, and, much more significantly, between the poorest households in Mexico. The so-called 'trickle down' mechanisms that have traditionally played an equalizing role in capitalist economies thanks to the welfare state in advanced economies since the early 20th century are precarious and continue to weaken in Mexico.[54]

Reyes Heroles estimated the difference between Mexican revenue and advanced, OECD member states in 2012 was as follows: the central (or federal) government in the average OECD member country collected around 20 percent of annual GDP, while Mexico collected 14 percent. The gaps become chasms at the subnational level. Thus, state or provincial governments in OECD countries on average collected 6 percent of GDP while Mexico's state's governments collected just 0.6 percent. Even worse was the municipal level, where the average for advanced OECD countries was 4 percent of annual GDP, while in Mexico it was just 0.2 percent. Last, another huge gap between Mexico and advanced OECD countries was that while the latter collected on average 8.4 percent of annual GDP for social security purposes, Mexico only collected 3 percent.[55] Reyes Heroles emphasized that this cumulative problem was strongly, if not just related to the Mexican state´s fiscal dependence on oil revenues, which has acted as expansionary fiscal policy by adding the 30–40 percent annual shortfall in the federal government's annual budgets, thus allowing the postponement of costly and unpopular measure such as the need to create efficient nationwide taxation authorities for each level of government.

Moreover, as shown in Figure 5.2, state capacity to redistribute income from taxation is, comparatively, very weak in Mexico. The data comes from the OECD and shows that in advanced capitalist countries inequality, according to the Gini co-efficient, which measures the difference between the proportion of income that goes to the top decile of a given population and the proportion that goes to the bottom decile of the same population, falls after taxation and state transfers.[56]

Therefore, in countries that have had a strong social-democratic tradition, such as Scandinavian nations, inequality is significantly reduced after the state taxes and transfers resources (Denmark's co-efficient falls from 0.400 to 0.250, while Sweden's falls from 0.380 to 0.280). The same happens in countries in southern Europe like Spain or Italy, and in East Asia like Japan. In English-speaking countries, which have a less social-democratic tradition compared with continental Europe, the Gini co-efficient still falls after taxation and transfers by the state. Even the USA, usually portrayed as a country of great opportunities ('the American dream') or great failures ('the American nightmare'), and therefore prone to high inequality, manages to reduce inequality (not as much as most of the other advanced economies) through taxation and state transfers (from 0.480 to 0.390). The only two Latin American countries that belonged to the OECD as of 2018 were Mexico and Chile. They are also the worst performers in this area. State taxation and transfers hardly make a dent in inequality (Mexico's went from 0.470 to 0.460 and Chile's from 0.490 to 0.470). So much for criticism about the heartless, savage capitalism that reigns in the USA. In contrast, in Latin America sluggish, rentier, crony capitalism, which in and of itself produces great inequality, is compounded by states with very weak progressive taxation and transfer capacity.

The data in Figure 5.2 is only for the year 2013, so no claims can be made about the evolution of state capacity in helping to reduce inequality since then. However, the Gini co-efficient numbers do not change significantly from one year to the next. They tend to move relatively slowly, because big changes in state capacity to tax and transfer in a progressive (or regressive) way are relatively rare. Much more often than not, this is a slow process which, nonetheless, can yield important improvements (if a less unequal society is a fundamental public priority—which it may not be necessarily) in time.

Therefore, fiscal weakness, as well as the precarious mechanisms the state has to redistribute resources in a progressive way lie at the heart of the problem of why, irrespective of Mexico's integration with its North American neighbors, a majority of Mexicans are not better off in 2018 than they were in 1993. This is not a problem that is specific to Mexico. Many studies have shown the weak capacity that governments in many developing countries have to transfer wealth and income effectively, in order that levels of inequality do not keep growing by simply allowing the free forces of markets to operate as they see fit. Latin America is considered the most unequal region in the world, and the data from Figure 5.2 illustrate one of the reasons why this is the case.

For the case of Mexico, the incapacity to tax the rich is a problem faced and known since at least President Echeverría's failure to create a more progressive taxation system in 1971–72. According to Cicero, in Mexico the issue that helped the most to cement loyalty and collective action among the major capitalists against the state since the 1930s was the fight against paying taxes. From this perspective, bankers' capital financed the creation of the PAN in 1939 and Manuel Gómez Morín, leader and co-founder of the main conservative party in Mexico, legitimized the party as a pragmatic vehicle to solve the most pressing problems the nation faced at any point in time. However, pragmatism in this context meant, first and foremost, the affluent avoiding or minimizing payment of tax in order that the state and its potential actions remained checked.[57] I understand this politico-economic position at least, given when it was created (toward the end of the 'socialist' presidency of Lázaro Cárdenas). Sadly, as it took root and gained adherents and power among well-to-do Mexicans ('*la gente bien*') it reinforced a severing of the social contract, according to which citizens have the right and are empowered

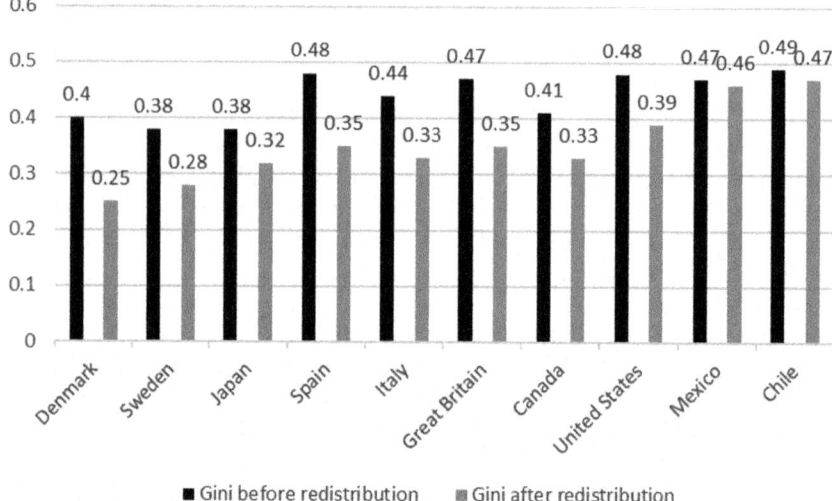

Figure 5.2. Capacity and Incapacity to Level-Off Inequality Across the World
Source: Data selected and elaborated by the author from the OECD, Income Distribution Database (IDD), http://www.oecd.org/social/income-distribution-database.htm, Accessed 30 January 2018.

to hold their authorities accountable because these authorities, first, emanate from citizens' electoral choice; and, second, because citizens pay politicians and public servants money to create public goods, pursue the public interest, and improve citizens' conditions within the rule of law. This is a far cry from what happened in Mexico, and has yet to happen. Lest this proposition be interpreted as an issue that was born in the 1930s, it is important to emphasize that clientelism, fiscal exceptions, venality, and the use of public power to pursue private gain is a trait identified with the Iberian world and its colonies. The problem is not new. Its roots are deep and wide.

Given the limits of taxing wealth and income, technocrats with great experience at the commanding heights of the Mexican economy have defended the VAT, inasmuch as it is a tax that is good for control purposes: it leaves behind a paper trail of who generates what amount of value, when and where, in order that fiscal authorities can go after them. Of special importance to understand the chronic fiscal weakness of the Mexican state Reyes Heroles emphasized the many tax exceptions created and accumulated for political purposes (electoral as well as employment-generation) in time. He calculated that more than 30 percent of potential taxes were not being collected as of 2012, thanks to privileges offered by successive governments to sectors like agriculture and trucking. Likewise, the level of property taxes collected in Mexico compared with its OECD peers is almost laughable. The logic for this deficit, in his view, had to do with Mexican mayors' three-year terms without possibility of re-election, which created disin-centives to raise and collect revenue from an electorate that had no way of rewarding or punishing mayors due to the no-re-election clause.[58] But after an electoral reform that will allow legislators and mayors' to be re-elected (but not President or governors), and which started in earnest in 2018, the dynamics of taxation collection and calculations for re-election prospects at the local level might help to start changing this dysfunctional system, which to all intents and purposes has been completely reliant on federal funding, and therefore subject to the perversions, complicities, and illegalities that such dependence has engendered.

Lest we end up with a general image about the Mexican state being weak across the board, it is important to add some qualifiers. Its weakness in extracting resources for taxation and general purposes such as the provision of public goods (security, high-quality education, healthcare, and housing, among others) is not equal in all areas, or in its relationship with different segments of Mexican society. First, the Mexican state retains a presence throughout the country's territory, however deficient and corrupt this might be in places. Having the institutional and human capabilities throughout a given territory is the most important prerequisite for a state to exist: person-nel and infrastructure can be changed (even if vested public-private interests do not make this an easy task). Instead, creating state presence institutionally and with human personnel in the first place in a given territory is harder and has taken thousands of years to become an (imperfect) reality.[59] This issue highlights why comparing Mexico with failed or quasi-failed states (say, Colombia in the 1990s) is wrong and has led, in turn, to wrong prognosis, diagnoses, and interventions since brutal, highly graphic violence started increasing in Mexico as the largest drug-trafficking cartels went after one another in the early 2000s.

Second, the Mexican state has retained the capacity to control some social groups more than others. Thus, since the first wave of liberalization between the late 1980s and the 1990s, successive governments from both the PRI and the PAN have been much more effective in controlling organized and unorganized labor's demands, vis-à-vis those of capitalists. The latter have been in the driving seat since the Mexican economy was opened up. Big business, both foreign and domestic, has benefited from Mexico's monetary policy of keeping an open capital account. This policy has allowed capital flows to enter and exit Mexico with relative ease. The end result has been that the country has benefited from liquid capital injections during good times, while having to scramble to keep a relative level of stability during periods of international economic crisis and uncertainty (like the bursting of the dot.com bubble in 2000 or the crash of the subprime mort-gage market in 2007–08, both in the USA). This happens time and again when capital exits the places where it gains high returns—like emerging markets, of which Mexico is one of the largest in the world—but risk of devaluation or of non-repayment is also higher than in safe, low-return, advanced economies.

The comparative strength of organized capital vis-à-vis labor in Mexico has yielded a continuation of pro-business policies. One of the most important examples, which shows the selective force of the Mexican state, and helps to qualify the notion of Mexican state weakness across the board, is wage policy. Wages are set nationally by the Comisión Nacional de Salarios Mínimos. A decentralized federal agency created in the 1960s, with a government representative and eleven representatives of capital and labor, respectively, it decrees by fiat the minimum wage level, which in turn is the reference point for many economic activities throughout Mexico.[60] This agency has been part of the bureaucracy dominated by the neoliberal policymakers. The end result has been a tight wage policy compared with capital gains. Economists talk about "wage repression,"[61] whereby real gains of wages are eroded compared to capital gains (those of stocks, bonds, and other securities, as well as those that are parked in foreign-denominated currencies like the US dollar and those that are indexed after major devaluations, like real estate) through an explicit national government policy that keeps minimum wages at a low nominal level.

Returns to capital have grown exponentially compared to returns to labor since the 1990s in Mexico. On the capital side, returns on Mexican stocks and bonds contained in the MSCI emerging markets index have outperformed the average of the index since 1989, which includes 24 emerging market countries around the world.[62] On the labor side, because China and Mexico have been rivals in their trade with the USA, particularly since China joined the WTO in 2001, it is legitimate to contrast the growth of Chinese wages compared to Mexico's. Thus, Chinese wages, having started at around one-quarter of the level of Mexican wage in 2000, had surpassed them by 2011–12.[63] This development probably made China less competitive compared with Mexico as a supplier of labor to the US market. However, this is no consolation in the sense that growing real wages (or their stagnation) are a good proxy indicator about improving quality of life, whereas stagnant wages reflect the opposite: a harsher fight for resources among the majority of formal workers (and the many below them) in a given population.

When gains to capital and labor in Mexico are compared since 2000, the relationship has been similar to the disproportionate and growing gains for capital compared with labor that economists have identified around the world since the 1980s.[64] Thus, the ratio of gains for capital compared to wages in Mexico since 2000 has been around five units gained by capital, for every 1.5 units gained by labor.

The wage repression policy, which has enriched capital at the expense of labor in Mexico, has been justified as a way to keep Mexico competitive compared with countries with higher wages. And keeping Mexico cheap on the labor costs side was part and parcel of the original NAFTA design. In this context, competitiveness through low labor costs is the logic that has been used to justify prospective job creation and economic growth in Mexico. From this perspective, the model of economic integration with North America set out by Salinas and his colleagues was biased in favor of capital and against labor. To get the model to work for Mexico, it had to apply permanent wage repression. Otherwise, the country would lose competitiveness within the North American partnership it joined.

The model has produced sustained growth and has allowed the Mexican economy to move up the value-added chain in several manufacturing activities. However, this has been done by favoring capital and suppressing labor's gains: the success of the model (growth and jobs in manufacturing) depends on anchoring labor's gains through low nominal wage increases, and not allowing them to be translated into higher living standards for a majority of Mexicans. The Mexican state has managed to continue implementing wage repression without a general breakdown of order, let alone civil war.

Why? First, tougher living conditions for a majority in a given population or increases in inequality by no means spark revolts or revolutions, even if they increase latent resentment and discontent. Second, it is difficult to know the real cumulative loss of purchasing power for the average Mexican since the 1980s–90s. There is no question that wage suppression has kept in check net income growth for formal manufacturing workers in Mexico. Subsistence agriculture was and continues to be hit severely. For this segment of the Mexican population, the main option has been emigrating from rural to urban areas, and, if possible, although increasingly more difficult, to the USA. It is very hard to know what has happened in the informal sector, although for the purpose of this work it is safe to say that this sector is characterized by irregularity, booms and busts, and no social rights. Relative to a majority of losers, the highly educated or those who started with significant factor endowments, i.e. part of the middle-middle, the upper-middle, and the upper classes, have benefited from recent developments. Their inclusion in average living conditions in Mexico bring the average living conditions up, due to the disproportionate returns to education (and to initial capital endowments) in an economy where the demand for professional, technical, and social skills has increased significantly since Mexico joined NAFTA. The ability to understand and speak basic English (let alone write it or converse in it fluently), became a clear dividing line between those who could benefit from labor opportunities, and those who were excluded.

Third and last, it is also very difficult to understand the net balance sheet of 'Mexico in NAFTA.' Winners extol its benefits. Losers condemn it. People in-between feel perplexed. While some sectors have lost significantly (subsistence agriculture is the main one) and others have won disproportionately (capitalists, professionals, merchants, and technicians connected to the supply chains of manufacturing goods that are re-exported to the USA) the net result is difficult to understand. A majority of Mexicans might have lost ground as producers (wage repression, abandonment of subsistence agricultural land). At the same time, they may have gained ground as consumers. This argument, according to which the lowering of trade barriers can inundate domestic markets with cheaper consumer goods (including food and clothes), thereby providing price deflation which can benefit a majority in a given population, is plausible. This phenomenon has been documented for other countries that pursued some degree of economic liberalization in removing trade barriers.[65] The bottom line is that nobody has done a proper analysis that contrasts the net costs and benefits for the Mexican population, both as producers and consumers of trade liberalization.

In conclusion, the opening of Mexico's economy since the 1980s has been asymmetrical. It has favored trade and capital liberalization, while clamping down on labor. In the domestic sector of the economy it agglomerated and concentrated productive activity in public and private monopolies or oligopolies. The state remained dependent on income from state-owned enterprises, most notably Pemex. The end result was a weakened state, growth in inequality, and the influence of powerful, concentrated economic sectors whose leaders had the financial, media and diplomatic means (i.e. the relationship with the US government and private business) to capture the Mexican state in order that it followed the so-called 'Washington consensus' range of policies. It is now more than 30 years since this process started in 1985. Many organized groups are naturally frustrated and their patience has run out time and again. However, the system has remained in place. Can it survive the elections of 2018? The victory by the left might suggest that efforts will at least be made to change it.

Notes

1 Data elaborated by the author from World Bank, Global Development Indicators Database, http://data.worldbank.org/country/mexico, Accessed 7 March 2014.
2 Gordon H. Hanson, "Why is Mexico not Rich," University of California, San Diego and National Bureau of Economic Research (NBER), September 2010, http://irps.ucsd.edu/assets/001/500330.pdf, Accessed 18 October 2014.
3 *Ibid.*, from Abstract.
4 Santiago Levy and Michael Walton, eds., *No Growth without Equity? Inequality, Interests, and Competition in Mexico*, New York: Palgrave, 2009.
5 Jaime Ros Bosch, *Algunas tesis equivocadas sobre el estancamiento económico de México*, Mexico: El Colegio de México, 2014.
6 David Ibarra, *Paradigmas monetarios en México*, México: UNAM, 2010; Francisco Suárez Dávila, *Crecer o no crecer: Del estancamiento estabilizador al nuevo desarrollo*, Mexico: Taurus, 2013; David Ibarra, *La crisis inacabada*, México: UNAM, 2013.
7 Arturo Rodríguez García, "Los hijos del privilegio," in *Proceso*, 25 May 2013, http://www.proceso.com.mx/343013/los-hijos-del-privilegio, Accessed 17 February 2018.
8 See the reportage series by Damien Cave, "Immigration Upended," in *The New York Times*, 2011–2012, http://www.nytimes.com/interactive/world/americas/immigration-upended-series.html, Accessed 22 February 2018.
9 See for example, Walter Scheidel, *The Great Leveler: Violence and the History of Inequality from the Stone Age to the Twenty-First Century*, Princeton: Princeton University Press, 2017.
10 In 2017, according to *Forbes* magazine, the richest Mexican billionaires were: 1) Carlos Slim (telecoms, construction, finance and other industries – sixth wealthiest individual in the world); 2) GermánLarrea (mining, railways – 82nd); 3) Alberto Bailleres (mining, top retail – 123rd); 4) María A. Aramburuzabala (Brewing,

finance – 250th), in *Forbes: the World's Billionaires*, April 2017, Accessed 7 January 2008, https://www.forbes.com/billionaires/list/6/#version:static.

11 Gerardo Esquivel, "Extreme Inequality in Mexico," Oxfam Report, July2015, Accessed 7 January 2018, http://www.pulsamerica.co.uk/2015/07/mexico-wealth-i nequality-four-richest-mexicans-worth-same-as-20-million-poorest/.

12 Esquivel, 2015, http://www.pulsamerica.co.uk/2015/07/mexico-wealth-inequality-four-richest-mexicans-worth-same-as-20-million-poorest/.

13 ECLAC, "Latin America is the world's most unequal region. Here is how to fix it, "https://www.cepal.org/en/articles/2016-latin-america-worlds-most-unequal-region-he res-how-fix-it, 25 January 2016, Accessed 6 December 2017; FocusEconomics, "Latin America: the Most Unequal Region in the World,"https://www.focus-econom ics.com/blog/inequality-in-latin-america, 16 June 2017, Accessed 6 December 2017; Open Democracy, "Why does Latin America remain the most unequal region in the world?"https://www.opendemocracy.net/democraciaabierta/why-does-latin-america-r emain-most-unequal-region-in-world, 12 June 2017, Accessed 6 December 2017.

14 Ariel Fizbein *et al., Conditional Cash Transfers: Reducing Present and Future Poverty*, Washington, DC: World Bank, 2009, https://openknowledge.worldbank. org/handle/10986/2597, Accessed 6 December 2017. This area of policy research, programs, evaluation and re-design for better implementation probably became the most used social policy tool in the course of the 2000s around the developing world, in part thanks to its embrace and diffusion by the World Bank. CCTs remain among the most powerful proven tools in the arsenal of policy interventions by international development experts at least up until the late 2010s.

15 IDB, "Latin America and Caribbean register middle class growth. Child poverty and inequality problems persist,"24 October 2016, https://www.iadb.org/en/news/ news-releases/2016-10-24/latin-american-middle-class-has-nearly-doubled%2C1161 1.html, Accessed 7 December 2017.

16 IDB, "Latin America and Caribbean register middle class growth. Child poverty and inequality problems persist,"24 October 2016, https://www.iadb.org/en/news/news-releases/2016-10-24/latin-american-middle-class-has-nearly-doubled%2C11611.html, Accessed 7 December 2017; Francisco H.G. Ferreira, *et al., Economic Mobility and the Rise of the Latin American Middle Class*, Washington, DC: The World Bank, 2012, http://elibrary.worldbank.org/doi/abs/10.1596/978-0-8213-9634-6, Accessed 24 October 2014.

17 Thomas Piketty, *Capital in the Twenty-first Century*, Cambridge MA, Harvard University Press, 2013.

18 Facundo Alvaredo, Lucas Chancel, Thomas Piketty, Emmanuel Saez, and Gabriel Zucman, *World Wealth and Income Database*, http://wid.world/world-inequality-la b/, 2015, Accessed 7 January 2018.

19 Enrique Krauze, *La presidencia imperial*, Mexico, Tusquets, 2001.

20 Eduardo Turrent, "Historia sintética de la banca en México", Mexico, Banco de Mexico, 2008, http://www.banxico.org.mx/sistema-financiero/material-educativo/ba sico/%7BFFF17467-8ED6-2AB2-1B3B-ACCE5C2AF0E6%7D.pdf, Accessed 7 December 2017.

21 Francisco Ibarra Palafox, *La privatización bancaria en México*, México, Siglo XXI, 2014, chapter 1.

22 Stephen Haber and Aldo Musacchio, "These are the Good Old Days: Foreign Entry and the Mexican Banking System," Harvard Business School, Working Paper 13–062, 10 January 2013, https://dash.harvard.edu/bitstream/handle/1/ 10208236/13-062.pdf?sequence=1, Accessed 8 December 2017, p. 51.

23 Haber and Musacchio, 2013, p. 60.

24 World Bank, Global Financial Development Report 2017/2018, https://openknow ledge.worldbank.org/bitstream/handle/10986/28482/9781464811487.pdf, Appendix A, pp. 121–126.

25 Dag MacLeod, *Downsizing the State: Privatization and the Limits of Neoliberal Reform in Mexico*, University Park: Penn State University Press, 2004, 162–163.
26 MacLeod, 2004, p. 168–70; Lawrence Wright, "Slim's Time: Who is Carlos Slim, and does he want the paper of record?"*The New Yorker*, 9 June 2009, https://www.newyorker.com/magazine/2009/06/01/slims-time, Accessed 11 January 2018.
27 MacLeod, 2004, 170.
28 Wright, 2009.
29 According to investigative journalists and the Swiss judicial investigation, Salinas' government adopted the approach of containing the main narcotics' syndicates by regulating all of them under the supervision of the president's older brother, Raúl, who made an inexplicable fortune of close to half a billion dollars and served ten years in prison accused of masterminding the murder of his ex-brother-in-law, Francisco Ruiz Massieu, a prominent PRI leader, who would have become the Leader of the Majority in the lower chamber of Congress (Cámara de Diputados) after the 1994 general elections.
     If such illegal capitalization of private firms started in earnest during the Salinas years, there is no reason to believe that it stopped after that. See *Proceso*, "En los setenta, Salinas Lozano 'introdujo' a Carlos y Raúl en el tráfico de drogas", 20 January 1999, Accessed 11 January 2018.
30 Economist Intelligence Unit, "Telecoms reform begins to show results," 30 October 2015, http://www.eiu.com/industry/article/673657251/telecoms-reform-begins-to-show-results/2015-10-30, Accessed 11 January 2018.
31 Joe Torres, Julia Love and ShekyEspejo, "Slim's America Movil wins telecom battle in top Mexico court," in *Reuters*, 16 August 2017, https://www.reuters.com/article/us-mexico-telecom/slims-america-movil-wins-telecom-battle-in-top-mexico-court-idUSKCN1AW2IA, accessed 11 January 2018.
32 Azam Ahmed, "Mexico Spends Big on Ads to Tame the News Media," *The New York Times*, 25 December 2017, A1; A10–11.
33 Proceso, "Azcárraga se declara priísta y soldado del presidente", 15 May 1982, http://www.proceso.com.mx/133473/azcarraga-se-declara-priista-y-soldado-del-presidente, Accessed 12 January 2018.
34 Rory Carroll and Jo Tuckman, "Spotlight falls on Televisa, Mexico's all-powerful TV station," in *The Guardian*, 26 June 2012, https://www.theguardian.com/world/2012/jun/26/spotlight-televisa-mexico-tv-station, Accessed, 12 January 2018.
35 *Proceso*, "En los setenta, Salinas Lozano 'introdujo' a Carlos y Raúl en el tráfico de drogas,"20 January 1999, Accessed 13 January 2018.
36 Jenaro Villamil, "Va reforma de telecom contra creaciones del propio gobierno," in *Proceso*, 16 March 2013, http://diario.mx/Nacional/2013-03-16_4d5e1fd4/va-reforma-de-telecom-contra-creaciones-del-propio-gobierno/, Accessed 12 January 2018.
37 Villamil, 2013.
38 Francisco Cruz and Jorge Toribio Cruz Montiel, *Negocios de familia: biografía no autorizada de Enrique Peña Nieto y el grupo Atlacomulco*, Mexico, Temas de Hoy, 2009.
39 Sin Embargo, "*The Guardian* revela que Televisa vendió a EPN plan para posicionarlo y hundir a AMLO; involucra a Fox", 7 June 2012, http://www.sinembargo.mx/07-06-2012/257208, Accessed 12 January 2018.
40 See the progressive perspective in Lorenzo Meyer and Isidro Morales, *Petróleo y nación: la política petrolera en México, 1900–1987*, Mexico, Fondo de Cultura Económica, 1990; Lorenzo Meyer, *Mexico y los Estados Unidos en el conflicto petrolero, 1917–1942*, Mexico, El Colegion de Mexico, 1981; Adolfo Gilly, *El cardenismo: una utopía mexicana*, Mexico, cal y arena, 1994; the conservative view in George W. Grayson, *The Politics of Mexican Oil*, Pittsburgh, PA: University of Pittsburgh Press, 1980.

41 Robert T. Deacon, "The Political Economy of the Resource Curse: A Survey of Theory and Evidence," in *Foundations and Trends in Microeconomics*, 7 (2, 111–208, 2011); Macartan Humphreys, Jeffrey D. Sachs, Joseph E. Stiglitz, eds., *Escaping the Resource Curse*, New York: Columbia University Press, 2007; Terry Lynn Karl, *The Paradox of Plenty: Oil Booms and Petro-States*, Berkeley, CA: University of California Press, 1997.

42 Steinar Holden, "Avoiding the Resource Curse: the Case of Norway," in *Energy Policy*, 63 (December 2013, 870–876).

43 Ana Lilia Pérez, *Camisas azules, manos negras: El saqueo de PEMEX desde Los Pinos*, Mexico, Grijalbo, 2010.

44 Excélsior, "Perfil de Joaquín Hernández Galicia, La Quina," 11 November 2013, http://www.excelsior.com.mx/nacional/2013/11/11/928036, Accessed 16 January 2018.

45 Martín Moreno, "Todo el imperio podrido de Carlos Romero Deschamps", in *Sin Embargo*, 25 February 2015, http://www.sinembargo.mx/25-02-2015/1260531, Accessed 16 January 2018; *Proceso*, "Romero Deschamps, historia de un líder menor", 24 September 2002, http://www.proceso.com.mx/245057/245057-romero-deschamps-historia-de-un-lider-menor, Accessed 16 January 2018.

46 Carmen Silvia Zepeda Bustos, "Privatizaciones realizadas durante el sexenio de Ernesto Zedillo", in *El Cotidiano*, 172, March-April 2012, 32–39, http://www.reda lyc.org/html/325/32523118004/, Accessed 16 January 2018.

47 SR Srocco Report, "PEMEX: Mexico's State Oil Company on the Verge of Bankruptcy and Collapse,"25 March 2017, https://us-issues.com/2017/03/25/pem ex-mexicos-state-oil-company-on-the-verge-of-bankruptcy-collapse/, Accessed 16 January 2018.

48 Ana Lilia Pérez, *El Cártel Negro: Cómo el crimen organizado se ha apoderado de PEMEX*, Mexico, Grijalbo, 2011.

49 Jesús Reyes Heroles, "Fiscal and Energy Issues in Mexico in a Presidential Election Year," Presentation at The Johns Hopkins University School of Advanced International Studies (SAIS), 5 April 2012.

50 On the side of supporters see Carlos Loret de Mola, "Lo major y lo peor de Felipe Calderón", in *El Universal*, 2 December 2010, http://archivo.eluniversal.com.mx/ columnas/87424.html, Accessed 16 January 2018; on the side of opinion against the measure, see Arturo Rodríguez García, "El golpe a Luz y Fuerza, ilegal de principio a fin", in *Proceso*, 26 October 2012, http://www.proceso.com.mx/323571/ 323571-el-golpe-a-luz-y-fuerza-ilegal-de-principio-a-fin, Accessed 16 January 2018.

51 Energy Information Administration, "Mexico,"16 October 2017, https://www.eia. gov/beta/international/analysis.cfm?iso=MEX, Accessed 19 January 2018.

52 Mexico, Secretaria de Energía, "Ronda Cero", March 2014, https://www.gob.mx/cm s/uploads/attachment/file/55590/Ficha_tecnica_R0.pdf, Accessed 19 January 2018.

53 Economia hoy, "Probable, una tercera subasta petrolera en 2018,"19 October 2017, http://www.economiahoy.mx/empresas-eAm-mexico/noticias/8687385/10/17/ Probable-una-tercera-subasta-petrolera-en-2018.html, Accessed 19 January 2018.

54 Jesús Reyes Heroles, "Fiscal and Energy Issues in Mexico in a Presidential Election Year," Presentation at The Johns Hopkins University School of Advanced International Studies (SAIS), 5 April 2012.

55 Ibid.

56 The Gini coefficient goes from 0 to 1, where 0 would mean perfect equality, i.e. same amount of income goes to the top as to the bottom, and 1 is perfect inequality, i.e. all goes to the top decile and nothing to the bottom one.

57 Author's interview with Cicero, 22 August 2011.

58 Ibid.

59 See for example James C. Scott, *Against the Grain: A Deep History of the Earliest States*, New Haven: Yale University Press, 2017.

60 Rogelio Gómez Hermosillo, "Quién fija el salario mínimo?" in El Universal, 8 December 2015, http://www.eluniversal.com.mx/entrada-de-opinion/articulo/roge lio-gomez-hermosillo-m/nacion/2015/12/8/quien-fija-el-salario-minimo, Accessed 19 January 2018.

61 Robert A. Blecker, "The North American Economies after NAFTA: a Critical Appraisal," in *International Journal of Political Economy*, 33 (3, 5–27, 2003); Irma Adelman and Edward Taylor, "Is structural adjustment with a human face possible? The case of Mexico," in *The Journal of Development Studies*, 26 (3, 387–407, 1990).

62 MSCI Emerging Markets Index (USD), https://www.msci.com/documents/10199/ c0db0a48-01f2-4ba9-ad01-226fd5678111, Accessed 20 January 2018.

63 Pan Kwan Yuk, "Want cheap labor? Head to Mexico, not China," in *Financial Times*, January 14, 2016, https://www.ft.com/content/bddc8121-a7a0-3788-a 74c-cd2b49cd3230, Accessed 20 January 2018.

64 FacundoAlvaredo, Lucas Chancel, Thomas Piketty, Emmanuel Saez, and Gabriel Zucman, *World Wealth and Income Database*, http://wid.world/world-inequality-la b/, 2015, Accessed 7 January 2018.

65 Andy Baker, *The Market and the Masses in Latin America: Policy Reform and Consumption in Liberalizing Economies*, Cambridge: Cambridge University Press, 2009.

6   Why Is Mexico so Violent? Governors, Caciques, and Cartels

The Fall of PRI Hegemony and the Rise of 'Feuderalism'

Introduction

Co-written with Albert 'Jim' Marckwardt

The reign of the Partido Revolucionario Institucional (PRI) in Mexico, spanning from 1929 through to 2000, is characterized as an era of a patronage-based hegemonic rule. As Nobel Prize winner Mario Vargas Llosa described it, Mexico had 'la dictadura perfecta', the perfect dictatorship—a dictatorship camouflaged to not look like one (to look instead like a democracy), with seemingly free open elections and freedom of the press. For the first 50 years the PRI steadily amassed monopolistic power. However, after the 1982 financial crisis that led to the 'lost decade' in growth and development the conservative and left-wing opposition strengthened as the leaders of large, medium-sized and small businesses joined the Partido Acción Nacional (PAN), and started competing for office in earnest.

Likewise, inside the PRI there was a growing number of malcontents who derided President Miguel De la Madrid's (1982–88) crisis management (i.e. prioritizing paying foreign creditors by cutting in a draconian way public investment and the main public services such as education, health, and housing). Many of them left the party in 1987 when President De la Madrid chose the young, pro-US, neoliberal technocrat, Carlos Salinas de Gortari (1988–94) as his successor. The end result was that the Mexican left, which had until then been fragmented among many small parties and movements, converged and joined efforts to fight the 1988 presidential elections as a block. Following the leadership of PRI grandees like Cuauhtémoc Cárdenas and Porfirio Muñoz Ledo, who left the party after the nomination of Salinas, the left came together in the Frente Democrático Nacional (FDN) with Cárdenas as its presidential candidate.

The 1988 election saw the PRI facing for the first time in its history strong contenders on both the right (Sinaloan entrepreneur Manuel Clouthier) and the left (Cuauhtémoc Cárdenas, son of the most popular Mexican president since the end of the revolution). The end result was a hard-fought election which, as seen in Chapter 3, was blatantly rigged as the Minister of the Interior halted vote counting and came out to tell all

Mexicans who had a television or a radio that the "the [computing] system [counting votes] crashed."

This was a momentous period for Mexico's political development. The doubtfully legally elected Carlos Salinas proceeded by officially saying that the years of PRI hegemony had come to an end, and that the country had to democratize. But he did not carry out this promise. What he did was to implement a process of selective political liberalization, which rewarded those who supported his revolutionary program to open up the Mexican economy, privatize most state sector firms, and integrate economically with the USA. Salinas's strong personal leadership meant that the PRI, despite being the party of many politicians who were doubtful about embracing neoliberalism, followed the President. The PAN, under the legislative leadership of Diego Fernández de Ceballos, also aligned behind the neoliberal revolution. In return, Salinas's government accepted for the first time in the PRI's history governorship victories by the PAN, starting in the state of Baja California in 1989 and later in Chihuahua and Guanajuato states. In contrast, the President was antagonistic and punished the Partido de la Revolución Democrática (PRD), the left-wing party created in 1989, and made up by the main parties and movements that had fought the 1988 elections under the FDN.

Thus, democratization of Mexico's long-lasting, resilient authoritarian political regime started as a highly controlled process from above by President Salinas. It was not democratization in fact, but rather selective political liberalization, given that Salinas was generous with his allies like the PAN, and his reluctant followers in the PRI, just as he was brutal toward his enemies, the PRD. For example, in the face of PRD representatives' protests during his last State of the Union address in September 1994, Salinas said "ni los veo, ni los oigo"[1] (I do not see them or hear them). This is exactly what happened during his six years in power, as hundreds of PRD members or sympathizers were persecuted and killed for opposing the PRI and what they considered fraudulent local, state, and federal elections.[2]

The process of controlled, selective political liberalization gave way to a genuine democratic opening as a consequence of the 1994–95 'tequila crisis', and recently installed President Ernesto Zedillo's (1994–2000) precarious political position. His 1996 political reform led to a more level playing field across the political spectrum, and democratization (as seen through increasing defeats for the PRI and victories not just for the PAN, but also the PRD) accelerated in the course of the late 1990s. Democratization occurred mainly at the expense of the PRI, which did not forgive Zedillo for weakening the party and reaching out to the opposition in general rather than just selectively. The disintegration of the PRI's political monopoly during this transition was the result of inadequate political responses to events outside of its control (such as the economic crises at the end of each presidency since 1976 or the indigenous Zapatista uprising in Chiapas which started in January 1994, or the assassination of the PRI's presidential candidate, Luis Donaldo Colosio, in the campaign trail in Tijuana in March 1994), as well as deliberate changes in the hegemonic paradigm implemented by the PRI (Salinas' selective political liberalization and Zedillo's more general democratic opening).

Inadequate political responses that chipped away at the PRI's hegemony included the inability to prevent the economic crises that devastated the country at the end of each *sexenio*; the exposure of almost unimaginable levels of enrichment through grand corruption by President José López Portillo (1976–82), his family and close collaborators and their families; the failed government assistance after the earthquakes that destroyed parts of Mexico City and killed thousands in September 1985; or, again, the enormous enrichment through grand corruption by President Salinas de Gortari, his family, and close collaborators and their families. These and other public events that worsened political and socioeconomic conditions for the average Mexican led to growing, mass public dissatisfaction with the PRI. At the same time, as mentioned above, the regime's leaders enacted deliberate changes which included various electoral reform bills and the PRI acknowledgment of victories by the PAN (during Salinas's presidency) and, later on, also victories by the PRD during Zedillo's presidency—for example, the first open election for mayor of Mexico City in 1997, which was won by Cuauhtémoc Cárdenas.

In contrast to the economic opening, privatization, and deregulation, all of which were designed and closely followed by neoliberal technocrats who started serving under De la Madrid and then came to dominate all economic policymaking, the political transformation lacked any true strategy, structure, or assistance from multilateral organizations. Instead, political opening and the birth of democracy took place through a series of events, many of which were unplanned and unpredictable. According to the World Bank, political opening and decentralization aim to give citizens or their elected representatives more power in public decision-making.[3] However, the transition in Mexico failed to accomplish the aforementioned goal, and instead, political power was transferred to a new group of political élites.

As the barriers to entry into the political arena came down, new entrants began to contest the regime's monopoly at both state and municipal levels. Many of these entrants were simply old actors who had operated within the centralized and structured hierarchy of the hegemonic PRI and now sought to increase their power independently in an increasingly pluralistic system. Many PRI leaders and members migrated to the PRD after what they considered as the betrayal of the party's historical mission (i.e. nationalism, protection, neutral position vis-à-vis the USA) during the Salinas and Zedillo administrations. Likewise, as the PAN started winning governorships, state legislatures, and more federal elective positions, many more conservative-minded or simply opportunistic PRI members left and joined the PAN and its rising star.

After the election of Vicente Fox of the PAN as President in 2000, the first non-PRI head of state since the rise of the PNR/PRM/PRI during 1929–2000, the barriers to entry continued falling. But a deeper process of social decomposition had also been taking place since the De la Madrid and Salinas years, whereby the only way that politicians and policymakers managed to retain control of the state and its most important function, namely the monopoly over the legitimate use of persuasion/force/coercion across the territory, was through illegal clampdowns and repression in many cases. The appearance of social peace and political order during the Salinas years was intimately tied to the president's personalization of power and the implacable way that he dealt with dissent and opposition.

Organized crime had made international headlines, in particular in the USA in 1985, during De la Madrid's presidency, when a Drug Enforcement Agency (DEA) official, Enrique 'Kiki' Camarena was brutally tortured, mutilated, and murdered by members of the Guadalajara drug-trafficking cartel. During Salinas's administration, in 1993, a Cardinal of the Catholic Church, Juan Jesús Posadas Ocampo, was murdered in broad daylight at Guadalajara international airport, in a case of mistaken identity. By the time President Zedillo came to power and the country collapsed financially in 1994–95 in what came to be known as the 'tequila crisis', petty as well as organized crime got out of control as it multiplied and gained notoriety both in Mexico and abroad. Kidnappings, muggings, burglary, and armed confrontations among criminal groups and between them and law enforcement groups (both police and military) grew significantly (or at least their public salience as reported by diverse media—and despite control mechanisms like the so-called *chayote,* or bribe).

The gradual descent into widespread violence and the state's inability to control it were intertwined with the years of democratization. As British author Ioan Grillo notes, the Mexican drug war is intimately tied to the country's democratic transition.[4] The weakening and hollowing of state power after the Salinas years created a process that lowered barriers to entry in the public sphere to organized criminal groups, fragmented power, and multiplied the actors and avenues capable of competing with the state over the use of persuasion, force, and coercion.

Although not exhaustive, the phrase 'Governors, Caciques, and Cartels' summarizes some of the main competitors the Mexican federal government had to start confronting in order to try and maintain a semblance of social peace and political stability from the second half of the 1990s. These powerful actors on the ground began to work together at the state and municipal level, creating a new political paradigm of order in their respective areas: 'feuderalism'.[5] The concept, derived from Mexico's constitutional federal order as well as from the notion of feudalism, under which Europe experienced during the early Middle Ages fragmented political power, frequent internecine conflicts and wars due to such fragmentation, and the relative autonomy of feudal lords who could do as they pleased in the territories they controlled, gained popularity among analysts, journalists, and scholars who study Mexican politics.

This chapter explores the correlation—not necessarily the unique causation—between the lowering of political barriers, state power fragmentation, and the proliferation of organized violence that gathered steam during Zedillo's presidency and then became embedded into public life in many parts of the Mexican territory under presidents from the PAN—Vicente Fox (2000–06) and Felipe Calderón (2006–12), and how it continued during the return of a president from the PRI, Enrique Peña Nieto (2012). This chapter presents evidence to help understand why political fragmentation instead of decentralization led to violence, by analyzing how the PRI regime maintained its monopoly with high barriers of entry before the proliferation of organized violence; how and why the party began to fragment and lose its power as the barriers lowered during the democratization period; and finally which actors—mainly governors, *caciques*, and cartels—created the new political paradigm of 'feuderalism' as the barriers evaporated, triggering an increase of organized violence throughout the country which state institutions could not contain.

PRI's Monopoly

To understand why the fragmentation of Mexico's monopolistic political system led to calamitous consequences, it is essential to first understand the mechanisms the party used to maintain power. Over several decades the PRI developed a top-down hierarchical hegemonic system. This system resembled a monopoly with high barriers of entry that denied other political parties from contesting the regime. Key elements of this power stemmed from its election policies that allowed the party to remain in power; its taxation system that gave the government resources to pay off clients (both argued by Frank Brandenburg)[6]; its use of security forces to keep dissenters in line; and its ties to the historical *cacique* system.[7] The party used these elements of power to maintain high barriers to entry, in contrast to a system of democratic rule with open elections.

Political Careerism

As Alberto Díaz-Cayeros writes, the PRI regime's 'mature limited access order' strengthened over the decades from its inception in 1929.[8] 'Limited access order' governments prevented the proliferation of violence where they operated by granting economic and political access to the local, state, or federal élites, thereby allowing them to receive rents, instead of opening up access to all.[9] In Mexico, the Constitution prohibited re-election at any level of government, limiting access to few. This golden rule, a result of the Mexican Revolution and politicians' and popular leaders' belief that the only way to stop another long-term dictatorship by a strongman like the one they fought against General Porfirio Díaz, became a very effective disciplining mechanism which in turn strengthened command-and-control orders emanating from the presidency. Given that every politician's political future depended on their superiors, all the way up to the President due to the no re-election law, rather than on citizens (constituents) rewarding good politicians by re-electing them and punishing bad ones by throwing them out, most politicians followed the political and bureaucratic commands from above. Acquiescence and good implementation of such central commands would then end up deciding the fate of politicians operating on the greasy pole of a system without popular re-election, but with advancement, in so far as they complied with and advanced incumbents' laws, rules, and interests. All those individuals who managed to enter the system had to play the game. All politicians focused their efforts on improving their reputation within the party, competing for jobs and opportunities to run for better political offices, all at the neglect of their constituents. Congress filled up with aspiring PRI politicians fighting to get ahead in their careers. For instance, Rubén Figueroa Figueroa, the Governor of Guerrero state during 1975–81 had previously served as a Senator in the national Congress during 1970–74 and before that in the House of Deputies (Cámara de Diputados) during 1964–67. This was hardly an exception, but rather the norm, which his son followed 20 years later. Career politicians are not a phenomenon unique to Mexico—this career exists in all countries and includes advanced countries like the USA or those of Western Europe. However, the difference was how the system fostered a lack of accountability on behalf of the constituents. A lack of re-election ensured that what mattered most to politicians was to be selected by the PRI's leaders, and in particular by the incumbent president and his close collaborators, in order to achieve higher office in the next round of elections. This mechanism ensured that the idea of representation and accountability to citizens as voters was practically non-existent.

This patronage-style political careerist path prevented any positive social contract between PRI politicians and voters from developing. Instead, the PRI focused on maintaining stability in the country through a hegemonic party system that granted nearly unlimited power to the president to autonomously fire governors, appoint senior politicians, name his successor, and decide the federal budget.[10]

Despite hegemonic rule, lower-level politicians did at times overstep their bounds and embarrassed the party. The punitive response from the incumbent President was always swift and harsh. In 1993 Rubén Figueroa Alcocér, the son of Rubén Figueroa Figueroa and PRI loyalist, was elected governor of Guerrero for a six-year term. Like his father, he previously served in the Senate in 1991–92, and in the House of Deputies in 1979–81. Unlike his father, however, his term as governor was cut short. On 28 June 1995 farmers from the Organización Campesina de la Sierra travelled to Atoyac de Álvarez to participate in protests. On their way, the Guerrero state police ambushed them, killing 17 people and injuring 21 more. The police immediately proclaimed self-defense. However, over the next several months the police were implicated in having planned and executed the massacre. By March 1996 the public believed that the Governor had orchestrated the police operation. Whether the accusations were true or false was irrelevant—the embarrassment was more than the party was willing to bear and on 12 March 1996 Rubén Figueroa Alcocer was forced to resign. In fact, during President Salinas's *sexenio* a total of 17 governors of the 31 nationally resigned under pressure from the President.[11] The will of the President was systematically stronger than that of the citizens.

A key factor perpetuating the PRI's control of the electoral process was the appointment of a presidential successor, a practise commonly known as el 'dedazo'. The term literally referred to the President pointing his finger to his chosen successor.[12] This was the ultimate hegemonic expression of the party in which the incumbent president decided autonomously who the next president of Mexico would be. Although a formal general election followed each nomination, no other party or independent candidate could compete with the PRI and its vast resources in the national election. The successor always won, traditionally with close to 90 percent of the vote. In 1976 López Portillo ran unopposed for president, winning all the valid votes. This result embarrassed the regime because such types of election and voter statistics were typical of totalitarian regimes at the time in communist countries like the Union of Soviet Socialist Republics (USSR), Cuba, or North Korea. Mexico, 'la dictadura perfecta,' was not communist, had many political parties, and was a 'free' country.

As a consequence, President López Portillo was forced to change the country's electoral system in 1977 by introducing a measure of proportional representation (a mixed system copied from the German system of the Bundesrepublik), alongside the existing first-past-the-post formula. The architect of the reform, PRI intellectual and leader Jesús Reyes Heroles, explained the need to have opposition in an hegemonic party system thus: "No queremos luchar con el viento, con el aire; lo que resiste apoya. Requerimos una sana resistencia que nos apoye en el avance político de México".[13] (We do not want to fight against the wind, the air; what offers resistance helps to support. We need a healthy resistance that supports us [the PRI] in Mexico's political development.)

Financial Carrots

While the election system helped propagate and retain the PRI's grip on power, its financial resources, funded through the national tax system, trade unions' contributions, and the earnings of the largest state owned enterprises like Pemex, the Comisión Federal de Electricidad, or state development banks including NAFIN, Banobras, and Banrural provided a critical carrot used to incentivize its clients. This system also minimized the public oversight of tax expenditures. As seen in the previous chapter Mexico has traditionally collected very little in the way of personal income taxes from its citizens, and instead relies heavily on value-added tax, taxation of formal wages, and taxation of some public corporations, but mostly of state-owned enterprises. Historically approximately 60 percent of its total revenue came from income tax and 40 percent from sales tax.[14] Of the total, about 40 percent of its tax revenue has come since the 1980s from one corporation, Pemex. As seen in the last chapter, this highlighted the importance of Pemex, the largest state-controlled corporation, as a financial carrot source for the PRI. Additionally, states and municipalities received most of their revenue from the federal government, further increasing the control of the President over lower-level governments. The most corrosive aspect of the system was that it weakened the social contract between citizens as taxpayers and their elected officials, as only a small percentage of the revenue came from private citizens. Instead of responding to the needs of their constituents, politicians focused expenditures on "political support through patronage and pork-barrel projects".[15]

Further highlighting the disconnection between the PRI-dominated regime and taxpayers, the Constitution allowed for a secret presidential discretionary fund for presidents to use at their will. Known as the 'partida secreta presidencial,' presidents used this fund frequently, with little accountability. President De la Madrid spent US $352m. from this fund during his *sexenio*. In fact, during a 14-year period from 1983 to 1997 a total of $1,340m. was spent from this account.[16] Acknowledging the little oversight that existed, De la Madrid in 2009 confessed in a television interview that Raúl Salinas, the older brother of President Carlos Salinas, personally embezzled half of the $857m. available to President Salinas.[17] The vast coffers of the national treasury allowed the PRI to continue to incentivize and pay its clients, in order to remain in power without due accountability.

Due to the great dependence of state and municipal governments on federal funding, the Treasury or Ministry of Finance became one of the essential sticks and carrots for presidents to use in favor of or against lower-level government officials. If a state governor or a city mayor followed the president's wishes, they would be recompensed. But if they questioned orders from above, rocked the boat or became a whistleblower against corruption and impunity, they would face financial starvation. This system was easier to run when all the main actors belonged to the PRI. Mexico became more plural politically in the course of the 1990s: this system of publicly financing rewards according to blind loyalty to the chief federal executive became much more controversial as members of different parties, whether from the left, right, or center, occupied positions at the three levels of government. Therefore, federal transfers became not necessarily more politicized (they had been during the years of PRI hegemony given the many groups or *camarillas* in the party that fought to advance their interests and power), but definitely more subject to partisanship: a PAN or PRD governor or mayor has to tread carefully if the Mexican president is from the PRI. Likewise, other combinations apply with the same logic, of which the end goal is to conform, be loyal, and follow the federal government's aims and objectives.

Security Stick

Just as important as the carrot was the stick in maintaining the hegemonic regime and the governments that emanated from it. The security forces played a vital role in fortifying the PRI's power throughout much of the second half of the 20th century. Although these forces (the military under the Department of National Defense and the Department of the Navy, and the police and its intelligence services under the Ministry of the Interior) existed as state institutions, they were loyal to the regime and served as its enforcement arms. Unlike developed 'open access order' countries, the public did not give the security system its legitimacy, instead, the regime did.[18] Similar to the nonexistent relationship between taxpayers and their elected officials, there was no direct social contract between security forces and the public. Instead, the security institutions depended on the party as much as the party depended on them. "The armed forces bolstered the top-down control exercised by the state."[19] And the party repeatedly used security forces to maintain power.

Tlatelolco Massacre

Examples abound of the PRI using the military to maintain its hegemonic rule, however, none is more infamous than the Tlatelolco massacre. On 2 October 1968, less than two weeks before the opening of the Summer Olympic Games in Mexico City, over 10,000 university students and civilians from across Mexico City rallied in the Plaza de las Tres Culturas to protest against the government's excessive expenditure on the Olympics, and to demand the release of political prisoners, and an opening up of society to mass political participation. Student protests had started earlier that year and had been dealt with heavy handedly by the authorities, with the result that the student movement had grown in numbers and intensity. On 2 October the demonstrators were violently confronted by the military, and by sunset the army surrounded the plaza with 5,000 soldiers and 200 armored vehicles under orders from the Minister of National Defense, Gen. Marcelino García Barragán. Gunfire erupted and hundreds of students were killed as well as thousands arrested and later tortured and imprisoned on trumped-up charges.[20]

In the immediate aftermath, the media reported that students fired at the soldiers from sniper positions, causing the army to retaliate with shots. In fact, on the following morning, the *El Día* daily newspaper published the headline "Criminal Provocation at the Tlatelolco Meeting Causes Terrible Bloodshed".[21] Over 30 years later and after several commissions to discover the truth, the consensus was that Presidential Guard snipers fired at the students, not vice versa. The tragedy underscored the regime's ability to control the media 30 years after the massacre. It was not until 1998, as the 30th anniversary of the massacre brought tens of thousands of demonstrators to the streets to protest against the continuation of authoritarian rule by the PRI, that President Zedillo established a congressional investigation in order to establish the truth. Apart from the Minister of Defense at the time, Gen. García Barragán, Minister of Interior Luis Echeverría Álvarez, who was elected President in 1970, were found to be the main executors of the massacre.

Ministry of the Interior

While the PRI regularly used military might to secure its power, it was the Ministry of the Interior that served as the primary stick for the regime acting as its "political interlocutor."[22] The Ministry of the Interior was often the training grounds for future Presidents, such as Lázaro Cárdenas del Río (1934–40), Miguel Alemán Valdés (1946–52), Adolfo Ruiz Cortines (1952–58), Gustavo Díaz Ordaz (1964–70), and Luis Echeverría Álvarez (1970–76). In fact, Minister of the Interior Francisco Labastida Ochoa had been President Zedillo's presidential candidate in the run-up to the 2000 elections, which he lost to the PAN's Fox. The PRI placed considerable importance on the Ministry of the Interior and its leadership to keep political stability and social peace in Mexico.

The primary entity underneath Ministry of the Interior responsible for political and public order was the Dirección Federal de Seguridad (DFS). Created in 1947, this agency maintained the internal security of the nation through investigations and enforcement. The agency was also used to control "dissent and monitor expressions of disagreement against the regime."[23] It was in essence a political police force.[24] After DFS involvement was proven in the kidnapping, torture, and murder of DEA agent Enrique 'Kiki' Camarena in 1985, the agency was disbanded. Carlos Salinas, anointed president amid general protests and allegations of fraud in 1988, and wanting to create a clean slate in the Mexico-US relationship, created the Center for Research and National Security (CISEN) in its place. This intelligence agency was supposed to be a professional, impartial agency, modelled on US intelligence agencies to monitor national security activities and report directly to the president. In reality, it broadly continued to operate like its predecessor, the DFS.

The power of the Ministry of the Interior, however, was not just limited to its security forces. As the secretariat also responsible for all government elections, in July 1988 it ran Mexico's presidential election as it had many times before. The three primary candidates were Carlos Salinas from the PRI, Cuauhtémoc Cárdenas of the PRD as the left-wing firebrand who united the Mexican fragmented left, and Manuel Clouthier from the PAN. As related above, the Ministry of the Interior, under Manuel Bartlett Díaz, engineered an electoral fraud that rippled across the world due to its cynical justification: a crash of the computing system counting votes, which observers noted was very convenient for the PRI. Many years later, former President De la Madrid admitted to falsely announcing that the electoral computer system had crashed.[25] By the time the alleged 'crashed' system had been restored, Salinas conveniently emerged the victor with only a fraction above 50% of the total votes cast. Three years later the Congress, led by an alliance between the PRI and the PAN, ordered the destruction of all the ballots.[26] Only a still effective totalitarian or a hegemonic party could have got away with such a blatant act of fraud.

At least two political heavyweights who spent decades at the center of power and decision-making in Mexico, whom I interviewed twice, separately, between 2011 and 2014, said that after the PAN came to power in 2000, it enacted a deliberate policy to weaken the Ministry of the Interior. From both individuals' perspective, this was far from an outrage. Rather, it was the logical conclusion that opposition political forces had formed about the oversized political control that the Ministry of the Interior had exercised, among others, against them. Thus, President Fox weakened the intelligence functions of the Ministry of the Interior, which were under the CISEN; he rolled back media surveillance, electoral management, and federal co-ordination with states and municipalities about order and stability, traditionally prerogatives of the Ministry of the Interior.[27]

What to many Mexican citizens and foreign observers, including me when I carried out these interviews, was a logical step to democratize Mexico (dismantling some of the formidable, unaccountable, violent, and discretionary means that the Ministry of the Interior had used to maintain political acquiescence and social peace) was to them one of the main reasons why Mexico had started experiencing barbaric violence and rule by rogue governors, *caciques*, and cartels, not just since the PAN won presidential power in 2000 (the Zedillo years, both said, had incubated state weakness and fragmentation).

Looked at from their perspective, the situation was not surprising. Their logic went something along these lines: the PRI kept peace and stability through a variety of mechanisms, and the Ministry of the Interior was a central one. To PAN or PRD members or sympathizers, the Ministry of the Interior and its activities kept them on edge and were the personification of evil. They were spied on, tracked, threatened, and in many cases they or their families and associates suffered coercion and violence perpetrated by the Mexican state and its arm, the Ministry of the Interior. When the PAN finally came to power when Fox was elected President, they distrusted the system they had inherited, and they clipped its wings. Democracy meant no more espionage or intimidation of legitimate political activity and participation.

However, by weakening the Mexican state's capacity to gather intelligence, monitor federal, state, and municipal politics, and assuming that a democratically elected president could somehow transform a very complex system that had responded to the carrots and sticks that Ministry of the Interior, among other arms of the executive branch of government, had executed during more than half a century, was naïve and irresponsible.

The Power of *Caciques*

Another contributor to the PRI's success was its ability to understand, work with, and even lead the *caciques* in Mexico. *Caciques* were local leaders steeped in Mexican culture and history who served as political mediators within the informal corners of Mexican society, connecting the central government to its citizens on the ground, in villages, towns, and small cities.[28] Although *caciques* tended to be farmers, small businessmen, professors, doctors, and even politicians, what they all had in common was they acted as the intermediaries and influencers between the locals and larger interest groups, such as governments, in their native regions. Their strength lay in their ability to rally their followers for different causes, typically personal, but also sometimes business and political. *Caciques* have played a significant role in Mexican history, dating back to the country's independence from Spain, and have existed at several levels, from the local and municipal level, to the state and regional level.[29] At the local and municipal level they communicated directly with residents within their circle of influence. In contrast, *caciques* at the state and regional level maintained contact, and oversaw and influenced lower level local and municipal *caciques*.

The strength of all *caciques* relied upon their ability to manage relationships throughout the Mexican social spectrum, from the common citizen to the political élite. At the citizen end of the spectrum *caciques* maintained 'political domination' over their communities by controlling the political and economic resources to which the community lacked access. By holding these resources ransom, they could influence their communes to vote in a manner that benefited the *caciques'* client interests. At the other end of the spectrum, *caciques* would provide electoral guarantees to both the party in power and the higher-level *caciques* in exchange for rents. As the PRI strengthened its political power during the 20th century, *caciques* correspondingly increased their alignment with the regime that provided them ample resources.

Due to a lack of regime change during the PRI reign, the *caciques* began to institutionalize themselves within the PRI and began operating vis-à-vis the state institutions.[30] This eventually led to the President also becoming the national-level *cacique* during much of the PRI's reign. Unlike *caciques* at the subnational level, the national *cacique* answered to nobody and possessed nearly limitless resources, granted to him through being the head of state; the head of government; and the head of the hegemonic party, the PRI. This intertwined relationship between the *cacique* system and the regime practically guaranteed the regime's votes, in exchange for rents for the local and regional level *caciques*.

The example of Marcelino García Barragán illustrates the creation of a *cacique* who, from the local and state level ended up at the apex of power as Secretary (Minister) of National Defense. García Barragán became a powerful regional *cacique* with close ties to President Cárdenas. A career military officer, García Barragán was ordered by President Cárdenas to 'modernize' and appease the coast of Jalisco state with his military forces. He eventually gained military control of that area and expanded his influence into the political and *cacique* arenas. In 1943 he was elected governor of the state of Jalisco. Although he only served as governor until 1947, his influence over the *caciques* in Jalisco continued for decades after he left office. In essence, he was the top regional *cacique*, maintaining such close ties to successive presidents that in 1960 he was reinstated back into the military as a General. In 1964 he was appointed as the Secretary of National Defense. While serving as the top military officer in the government, he maintained oversight of the *caciques* in his region. "Almost all decisions about who should be municipal president or who should lead the peasants, as well as who should be included in the lists of candidates, fell on his shoulders."[31] This continued, despite causing the tragedy of the Tlatelolco Massacre, until his death in 1979. Throughout his reign as undisputed *cacique* in important parts of Jalisco, he always subordinated himself to the national *cacique*—that is, the sitting president of Mexico, and provided the PRI with votes in exchange for handsome rewards such as his appointment as Secretary of National Defense. During the PRI hegemonic rule, *caciques* worked "with and through state-controlled institutions."[32] However by the early 1980s, social, economic, and political forces began to challenge this once untouchable paradigm, and the assassination of a US federal agent rattled this arrangement and forced some important changes.

A Critical Juncture? The Case of the Assassination of DEA Agent Enrique 'Kiki' Camarena

The murder of US Drug Enforcement Administration (DEA) Agent Enrique 'Kiki' Camarena in Guadalajara, Mexico in February 1985 highlights the extent to which the political regime under PRI hegemony could even be trusted to help with large-scale operations with geopolitical implications during the late years of the Cold War. Camarena had served in the DEA for 10 years and in 1984 began working with Mexican authorities to destroy hundreds of hectares of marijuana that belonged to maverick drug-trafficker of the Guadalajara Cartel, Rafael Caro Quintero. The commonly held belief is, that after Camarena reported the discovery of this plantation in the state of Chihuahua (at the ranch El Búfalo), the DEA and Mexican authorities intervened, found, and destroyed the crop and packaged marijuana with a street value of around US $2,500m. Caro Quintero decided to kidnap and kill Camarena, in retaliation. The real story is more complex and involves senior Mexican authorities during President De la Madrid's administration, the US Central Intelligence Agency, funding (from the sale of narcotics) and training for the right-wing 'Contra' rebels in Nicaragua (using Mexican territory and weaponry sent to Honduras) to try to bring down the Sandinista regime in Nicaragua.[33]

When the discovery of Camarena's tortured remains and the body of a Mexican pilot who had flown with him during his investigations in Mexico made the headlines, there was an uproar in the USA. The US public was given the gory details about Camarena's fate. That a DEA agent, American patriot, husband, and father had been brutally tortured and murdered by drug-traffickers hit a raw nerve. The US government immediately protested, demanding that the Mexican authorities bring Camarena's killers to justice.

As a consequence, the largest joint criminal investigation between the two countries to that date was launched.

The Mexican government dithered because top politicians, and military and law enforcement personnel were involved. Caro Quintero, who fled to Costa Rica, was eventually apprehended there and returned to Mexico. His senior associate Ernesto Fonseca Carrillo, also known as 'Don Neto,' was also arrested, and both were imprisoned. The kingpin of the group, however, Miguel Angel Félix Gallardo, also known as 'El Padrino,' continued to run the largest-scale operations transporting cocaine from Colombia to the USA. Under increasing pressure from the Mexican government, Felix Gallardo ordered all members of the cartel to keep a low profile. By 1987 he felt the best way to maintain his operations was to divide up his Guadalajara Cartel into smaller operations run by seven different families (the splitting-up of cartels would later result in the cartel wars.) El Padrino's actions as a result of increased pressure from the regime demonstrated the hegemonic power the PRI retained when it needed. In fact, the regime's power was so strong that "PRI presidents dictated the corridors for shipping narcotics to prevent attacks on civilians".[34] Everything was controlled from the center, and kingpins lived to operate and make fortunes as long as authorities wanted them to.

With the change of government in January 1989 in the USA, President George H.W. Bush prioritized fighting the cocaine trade from Colombia. Under sustained pressure from the new USA administration, the new Mexican government under President Salinas acted quickly to apprehend Gallardo. In April 1989 Gallardo was captured without resistance at a restaurant in Guadalajara. The chief of the federal judicial police, Guillermo González Calderoni, simply scheduled the meeting and Felix arrived at the restaurant as scheduled. They had known one another and had shared many meals and attended events for years.[35]

The swift action in capturing those responsible, including the head of the cartel, highlights the power of the PRI regime. The drug-traffickers were allowed to operate, but they were also ring-fenced and controlled by the top command at the Ministry of the Interior (and within it the DFS), the military services, and the governors of the states where they operated. In turn, all these actors followed a strict and effective command-and-control chain under the PRI pyramid of power.

Democratization and State Effectiveness: a Necessary Trade-Off?

The series of events described above are in stark contrast with the gradual loss of control over drug-traffickers and organized crime that the Mexican state suffered in the course of the 1990s, and the complete loss of control that happened after alternation in power and the PAN took over the presidency in 2000. The cases of El Chapo Guzmán (Sinaloa), El Chayo Moreno (Familia Michoacana), Heriberto Lazcano (Los Zetas), among others, exposed the breakdown of the tight, effective command-and-control chain.

Does this mean that there is a necessary trade-off between the democratization of an authoritarian regime and the weakening and fragmentation of the state where political regime transition took place? Not necessarily. The cases of Chile, Spain, Uruguay,and South Korea, to name a few, show that the fall of authoritarian rule and the installation of democratic regimes did not lead to a weakening and fragmentation of the state over its monopoly over the legitimate use of persuasion, force, and coercion. However, there are also other cases where the fall of authoritarian or totalitarian rule did weaken and fragment the state. The case of the collapse of the USSR and the Boris Yeltsin years in the 1990s is usually invoked. Other cases of state fragmentation and proliferation of non-state actor violence are Brazil and the Philippines. The bottom line is that there is no general rule that can be applied. The case of Mexico is one which, sadly, led to state weakening and fragmentation.

Importantly as this work has shown, such weakening and fragmentation did not coincide strictly with the transition to democracy in Mexico. It started after the 1982 economic collapse and the so-called 'lost decade' that followed it. Later, the state recuperated strength and effectiveness through a significant personalization of power under President Salinas. However, his last year in power, 1994, with the uprising of the Zapatistas, the murder of the PRI's presidential candidate and of the party's Secretary-General, and the collapse of the economy which created the 'tequila crisis' destroyed any possibility to restore state cohesion and effectiveness. The last PRI administration before party alternation, under President Zedillo, followed by the two PAN presidencies under Presidents Fox and Calderón, and lastly the return of the PRI under President Peña Nieto from 2012 took place in a situation of post-hegemony rule by a single party (the PRI), and conditions on the ground, fed by fragmentation and weakening of the central state, allowed for centrifugal forces, which we have dubbed 'governors, *caciques*, and cartels'—shorthand for those and other politico-economic forces that managed—to operate with varying degrees of autonomy and against the central state, which were unthinkable during the years of hegemonic rule under the PRI. It is therefore more appropriate to say that democracy did not create the weak, fragmented state that lost its monopoly over the legitimate use of persuasion, force, and coercion. The decentralized ruling mechanisms of Mexico's electoral democracy accelerated the weakening and fragmentation of the state. However, its roots can be traced back to the 1982 crisis and the subsequent years of austerity, as well as to the personal maneuvering and personalized style of rule under President Salinas, who tried to manage the pace of political and economic liberalization in a selective manner. To his surprise, events on the ground surpassed his capacity to keep everything under firm control and the politico-economic events of 1994–95 dealt the PRI regime and the Mexican state a knockout blow from which there was no return. The fight to retain hegemonic control was lost, and Mexico became a much more complex, plural, and uncertain nation-state. Democracy was thus born handicapped in

Mexico. Centrifugal forces, led by governors, *caciques*, and cartels, among others, successfully challenged the state's monopoly over the use of persuasion, force, and coercion, which has continued to be the case.

The New Political Paradigm: 'Feuderalism'

As the barriers to entry fell for actors (in the public sphere such as governors and *caciques*, and also in the private sphere, such as as cartels and other organized criminal syndicates) to exercise persuasion, force, or coercion in the public sphere, due to the weakening of the Mexican state after the 1980s 'lost decade' and then the 'tequila crisis', these powerful new actors strengthened and challenged the nation's federal authority and legitimacy. Given a fragmented regime, these subnational political actors felt less accountable to the national government. Without a strong history of democratic accountability to its citizens, subnational governments acted in a void of legitimacy. They were increasingly free to operate independently, but were also susceptible to the growing power of other emerging non-governmental actors that were beginning to operate freely with impunity from the regime and its weak government institutions. Once the PRI was dethroned, governors, *caciques*, and cartels coalesced to create a new order—a 'feuderalist' state.

The transition to the new 'feuderalist' order was a gradual one, coinciding with the fragmentation and lowering of political barriers into the political monopoly enjoyed by the state under the stewardship of hegemonic political rule under the PRI. It was not immediate upon the assumption of Vicente Fox of the PAN as President on 1 December 2000. Subnational actors began testing the old PRI hegemonic system during the fragmentation period. For example, the Zapatistas declared war on the state; governors and their officials began to operate independently without regard to the central authority in Mexico City; *caciques* found an intermediate zone of action whereby they could benefit materially and in terms of power and influence by playing federal demands off against local demands, needs, and explosions of violence; and cartels expanded their business with assistance from *caciques* and corrupt politicians.

Zapatistas Uprising

In much the same way as governors, *caciques*, and cartels would challenge the government's monopoly on violence, the Zapatistas also contested the weakened PRI regime publicly—an unimaginable state of affairs just a decade earlier. Established in the state of Chiapas in southern Mexico, the local indigenous population of Mayan dissent formed the Ejército Zapatista de Liberación Nacional (Zapatista Army of National Liberation—ELZN) to confront the economic inequality facing their state. The mainly agrarian populace had long felt neglected by the economic opportunities that other parts of the country experienced. The ongoing negotiations for the creation of

the North American Free Trade Agreement (NAFTA) inflamed that senti-
ment. An important milestone was the official 'celebration' in 1992 of the five
centuries since Christopher Columbus touched land in the Americas (1492).
What for many was a cause for celebration was a cause of shame, resentment,
and a rallying cry to reassert a non-Western-centric perspective on the clash
between Europeans and native Amerindians since the last decade of the 15th
century.

In Mexico, sensing the PRI's tenuous grip on power, on 1 January 1994—the
same day as NAFTA officially entered into force—the EZLN declared war on
the Mexican state. Its aim was to initiate an armed revolution in Mexico that
would oust a regime they felt was out of touch with the needs of the people.
With an army of 3,000 insurgents, the EZLN seized several towns in the eastern Altos de Chiapas region, including Ocosingo, Las Margaritas, Huixtán,
Oxchuc, Rancho Nuevo, Altamirano, and Chanal. However, the EZLN
underestimated the capability of the regime's security capability and its willingness to use it, and on the next day the Mexican army, along with elements
of Grupo Aeromóvil de Fuerzas Especiales (Special Forces Group—GAFE),
counterattacked. The EZLN suffered heavy casualties at the hands of the military, and by 12 January, a ceasefire was reached. President Salinas was criticized vociferously by international human rights groups as it was common
knowledge that the majority of insurgents carried wooden weapons pretending
to be rifles, and were completely outgunned by the GAFE. The Catholic Dio-
cese, under Archbishop Samuel Ruiz Cruz, a long-time sympathizer and pro-
tector of indigenous communities in Chiapas state (where workers in agriculture
are repressed, and commercial operators exploit the environment, particularly
for rare timber), helped to broker a ceasefire and then continued to work
toward a peace agreement which eventually granted rights to their communities, such as choosing their governing authorities, management of their natural
resources, and the way they lead their everyday lives..

However, in February 1995, under President Zedillo, the Mexican army
broke the ceasefire and took control of the remaining land given to the
Zapatistas during the previous negotiations. Although the uprising was largely unsuccessful, it demonstrated the willingness of groups openly to oppose
the PRI during what appeared to be the beginning of a true democratic
transition period (given the 'tequila crisis' and Zedillo's weakness within the
PRI). Cartels also sensed the lowering of barriers and the changing paradigm,
thereby increasingly challenging the regime.

Intensifying Cartels

Arellano Felix, 'El Padrino', became the first major drug "boss of all
bosses".[36] Born in 1946, he began his career as a judicial state police officer in
Sinaloa. In his first assignment in 1963 he protected the PRI Governor, Leo-
poldo Sánchez Celis, giving him access to all the powerful *caciques* and
influential figures in the state. By the 1970s he had become intimately involved

in the transportation of drugs into the USA. His competitive advantage was his close relationship to the PRI leadership in his state, and his close connection with the Colombian cartels in transporting the most lucrative contraband, cocaine. Preceding Arellano's rise, Colombian cartels had grown in size and influence, giving the Colombians their largest profit margins. During the 1970s and 1980s, cocaine was the recreational drug of choice for those who could afford it in the USA. These drugs were primarily transported from Colombia through the Caribbean Sea and into Miami, Florida. However, from the early 1980s President Ronald Reagan began cracking down on the Florida route, and his successor, President George H.W. Bush, prioritized shutting down the Caribbean route, and going after Mexican kingpins who did business with their Colombian counterparts. Eventually, as Ioan Grillo wrote in his monograph on the Mexican drugs war, *El Narco*, "American agents figured out how to shut down the Florida smuggling corridor completely."[37]

Gallardo and the Guadalajara Cartel seized on the opportunity about the Caribbean route shutdown and created a Mexico-US corridor along western Mexico where eventually nine-tenths of the cocaine into the USA would transit. As a trusted government servant of the PRI, Gallardo leveraged this relationship and the party granted him permission to grow his illicit business unchecked. The "dominant PRI party developed almost tributary relations with organized crime groups."[38] In fact, Gallardo had the protection of the chief of DFS, Miguel Nazar Haro, in conducting his operations. Despite his growing power, "El Padrino" understood his limits if pressured by the PRI, which he began to feel after the death of Camarena. This led him to split up his cartel in 1987, two years after the assassination of the DEA agent.

In essence, Gallardo broke up his monopoly just as the government was doing with its state-run corporations, transforming the illicit monopoly into an oligopoly that could gain efficiencies and survive a government persecution. Much like Salinas's economic liberalization, "El Padrino" implemented cartel liberalization.

The new smaller cartels had designated territories or "plazas." From west to east, the smuggling corridors into the USA were delegated to trusted and proven members of Gallardo's conglomerate. The Tijuana corridor was handed to the Arellano Félix brothers, (nephews of "El Padrino") to eventually become the Tijuana Cartel; the Sonora corridor to Joaquín "El Chapo" Guzmán, which would become the Sinaloa Cartel; the Ciudad Juárez corridor to Amado Carillo Fuentes, which would become the Juárez Cartel; and the Ojinaga, Chihuahua corridor to the new DFS Commander Rafael Aguilar Guajardo, eventually merging with the Juárez Cartel after Rafael was murdered in 1993 by Amado Carillo.[39]

This agreement worked well and lasted for a few years, but by the mid-1990s, the diminishing power of the PRI could not contain the disagreements and ambitions of the smaller cartels, as they competed for lucrative new smuggling routes. Violence ensued on the streets. The cartels resorted to resolving disputes by combating each other with waning regard to government repercussions or public safety. One of the largest and most violent disputes arose between the Arellano Félix brothers' Tijuana Cartel and Joaquín "El Chapo" Guzmán's Sinaloa Cartel over routes into California, USA. In 1992 (during the presidency of Salinas), the increasingly fierce competition led Sinaloa Cartel gunmen to kill six members of the Tijuana Cartel in a discotheque in Puerto Vallarta. This incident made international news. Puerto Vallarta happens to be a city with a significant number of US expatriates and retirees.[40] The Tijuana Cartel did not blink. In turn, the Arellano Félix brothers upped the stakes and emphasized a tactic they had used previously to scare their rivals, society, and, ominously, the state. This tactic involved killing rivals and leaving their bodies wrapped with a sheet on the streets for everybody to see. This intimidation tactic was a significant escalation of violence among the cartels. Furthermore, this happened during the still supposed 'managed' period of state-drug trafficking relations under President Salinas and his elder brother, Raúl. The Arellano Félix brothers would not sit quietly after an attack of that magnitude, and responded aggressively a few months later.

Assassination of a Cardinal and the Proliferation of Organized Violence

On 23 May 1993 the Cardinal of Guadalajara Juan Jesús Posadas Ocampo, one of only two Catholic cardinals in Mexico (the other one in Mexico City), was assassinated in the parking lot at Guadalajara international airport. In total, 26 shots were fired into the car, killing six passengers. Signalling a growing and out-of-control drug war, the horrific assassination in broad daylight sent shockwaves of fear throughout Mexican society and the international community. Although it is possible the Cardinal was the intended target, it has been suggested that, more than likely, the Tijuana Cartel was targeting Joaquín "El Chapo" Guzmán, who was riding in a similar vehicle near the airport.[41] In fact, Ramón Arellano Félix (the eldest sibling and boss, whose behaviour has been described as 'psychotic') and his brothers (all nephews of "El Padrino") personally led the assassination group at the airport. It was clear that the drug cartels were beginning to impose violence publicly with little regard to government interference, thereby challenging the Mexican state's monopoly on violence. Much of the rising violence was directed toward competing cartels fighting for turf associated with money-making drug routes. The break-up of the monopoly and assignation of areas of control orchestrated by "El Padrino", organized under fear of government encroachment in around 1987, was clearly falling apart by 1993. Ironically, after the Arellano Félix brothers failed in their assassination attempt, authorities in Guatemala captured "El Chapo" two weeks later (a scapegoat was needed to show that the Mexican state had everything under control), and extradited him to Mexico where he received a 20-year prison sentence. The end result was that the Arellano Félix brothers were given carte blanche to keep operating, while President Salinas and the state's control apparatus got a short-lived victory, at least in the eyes of domestic and international public opinion.

Nonetheless, the assassination of Cardinal Posadas Ocampo showed to the world that drug violence was on the rise, and the Mexican state was becoming less capable of containing the violence. This was in sharp contrast to the Mexican regime's response to the death of DEA Agent Camarena, just a few years before. With El Chapo arrested and out of the way, the Tijuana cartel looked to expand by trying to knockout the Juárez Cartel.

Weakening PRI Regime-Government

Another example of the growing power of the cartels was evident in the scandal over Gen. Guitérrez Rebollo. Appointed in 1996 as the 'Drug Csar' in charge of the National Institute to Combat Drugs under President Zedillo—the equivalent of US President Clinton's Drug Csar, Gen. Barry McCaffery—he was quickly found to be colluding regularly with the cartels. Immortalized as the corrupt general in the 2000 movie *Traffic*, Gutiérrez Rebollo aided Amado Carrillo Fuentes in Ciudad Juárez for over seven years by protecting the shipment of drugs and providing him with intelligence information. In fact, this arrangement led to defeats by the Juárez Cartel at the hands of the Arellano Félix brothers' Tijuana Cartel, the two most powerful cartels at the time. Unfortunately for Gen. Gutiérrez Rebollo, the Secretary of National Defense Enrique Cervantes Aguirre became suspicious of him soon after his appointment, upon discovering that the general was renting lavish apartments in Mexico City's affluent neighborhood of Polanco, which a senior military officer could not afford (among other pieces of evidence). In February 1997 Gutiérrez Rebollo was arrested and sentenced to 40 years in prison. However symbolic, his arrest proved only that new non-PRI entities were growing in influence. The ever-expanding 'war on drugs' became a fight to gain more control, given the lack of strong government presence.

The Gulf Cartel

Following the rise of the Guadalajara Cartel and its subordinate cartels in the late 1970s and early 1980s in western Mexico, the Gulf Cartel along eastern Mexico in the late 1980s and early 1990s also flourished. Originally focused on bootlegging, the cartel diversified into the cocaine business under the leadership Juan García Abrego, with the authority given to him by Raúl Salinas, President Carlos Salinas's elder brother, and a connection to import several tons of cocaine from Colombia from the Cali Cartel. By the early 1990s the cartel was generating somewhere between US \$1,100m.–\$1,600m. in cocaine revenue through the newly established eastern corridor that flowed through the Yucatán Peninsula, to the states of Campeche, Tabasco, Veracruz, Tamaulipas, and Nuevo León, before entering the USA.[42] This agreement provided Colombian cartels with an alternate route to the Guadalajara cartel's western Mexico corridor. Unlike the Colombians, García Abrego could facilitate the smuggling operations by directly leveraging his close political ties with the PRI. Guillermo González Calderoni, the commander of the Mexican Federal Police, famed for having solved the Camerana case, by arresting Arellano Félix, but later gunned down in Texas in 2003[43], endorsed the flow of drugs by the Gulf Cartel. It helped that Calderoni was a childhood friend of García Abrego's older brother Mario, both having grown up in the town of Reynosa.[44]

Unfortunately for García Abrego, he became the first Mexican to be added to the US Federal Bureau of Investigation's 'Most Wanted' list. His cartel's success was short-lived, as in January 1996 he was arrested in Monterrey and extradited to the USA. Within months Osiél Cárdenas, known as "El Mata Amigos" (the Friend Killer), killed his way to the top of the organization. As the Gulf Cartel grew under his leadership, so too did Cárdenas's arrogance. Ignoring the lessons of Arellano Félix, Don Neto, and Caro Quintero after assassinating DEA agent Enrique Camarena, in 1999 (during Zedillo's tenure), Cárdenas and a large contingent of cronies with AK-47 machine guns surrounded an SUV filled with US federal agents in Matamoros. He approached the vehicle, with diplomatic plates, threatening them and yelled "You gringos, this is my territory. You can't control it. So get the hell out of here!"[45] Four months later a US federal Grand Jury indicted Cárdenas and a US $2m. bounty was placed on him.

Fearing a similar fate to García Abrego, Cárdenas recruited one of GAFE's own officials, Arturo Guzmán Decena, to assist him in fighting off aggressors, in order to remain in power. Guzmán had fought the Zapatistas just a few years before as a member of GAFE, and was at the time ironically serving in Tamaulipas state to fight the drug cartels. In fact, just a few months before in 1996, GAFE had apprehended García Abrego. Underscoring the overall government breakdown, Guzmán created his new paramilitary group in 1999 by recruiting more than 30 members of this élite military force to work with the Gulf Cartel and help protect the smuggling of contraband into the USA.

Ironically, the USA had helped Mexico create GAFE in 1990 as an attempt to develop Mexico's military special forces. Guzmán named his group 'Los Zetas' and became the main security force for the Gulf Cartel. Even soldiers in Mexico's élite military force could now be corrupted. The cartels' growing influence had no bounds. By the end of Zedillo's *sexenio*, multiple groups including more cartels than before, *caciques,* and even state governors were sensing the loss of power of the regime at the center. This discovery opened up more avenues for feuderalism to surface and gain strength. When the PAN took over the Mexican presidency in 2000, the new regime could not control the newfound power of these subnational players under the emergent feuderalist state, and organized violence soon erupted into the public sphere as never before, as competition among these players grew.

PAN Tries to Redefine Mexico

The inauguration of President Fox in December 2000 accentuated the crescendo of the democratic transition and the beginning of what turned out to be 12-year rule by the PAN. However, the euphoric public, optimistic about the possibilities of a new democracy, quickly realized that Fox lacked a well-defined vision of the future. Moreover, his absent strategy, coupled with a misunderstanding of how the state institutions operated, changed the paradigm by which the country had operated during most of the previous century. As Grayson observes, "when the PRI's almost 71-year monopoly over political power was broken at the national level in 2000 by the victory of PAN presidential candidate Vicente Fox, the old lines of tribute/bribery broke down as well and unleashed a wave of internecine violence among trafficking organizations as they struggled among themselves for control of cocaine transit through their country".[46] In fact, less than two months after the inauguration, El Chapo Guzmán escaped a Mexican maximum-security prison after seven years of imprisonment.

Exacerbating this increasingly contested environment, the lack of a direct social contract between the security system of Mexico and its citizens created an environment for the proliferation of organized violence. Mexico lacked a true legitimate state monopoly on the means of violence, "a condition in which a state's security forces operate lawfully under a legitimate civilian authority".[47] Instead, the security forces during much of the 20th century served the regime. As a result, when the PRI regime lost its hegemonic rule and its monopoly in Mexico, the security forces, which had maintained their loyalty primarily to the regime, lost their ability and desire to prevent the proliferation of violence that ensued. Some elements of the security forces even became willing participants in the violence.

Governors in a Feuderalist State

The changing of the guard from the PRI to the PAN signaled to the governors, *caciques*, and cartels a complete change in the existing order: no federal oversight or national cacique. With a weakened federal regime under the PAN, the state governors incorporated the previous federal hegemonic patronage-based model within their states, giving rise to 'feuderalism.' In much the same way as the PRI had maintained power through its election policies that promoted careerism with no social contract, its taxation system (dependent on state-owned enterprises contributions to the federal public purse) that allowed politicians to pay off clients, and the loyalty of security forces and ties to the *cacique* system, the state governors incorporated much of the same. As Jorge G. Castañeda writes, the rise of a feuderalist state was fuelled by two factors.[48] First, the understanding of how a democracy worked was based on the previous PRI model of clientelism between the politicians and powerbrokers. The lack of the federal PRI regime led the state governors to incorporate a similar model at the state level. Second, with little oversight from above, the large transfer of tax funds from the federal government to the state government gave governors increasing resources and power over their territories with which to pay funds to clients. As states and municipalities charged little to no taxes, politicians did not need to appease taxpayers in their constituencies. Instead, they used the tax revenue they received from federal government transfers to maintain power. State governments paid off their political clients—the clients that placed politicians in their positions— and were rarely required to justify their expenditure to local taxpayers: most of the resources they receive come from the federal government, but they are not audited by it. Rather, they are audited by their state legislature, in many cases loyal to and subservient to the governor. This freedom to spend money has been a key element of feuderalism. In addition, the lack of consecutive re-election continued to aggravate the disconnection between elected officials and their constituents, much the same as at the national level before. Governors during the era of feuderalism increased their political power without a strong federal government, living "extravagantly and either turning a blind eye to narco-trafficking or colluding with the cartels."[49]

Similarly, without strong federal leadership, *caciques* at all levels reverted to a more traditional role of operating independently from the national regime by strengthening its bond with power players at the state and municipal level. The key attribute *caciques* maintained was a long list of contacts, which could be leveraged for various motives. In addition, many of them also owned large expanses of land, all with an army of *campesinos* or peasants that worked for them. *Caciques* could translate these assets into political power to help elect local and state-level officials, and to collaborate with criminal organizations to grow or store large amounts of contraband, all for a fee. In fact, both subnational politicians and cartels depended on their relationships with *caciques* to remain successful.

The new feuderalist paradigm created a new challenge. Although state governors hoarded significant power, it paled in comparison to the power— granted to them by discretionary spending and the monopoly of violence—of Mexican presidents during the PRI hegemony. Therefore, the difference between the power of a governor in relation to the power of the *cacique* system and cartels was significantly less than it had been under PRI presidents. The feuderalist state therefore exists as more of a symbiotic agreement between governors, *caciques*, and cartels instead of under the oversight of the federal regime and national *cacique*. Therefore, given a more level footing between stakeholders under feuderalism, existing agreements could now be constantly renegotiated. Moreover, different emerging actors could threaten an existing agreement through various means. These included offering more lucrative deals or threatening the use of violence to change the terms.

Adding to the problems, state governors lacked a strong security arm. Although states and municipalities had their own police forces, their capabilities were rather weak in comparison to the federal level security forces controlled by the President. The military and federal police did not answer to the governors, and governors increasingly found themselves in a bind when negotiating with ever-stronger cartels. As the cartels grew in strength, governors became increasingly susceptible to corruption. In sharp contrast to the system under the PRI hegemony where the government infiltrated the cartels, under feuderalism, the cartels began infiltrating the state and municipal governments. Therefore, the governors worked closely with cartels and *caciques* to maintain power.

In Tamaulipas state, for example, politicians regularly worked explicitly or implicitly with the Gulf Cartel. Tomás Jesús Yarrington Ruvalcaba served as the PRI governor from 1999 to 2005 working closely with the Gulf Cartel under the feuderalism paradigm. Much the same as Raúl Salinas, he facilitated the shipment of drugs and laundered money for the cartel. He continued this collaboration even after he left office. In fact, seven years after leaving office he was accused of plotting the assassination of the leading PRI candidate for the governorship in Tamaulipas.

In June 2010, Rodolfo Torre of the PRI was leading in the polls by 20 points in Tamaulipas state. With the election just six days away, the candidate along with four of his staff were assassinated in an SUV on their way to a rally near Ciudad Victoria, the capital city of his state.[50] The Gulf Cartel, along with the former governor, were found to be the culprits in the murder, although the motive remained unclear. As Casey writes, either "Mr. Torre was an honest politician who posed a threat to drug gangs; Mr. Torre had struck a deal to protect one gang and was killed by a rival gang angry at being cut out; or a cartel killed him just to make life more difficult for a rival gang that controls turf in the state."[51] Irrespective of the motive, the fact that a former PRI governor would kill a member of his own party demonstrated the growing influence of cartels over governors. The cartels were willing to retaliate against the government when necessary.

During the PAN governments of 2000–12, cartels lost complete regard for the federal government and became solely focused on growing their businesses, leading to the eventual Drug Cartel War. This is not to say that the Fox administration was guilty of inaction. On the contrary, Fox succeeded initially in killing and capturing some of the most prominent cartel bosses. In 2002 police forces killed Ramón Arellano Félix of the Tijuana Cartel, and later that year captured Ramón's brother, Benjamín. In the following year Fox had yet another tactical victory: Osiél Cárdenas, leader of the Gulf Cartel and the key orchestrator in the creation of Los Zetas, was captured and extradited to the USA. However, all of these tactical successes left a power vacuum and any previous agreements between cartels evaporated. Thompson writes: "The more experienced drug kingpins, Mexican prosecutors said, were more willing to reach peace among themselves, to respect one another's territories and to stay out of sight in order not to cause trouble for local authorities."[52] With many of the principal actors gone, a subsequent war would erupt as cartels fought to satisfy the tenacious appetite for drugs in the USA. As former Deputy

Attorney José Luis Santiago Vasconcelos (killed in a suspicious aircrash that also claimed the life of the Minister of Interior, Juan Camilo Mouriño, in 2008) recounted in an interview, "the only leaders who can contain the violence are the ones who are in jail. The structures they used to maintain—of corruption and obstruction of justice—when we took those away, they were forced to use violence."[53]

In summary, governors became the linchpin between law an order on one hand, and criminality on the other. Criticism of state governors' abuses is not a new phenomenon related to Mexico's transition to democracy or to the fall of the PRI from power. The main difference between the years of PRI hegemony and the period of so-called feuderalism is that during the former, governors were kept in check by the president. Governors stepped down at the president's will. This control mechanism created a check on their power. Instead, since the Zedillo years as the center has weakened governors have emerged as stronger powerbrokers and top dogs in the states they rule.

Without the restraining capacity of a federal government Mexican civil society groups stepped up to the plate and started exhibiting, reporting, and denouncing state governors' abuses. Interestingly, another force that put pressure on Mexican governors was the US government. Such pressure was directed first and foremost to combat narcotics, an area in which many Mexican governors have been implicated. In fact, the first governor to be arrested, charged, and jailed for criminal activities (connected with narcotics-trafficking) was Mario Villanueva, who governed the state Quintana Roo between 1993 and 1999. In 2001 he was arrested on a tip-off from the DEA. He was charged in Mexico but was then extradited to the USA, where he ended up being sentenced, after co-operating with authorities, to a reduced sentence of ten years in prison by a New York court in 2013.

Several years went by before other governors started being investigated and persecuted for criminal offences. That the first governor jailed was tracked by US authorities and ended up serving a sentence in the USA suggests that corruption and impunity have allowed many governors to escape facing the law, because Mexican authorities have more often than not been bought off. However, an important change in this critical area of Mexican governance took off in the course of the 2010s. Mexican society's well-organized and increasingly vociferous tone and capacity to expose governors' corruption via social media, forced the government of President Peña Nieto to act and start going after outgoing governors who had committed a variety of crimes while in office. In particular, as corruption became a critical priority for a majority of Mexican voters in the run-up to the 2018 presidential elections, the Peña Nieto government arrested four former governors of his own party (the PRI) in the course of 2017 (two former governors of Tamaulipas, one of Veracruz, and another one from Quintana Roo).[54]

Some analysts of Mexico estimated that in early 2018 there were around 16 governors of all main parties under investigation. If this is the case, an important link in the creation and proliferation of misplaced monopolies in

Mexico might start being checked and limited. This would be good news. But it is important to remember that such investigations and persecutions are still selective. They respond to a politico-electoral logic (as with the four former PRI governors arrested by Peña Nieto's government in 2017) rather than to the impersonal application of the rule of law. The case of former governor of Chihuahua state, César Duarte, who is accused of misappropriation of several million dollars to funnel into the PRI's mid-term elections of 2016, is emblematic. Having fled to El Paso, Texas in 2017, where his daughter lives and has dual nationality, the Mexican government sat on its hands despite the widespread, intense pressure from public opinion to get Peña Nieto's administration to request Duarte's extradition. Even if and when Duarte is caught, the case illustrates the selectivity with which a federal government (it can be from any party) can act, depending on the damages that public revelations about the crimes committed by the former governor could have on its party's national brand and reputation.

Even if there has been a measure of checking the power and abuses of some former governors in Mexico, cartels keep running amok, as I explore in the section below.

Cartels Challenge the PAN and the Return of the PRI

After Osiél Cárdenas was captured, Los Zetas began flirting with the idea of breaking from the Gulf Cartel. Simultaneously, the Sinaloa Cartel began drafting plans to take over the Gulf Cartel's most profitable smuggling route into the USA, the Nuevo Laredo corridor. Across the border from Laredo, Texas, which is a short drive via interstate highway to Dallas and Houston, Nuevo Laredo was the busiest port along the border, through which over 70 percent of cocaine and methamphetamines entered the USA.[55]

In preparation for the siege, El Chapo recruited Edgar Valdez, known as 'La Barbie' for his light skin, blondish hair, and blue eyes, from Laredo, Texas and dispatched a group of hitmen to work under his command—in essence a new armed wing for the Sinaloa Cartel named 'Los Negros' that would counter the Gulf Cartel's prized Zetas. 'La Barbie' travelled to Mexico City and bribed the Federal Police commander with US $1.5m. in exchange for protection as Los Negros tackled the Gulf Cartel. However, within a few months, the Gulf Cartel assassinated the commander, marking the beginning of a new war.[56]

Sensing the upcoming battle over Nuevo Laredo, Los Zetas held off from any ambitions to secede and instead helped the Gulf Cartel fight off 'La Barbie.' In the fall of 2004 the Sinaloa's Negros collided with the Zetas in the first of many violent battles that would define the Mexican whirlwind into anarchy in many hot spots controlled by the contending cartels. Using military-grade weapons and grenades, the two openly fought on the streets during daylight hours.[57] Unlike previous drug battles, both sides were intentionally brutal in order to intimidate the enemy and public. As Steven Dudley wrote,

"The Zetas battle with Barbie heralded a significant change in the underworld in which members' families were targets and media would be used as a tool to fight the wars."[58]

In the end the Sinaloa Cartel was no match for either the élite military fighting style of the Zetas, and the Nuevo Laredo police force which the Zetas had corrupted for protection. The Sinaloa Cartel retreated, although only temporarily. President Fox eventually reacted and deployed a battalion of soldiers to recapture the streets from the cartels, but by that point the fighting had largely subsided. With the first major battle between eastern and western Mexican cartels over, a more aggressive tone for future battles was established.

As the Sinaloa Cartel and the Gulf Cartel (the latter defended by the Zetas) continued their battles elsewhere, they began targeting each other's families. Nothing was off limits anymore in the fight for power. 'La Barbie' killed the brother of Miguel Treviño Morales, the Zetas' leader in Nuevo Laredo. In response, the Gulf Cartel murdered El Chapo's brother. This back and forth continued to escalate, with multiple family members from both cartels assassinated. This practise became so extreme, that a member of the Zetas even kidnapped and raped La Barbie's granddaughter.[59]

The Zetas decided to take over some of the smuggling routes for themselves and a new drug war was carried out in the streets, between the Gulf Cartel and the Zetas. The Zetas "assumed the role of being the No. 1 organization responsible for the majority of the homicides, the narcotic-related homicides, the beheadings, the kidnappings, the extortions that take place in Mexico".[60]

There was no statistical increase in homicides per 100,000 inhabitants during Fox's years in government. If anything, the trend went slightly downwards compared with previous statistics. (As a result of recent violence, the Mexican federal government, through its Instituto Nacional de Estadística, Geografía e Informática—INEGI—started collecting data about homicides per 100,000 inhabitants in 1997.) Still, there is no doubt that feuderalism spread and deepened during his presidency, and this led to the eventual escalation in homicide during his successor's government. Fox was succeeded by Felipe Calderón, also of the PAN, in 2006. Once in office, President Calderón used the state of anarchy and his contested legitimacy, due to widespread claims of electoral fraud against Andrés Manuel López Obrador in the 2006 presidential elections, to stamp his authority on the national scene once and for all. As a result, around 10 days after he took over the presidency on 1 December 2006, he instituted a new approach to confronting the cartels, fighting them directly on the streets. President Calderón officially declared a 'war on drugs,' something no Mexican president had ever done before. As a consequence of President Calderón's official declaration of the war on drugs, homicides in Mexico between 2006 and 2011 increased nearly sixfold, from 2,221 to 12,366. Beforehand Calderón's presidency, these numbers had remained relatively stable or even fell slightly year on year.

Calderón's 'war on drugs' was a far cry from how the PRI had managed cartels during its hegemonic rule. More than 50,000 military and police elements were deployed to go after kingpins, interdict the traffic of narcotics, and safeguard towns and cities that experienced turf wars among the competing cartels to establish their 'plazas.' Another critical innovation was that the Mexican government asked officially for help from the US government. President Calderón and President George W. Bush met in the city of Mérida, Yucatán in March 2007 and declared their joint pledge to beef up Mexican security forces for the pursuit of the 'war on drugs.' A year later the US Congress started disbursing aid in the form of hardware (weapons, airplanes, and helicopters), training, advising, and ramping up intelligence capabilities by US military forces and military contractors, and after 2010 also support and advice on institutional reforms to Mexico's police forces and the Mexican criminal justice system. Between 2008 and 2017, the USA had spent around US $1,800m. in the so-called Mérida Initiative.

Such close, broad, and deep co-operation between Mexico and the USA in security policy was unprecedented. It divided Mexican public opinion and created a sense that Mexico would end up being dependent on and dominated by US military might, as had become the case in Colombia since that country and the USA signed the so-called 'Plan Colombia' in 2000. Another criticism of US–Mexico co-operation in the 'war on drugs' was that for all the growth in Mexican security forces' firepower and more effective operations thanks to such co-operation, Mexico's law enforcement and criminal justice institutions became (and remain) so corrupted that the end result would be more intense and violent confrontations between drug cartels and state forces, but without the institutional capacity to process in a legal, fair way, all those detained and arrested. Moreover, the state forces, many of which were (and remain) in the pay of the cartels, ended up being strengthened and empowered not just to fight organized criminals, but also to fight among themselves and in many cases against innocent civilians who dared to become whistleblowers or found themselves in the wrong place at the wrong time, as contending forces—usually a mixture of cartel gunmen and state security forces on both sides—battled it out.

Calderón was rightly criticized for starting the war on drugs without a well-thought out plan or the necessary means to achieve his objectives—something akin to kicking a hornets' nest without wearing protection against their sting or having insecticide to kill them. The president declared the 'war' in the knowledge that Mexico's law enforcement and criminal justice capabilities were weak, ineffective, and ready to put justice up for sale to whoever could pay more or deploy more influence through lawyers or political influence. The plan did not contain basic markers, such as what might constitute victory for the state or how the government would manage and exit strategy from the conflict. The result was that gruesome violence and insecurity simply increased in a deadly spiral, which was apparently open-ended.

The government renamed the conflict a 'war on organized crime,' in order that the population might temper its opposition to it (after all, citizens around the country were being kidnapped for ransom and the practice of extortion started growing and targeting not just big businesses, but also small and medium-sized firms, and even informal workers in the streets). However, as the deadly violence continued to increase, many groups, communities, civil institutions, intellectuals and students started opposing the conflict in public. But President Calderón would not budge and he stayed the course despite large year-on-year increases in deaths, disappearances, and turf wars in many villages, towns, and cities around the country.

Some people might argue that Calderón's strategy, knowing or unknowingly, would help to raise barriers to entry to non-state forces, in order that the state could recuperate its monopoly over the legitimate use of persuasion, force, and coercion throughout Mexican territory. This is a reasonable point of view. However, given that the state did not possess the means to achieve this end (i.e. eliminating or dramatically weakening organized criminal groups), this process, which might potentially have strengthened and reversed the fragmentation of authority and power at the center of the Mexican polity, in fact achieved the opposite. As cartel kingpins fell, their organizations started internecine wars over leadership succession. Some of the cartels splintered and this led to a proliferation of smaller groups, which were more difficult to trace, follow, and catch. As more narcotics were interdicted and there was lower supply in the streets, their price increased, which allowed the cartels to make more money with which to keep corrupting authorities, buying more lethal weaponry, and planning larger-scale operations. As narcotics operations showed some success, many of the splinter groups who left the cartels diversified into other illegal activities such as kidnapping, extortion, prostitution rings, human smuggling, the sale of weapons, and hitman services.

All in all, Mexico was, on average, more violent and more insecure when Calderón finished his term in 2012, than when his predecessor Fox did in 2006. The Pandora's box that was opened through the official declaration of a 'war on drugs' ended up lowering the barriers to entry both for non-state actors, as well as corrupted state actors, to operate with relative impunity around Mexico in pursuit of their illegal businesses and the super-profits that they yield. It would be erroneous to think that the entire country fell into a state of anarchy and violence. In fact, a majority of cities and towns in Mexico did not fall into the vortex of violence which begat more violence almost *ad infinitum*. What predominated were (and this continues to be the case) hot spots, that is, specific cities, towns, crossroads, mountainous, or desert areas which are strategic routes for transporting narcotics or migrants to the USA. The number of human rights abuses perpetrated by organized criminals as well as state forces soared after 2006, but the rotten criminal justice system was incapable of dealing with them. The system was and continues to be dominated by impunity. The words impunity and corruption were not new to Mexicans' everyday lexicon, but their utterance became a constant lament, and one that did not diminish, let alone stop after Calderón stepped down and the PRI returned to power in 2012.

By 2012 the average Mexican felt scared and insecure, and wanted change after two PAN administrations. The logic used by many to return the PRI to power was poor, but understandable under the circumstances. A phrase that colonized small talk, as well as mainstream and social media in the run-up to the 2012 elections was, "To fight the mafia you need the mafia," an unsubtle reference to the PRI's supposed capacity to keep organized crime under control. Mexicans wanted the new government to put the lid back on the Pandora's box. However, they were in for a surprise because, as discussed above, the system the PRI inherited was already very different, more complex, uncertain, and random than the one it used to dominate and lord over.

President Peña Nieto started his term in office on 1 December 2012. He had stated that there would be changes to the war on organized crime. His government would change some of the metrics that helped to assess and monitor success or failure. Under Calderón, the metrics used to monitor success were the number of kingpins detained or killed (so-called cartel decapitation), the volume of narcotics and weapons interdicted, and the number of cartels' shocktroops detained or killed. The result, as discussed above, created the unintended consequence of splintering cartels and creating more fragmented, lethal violence, as well as higher profits from smaller volumes of narcotics sold, as well as a diversification by criminals into other illegal activities, primarily kidnapping for ransom, extortion, and the smuggling of things other than narcotics—weapons and economic migrants, among others.

Peña Nieto's advisers decided to declare officially that the main metric of success for them would be a fall in the number of murders per 100,000 inhabitants. US authorities were concerned about this change. The author of this book was consulted on various occasions by several US federal agencies about the extent to which this change might jeopardize the strategic partnership forged under the Mérida Initiative. Like many other analysts of Mexico, I believed that the situation on the ground was so violent and volatile that a sudden call to the military to return to their barracks or the police to return to manage traffic in the streets was unfeasible. An about-face turn, given conditions on the ground, was not viable. Subsequent actions by the government proved that this judgement was correct. Operations continued, the sense of permanent mobilization among the military and police forces remained their day-to-day working dynamic, and the strong, intimate relationship forged by Mexico and the USA during the Calderón years was not affected. If anything, it continued to grow.

A key difference between President Calderón and President Peña Nieto was the public relations management of the war against organized crime. While President Calderón had been a convinced crusader who paraded kingpins in front of national television cameras, and made the conflict his signature policy, President Peña Nieto got a little help from his media friends, in particular Televisa, which became the power behind the throne. The idea was to focus mainstream broadcasting away from the war on organized crime. The President would be shown only 'selling' Mexico abroad in international fora such as Davos or regional and international summits such as Asia-Pacific Economic Cooperation, the Summit of the Americas, or the G-20. From this perspective, President Peña Nieto would be a head of state-cum-salesman who would attract foreign investment for the ambitious agenda to open up several sectors of the Mexican economy to competition (reviewed in chapter 5). The nasty, dirty work of the day-to-day gruesome violence would be managed by the Ministry of the Interior and it would stop being the main headline in every single news broadcast as had been the case during President Calderón's tenure.

This strategy worked early on. It is difficult to tell yet if numbers were fabricated or if there was a real fall in the homicides per 100,000 inhabitants in Mexico, but the official figures between 2013 and 2015 showed lower levels of homicides. To have a relative understanding of the problem, consider that Mexico suffered eight or nine violent deaths per 100,000 inhabitants in the late 1990s. The figures for the safest countries at that time, including France, Switzerland and Japan, were between just one and two violent deaths per 100,000 inhabitants. In contrast, the figure for very violent countries such as some in Central America such as El Salvador and Honduras were between 60 and 80 violent deaths per 100,000 inhabitants. For Mexicans, the shock was the jump in violent deaths in a relatively short period of time. Having stood at eight or nine violent deaths per 100,000 in the late 1990s, the number more than tripled to between 26 and 30 violent deaths per 100,000 during the latter part of President Calderón's administration in 2010–12). Furthermore, whatever improvements in this metric took place during the first half of Peña Nieto's presidency, it went into reverse during the second half, from 2015. Crime, violence, and its depiction on social media—which could not be controlled by Televisa—returned with a vengeance.

Splinter groups from the main cartels became more audacious in their kidnapping and extortion operations. The larger cartels continued to operate and were now challenged by a new generation of so-called 'narco-juniors,' whose families have been in the narcotics business for generations, and they claimed top place. The case of the Cartel Jalisco Nueva Generación illustrates the problem that no matter how many security officers the Mexican state deploys with the help of the USA, there remains in Mexico a huge industrial reserve army (i.e. millions of young men and women who are poor, whose life chances look grim, and who are therefore willing to play the lottery of joining the illegal underworld). In 2020, more than 40 percent of the Mexican population will be under the age of 30. As long as super-profits fuel organized crime and the Mexican economy is unable to provide opportunities to the younger generations, some of them will continue to want to play the lottery. There appears to be no end in sight to the war on organized crime.

By 2016–17 the trend of lower homicide statistics under Peña Nieto had reversed, particularly in the course of 2016–17. The year 2017 breached the previous national annual high of murders per 100,000 inhabitants, which happened in 2010–11, toward the end of Calderón's government. Cities where lethal violence seemed to have abated, such as Tijuana, experienced new highs as well: around 900 homicides occurred there in 2009 and close to double that number, around 1,700, in 2017. In the case of the Peña Nieto government, therefore, we are confronted with a 'U'-type curve in terms of homicides per 100,000 inhabitants during his six-year tenure.

From this work's analytical perspective, barriers to entry into the public sphere to threaten, extort, beat up, or kill people in Mexico were not raised during Peña Nieto's government. Likewise, state violence against Mexican society continued unabated. Journalists, as described above, have been the most visible category of individuals who continue disappearing and being murdered, both by cartels and by state security forces. But the violence has been also more general, hence the randomness of an innocent or a group of innocent civilians being caught in the wrong place at the wrong time has remained a chilling reality in a country that is not experiencing a conventional war or civil war.

The next subsection illustrates in some detail how feuderalism, accompanied by lethal violence, corruption and impunity, has operated in some Mexican states.

Morelos in the Thick of Violence

Home to Emiliano Zapata and the core of the agrarian revolution since the early 20th century, Morelos state is one of the most socioeconomically unequal territories in Mexico. More importantly for organized criminal activity, it is a bridge that connects the Guerrero coast (a hotbed of the cocaine trade) and mountains (heroin and marijuana) to the large market that is Mexico City, as well as its transportation further north to the USA.

I know and have been involved in the quotidian life of a significant number of families in the capital city of Morelos state, Cuernavaca, since I was nine years old. A paradise thanks to its year-round mild climate, exuberant flora, topography, and historical monuments, ruins, as well as its many English-language schools that have attracted tens of thousands of Americans and Europeans since the 1960s[61], the state got caught up in the vortex of the 'war on drugs,' created by the main fighting groups that operated there, and the terrible spillover of their barbaric violence. The capital city has been a very convenient base of operations since at least the 1990s, when Amado Carrillo Fuentes, the so-called Señor de los Cielos (Lord of the Skies), and the most wanted drug-trafficker by US authorities in the mid-1990s was a next-door neighbour of the state governor in his mansion. Carrillo Fuentes supposedly died while undergoing plastic surgery intended to change his facial identity, in order to evade detection, in 1997.

The exodus of upper-middle class families from that city since the mid-1990s, but particularly in the course of the 2000s, is well known among locals and their acquaintances. It should not be surprising. The state became a battleground between several cartels fighting to control the transit of narcotics to Mexico City and further north. Cuernavaca was the location where one of the most Hollywood-like successful kingpin elimination operations took place, in December 2009. The leader of the Beltrán Leyva Cartel, Arturo, 'El Barbas', was killed in a secret operation that included Mexican Navy operatives and US advisors (excluding the Mexican Army, because El Barbas had bought off the high command stationed in that city, and had managed to escape several operations thanks to tip-offs from them), and which included Marines dropped in by helicopter into a residential tower who killed the kingpin, as well as arresting some of his accomplices.

After this operation, Cuernavaca became a no-man's-land. The Beltrán Leyva Cartel splintered and the capital city suffered curfews as contending cells, one of them led by La Barbie, fought for supremacy of the streets. At times the contending factions, trying to ingratiate themselves with society, broadcast on radio to the population times and places that innocent civilians should avoid because the splinter groups had pre-arranged gun fights to show who was supreme. Police forces did not intervene. The city became one of the most dangerous places to inhabit, due to an explosion of extortion and kidnapping.

Between 2013 and 2014 a particularly perverse phenomenon unfolded. Medics and nurses started being kidnapped in a systematic way. The fighting factions of the different cartels trying to control the traffic of narcotics between the coast of Guerrero and Mexico City were responsible. Their aim was twofold: by kidnapping individuals who could keep people alive (medics and nurses) they got the means to treat their wounded troops, who could not be taken to hospitals or clinics due to the risk of being apprehended and arrested by authorities; on top of that they demanded from the families of kidnapped doctors and nurses exorbitant ransoms to set them free: two birds killed with one stone. Many doctors shut down their surgeries and left the city. The heads of police in the state were able to tell some of these doctors the exact time when it was safe to return, suggesting a high level of collaboration between the cartels and security apparatus. What does the experience of Morelos show? In terms of the 'barriers to entry' and 'misplaced monopolies' framework I proposed, it reflects the collapse of barriers to non-state actors to enter the public sphere, and their capacity to command the acquiescence of more than half a million people through the airwaves, for example, to show who is in charge of matters of life and death. Statistically Morelos remains one of the poorest performing states economically over the last decade and one of the most unequal as well: a few very rich households, a squeezed middle class, and the majority of the population poor, and trampled upon.

Morelos is one of the few states that in recent times have had governors from the main three parties: the PRI, the PAN, and the PRD. As shown in

Chapter 5, a crucial weakness in the Mexican federal system is the almost negligible tax-raising capacity of municipalities and states. Depending for basic
funding on the federal government can be a blessing (if the President's party in
power is the same as that of a governor) or a curse, if they are from different
parties. Given these conditions, Morelos's government capacity deteriorated
during the governorship of Graco Ramírez (PRD) and President Peña Nieto
(PRI). However, having a president and a governor from the same party does not
guarantee federal support or at least the effectiveness of such support. In Morelos state there were two PAN Governors –Sergio Estrada Cajigal (2000–06) and
Marco Adame Castillo (2006–12) – at the same time the Mexican presidency
was held by the PAN, first under Fox and then Calderón. Kidnappings and
public violence, traditionally high in Morelos, got worse during 2000–12, as
kidnappings, executions, gun fights, and extortion overwhelmed all authorities.

Irrespective of the effectiveness of federal support to states, there is growing
evidence that shows that Mexicans' basic welfare, including security, education, health, and waste disposal is politicized, and the federal Treasury holds
the reins. There are many stories that confirm this federal lottery. In 2018 the
story that grabbed domestic and international headlines was about the country's largest state, Chihuahua, which borders the USA. The federal Treasury
withheld more than US $800m., which funds the social services mentioned
above, because the incumbent governor, Javier Corral (of the PAN),
denounced massive misappropriation of public funds by the previous governor, César Duarte (PRI), to fund PRI electoral campaigns. As mentioned
above, Duarte escaped to El Paso, Texas, where his daughter lives. President
Peña Nieto procrastinated in the face of the public's demand for Duarte's
extradition to answer for such misappropriations, and be judged in Mexico.
This is one case among many, whereby governors of the party in power at the
federal level misappropriate resources for electoral and self-enrichment purposes, and receive the center's blessing, while governors from opposition parties are starved of resources or threatened to be if they denounce acts of
corruption that can hurt the party of whoever controls the presidency.[62]

Coahuila: *Pocitos* of Wealth and a Terrified Population

Home to both Francisco I. Madero and Venustiano Carranza, Coahuila is a
Mexican state that shares a border with the USA along the Río Bravo (or Rio
Grande as it is known in the USA). Texas and Coahuila used to be a single
state in early independent Mexico. The first time I went to Coahuila I was a
teenager. My paternal grandfather's family were among the founders of
Sabinas in the 1870s, a town located in the middle of the desert. The town
was only viable for human habitation thanks to the water from the Sabinas
River. It is also located among some of the greatest coking coal and shale gas
and oil reserves in Mexico. This small, unassuming town has lived off the
exploitation of coal and commerce for more than 150 years, given its proximity
to the US border.

The rise of Los Zetas (around 2008–09), the once enforcement-arm of the Gulf Cartel, and whose leadership was made up of deserters from GAFE and the federal police, led to the extension of organized criminal activities from their home state of Tamaulipas, to neighboring Nuevo León, Coahuila, and several other states in only a brief period of time. The Zetas started terrorizing the population in hundreds of villages, towns, and cities in northeastern Mexico. In Sabinas they started forcing small coal producers to help them. The small coal mining operations, known as *pocitos,* began to be used to hide narcotics. Their operators were forced by the Zetas to pay *derecho de piso* (protection money in typical mafia fashion). They also became an effective decentralized network of hiding places in the middle of the inhospitable desert.

The operators of *pocitos* were offered the bargain '*plata o plomo'* (silver or lead). Those who chose the former have made millions of dollars. In contrast, many of those who did not budge were killed, often along with family members. By the early 2010s some incredible marble masonry mansions started appearing in what for more than one and a half centuries had been a modest village, then town, and later small city without the means for the vulgar, in-your-face splendor that struck anyone visiting Sabinas. I remember several people saying, "Those mansions look a bit like those that Saddam Hussein had and were shown on television after the US invasion of Iraq, don't they?"

Life in the city was meticulously regimented. Uttering the word 'Zetas' could get people killed. The local argot for the organized criminals who had taken control of their city was '*los malosos*' (the baddies). I did not know what to make of it: laugh, cry, a mixture of both? The phrase 'the baddies' is usually heard in the sandbox of pre-Kindergarten schools. Municipal and state police were regularly seen acknowledging the Zetas who lived or came regularly to Sabinas. Locals had to brief outsiders about signs and signals that meant impending peril. Thus, cars on the road at night with blue lights were to be ignored or, even better, shunned. A car with these characteristics stopped one evening at a convenience store and two individuals jumped out of the car and entered the store. Around a dozen individuals shopping there suddenly froze. Outsiders who were visiting Sabinas and found themselves there recounted how they saw the terrified faces of shoppers as time seemed to go into slow motion. The two individuals were there just to buy beer, which they did, and then left quickly. I was told that the perception of slow motion amid an adrenaline high subsided slowly, and all one could hear were the whispers among clients and shopkeepers. When the leader of Los Zetas, Heriberto Lazcano, 'El Lazca', was hunted down and killed in October 2012, his body was taken to a mortuary in Sabinas—the town made international headlines after the body was stolen from the mortuary by some of his colleagues.[63]

In 2018 Sabinas is still a haunted city. Collaborationists continue to make a lot of money, while individuals who resist, and their families, remain under threat, and live a life of constant paranoia. Still, Sabinas has done well in relative terms. The town of Allende, 32 miles from Piedras Negras, by the US-Mexico border, suffered a massacre that could easily be compared to that of a village or town in a country suffering a civil war. During 18–20 March 2011 Zetas squadrons attacked the town and destroyed many of its houses and basic infrastructure. Official Mexican authorities claimed that 28 people had been killed. However, eyewitnesses during the two-day massacre said that around 300 bodies were burned, not just in Allende, but also in nearby cities like Piedras Negras, Ciudad Acuña, and the area of Cinco Manantiales. The motive? Apparently lieutenants of a top Zetas leader—the bloodthirsty Z-40, Miguel Angel Treviño—whose relatives lived in Allende, double-crossed him and escaped to the USA with millions of dollars from the business. On top of that, they started co-operating with US authorities by pointing at some of the main individuals in the private army known as the Zetas.[64] Retaliation was swift, deadly, and no Mexican state authorities intervened during a 48-hour massacre, of which many people were aware as it was happening at the time.

This is another case of misplaced monopolies, and one that continues in a low-intensity but permanent state of lawlessness and wealth concentration by the politicians, businessmen, and organized criminals who play the game. Coahuila is also one of fewer than five states in Mexico which until 2018 had never experienced alternation in power, that is, the PRI has yet to lose the governorship since Mexico became a democracy in the late 1990s and early 2000s. The state might have been punished financially when the PAN held Mexico's presidency between 2000 and 2012. A big controversy regarding the large rise of the state's public indebtedness erupted during the governorship of Humberto Moreira (2005–11), of the PRI, which overlapped with the presidencies of Fox and Calderón, of the PAN. However, and following the logic that the central government supports the governors that come from its own party, this is not a mechanical or automatic decision. It depends on state governments' leadership going along and supporting the center's decisions and *modus operandi*. Sometimes members of the same party can disagree and decide not to co-operate with one another. Meanwhile, the population of Coahuila remains a frightened, cowered society.

Michoacán: Land of Beauty, Cornucopia, and Egregious Violence

The state of Michoacán is where President Lázaro Cárdenas del Río was born. The wealth of the state's ecology was well known and exploited by the Spanish during colonial years. The original owners of that rich land, the Purépecha nation and culture, was never conquered by the Aztecs. They submitted to the Spanish. Among them, the first bishop of Michoacán, Vasco de Quiroga, known as 'Tata' Vasco, tried to emulate Thomas More's *Utopia* in and around Lake Pátzcuaro. The state and its capital city, Morelia (named after independence insurgent leader, José María Morelos y Pavón, who was born in that city), previously known as Valladolid, was an enlightened city where pro-independence civilians, military, and Church leaders plotted in favor of Mexican independence from Spain from the latter part of the 18th century.

To foreigners, Michoacán is known first and foremost for its avocados and other tropical fruit (mango and papaya), as well as for the survival of pre-Columbian traditions like the Día de Muertos (Day of the Dead) and the many marigolds they use to celebrate that day, as well as for its artisanal works using feathers, wood, and natural colors for their festive masks, as well as its cuisine. Such apparent bounty is grossly misallocated. Like Morelos and Guerrero (see below), it is one of the states with the most unequal distribution of wealth and income in Mexico.

Half of my family (my two grandmothers) is from Michoacán. I have made dozens of visits since I was a child to Morelia, Uruapan, Tancítaro[65], Zamora, and Sahuayo, among people I hardly knew but who were as kind to me as the cornucopian landscape I observed. In contrast to the other places I have written about—at least from personal experience—threats, kidnappings, and extortion already existed as far as I could tell in the 1980s, although they increased significantly in the second half of the 1990s. Family members and avocado producers were kidnapped and freed, but not before being roughed up, sometimes badly, and, of course, a hefty ransom had to be paid to spare the kidnapped individual from more abuse. They were not all so lucky: an uncle died in a suspicious car accident, while a cousin was gunned down outside his home.

Still, conditions 20 or more years ago were far from what they became in the course of the 2000s. Most of the moneyed families from cities like Uruapan left Michoacán and relocated to Guadalajara in the course of the 1990s and 2000s. Those who stayed have continued to experience the *derecho de piso* and the *plata o plomo* bargain constantly. I have heard from older men, whose daughters and wives were 'selected' by well-established kingpins in the area and were bought by however many thousand dollars to become brides who were then taken to the USA. Where? I have no idea and do not want to know. And they were the lucky ones. In many cases, as has been amply documented after several villages and towns rebelled (Las Autodefensas, a vigilante phenomenon that took off in parts of Guerrero, México state but mainly Michoacán) against the drug-traffickers and their alliances with local and state authorities, girls, young women, and wives were taken from their homes by the organized criminal groups never to be seen again, or raped for periods of time and then returned to their families.[66] According to the Autodefensas, it was not the *derecho de piso* or the *plata o plomo* bargain that triggered their societal rebellion, but the outrage of the violation of the intimacy and dignity of the home.

Federal and state governments have poured millions of US dollars into Michoacán to try and improve these inhuman living conditions. The truth is that people continue to live in fear and they are unable to tell if their supposed friends, who keep watch, are straight or crooked members of the state or federal police, let alone the Caballeros Templarios (previously the Familia

Michoacana) organized criminal group. And this is the intimate pain only of the people I know. From the macro, geopolitical perspective, who can forget the billions of dollars that have been made from the traffic of iron ore (from Michoacán) and pseudoephedrine—used as a precursor to cook crystal meth—(from China) in the port of Lázaro Cárdenas?[67]

Former President Calderón and his family are from Morelia, the capital of Michoacán; the Cárdenas clan, descendants of the popular progressive president Lázaro Cárdenas, who was born in Jiquilpan, Michoacán, and who own many properties and interests in that state, among them a large hacienda close to Apatzingán, which is home to one of the founders of the organized criminal group La Familia Michoacana, Nazario, 'El Chayo' or 'El Más Loco', Moreno. These and other facts explain the Mexican federal government under President Peña Nieto's response in that state. The President has diverted millions of dollars to placate Michoacán state since 2014. In this sense, Michoacán is different from the cases of Morelos and Coahuila, where there has not been federal intervention and occupation as a consequence of state paralysis and ineffectiveness, if not temporary collapse. Consider, among other things, that in Michoacán the brother of ex-Governor Leonel Godoy (2008–12), once leader of the PRD at the national level as well as Deputy and Senator in the federal Congress for that party, was linked to the main organized criminal group in the state, and in central Mexico, the Familia Michoacana. Governor Godoy asked publicly and officially for his brother to turn himself in.[68]

While somewhat improved, conditions for the average citizen in Michoacán remain precarious and dangerous. Michoacán keeps haemorrhaging its human and natural wealth, its people forced to pay *derecho de piso* or the *plata or plomo* bargain. However, unlike the cases of Morelos or Coahuila, the federal government's intervention reduced the descent of chaos into a failed state in Michoacán. Why has this not happened in other states? Because of a mixture of visibility (and therefore reputational damage), politics, and the fact that the federal government simply does not possess the resources to carry out interventions like this in three or four of the other most violent states affected organized crime.

Guerrero: Every Square Foot of Land Costs Lives

A turbulent state since colonial times, Chilpancingo (which later became the capital of Guerrero state), hosted a congress that promulgated Mexico's independence from Spain in September 1813, under the leadership of insurgent José María Morelos, the same founding father born in Valladolid, later Morelia. Independence or emancipation floundered, however, because the insurgent army of which he was leader was unable to defeat the Spanish army, and Morelos himself was captured and executed in 1815. Nonetheless, the state of Guerrero, although one of the poorest in Mexico, has played important roles in contestation against established powers, be they Spanish or later Mexican. The contrast in material wealth between the coast, particularly rich Acapulco, and the very poor sierra, where Mixtecs remain some of the poorest people in Mexico, cannot be emphasized enough.

In modern times Guerrero was the home of the most famous rural guerrillas who fought the PRI regime in the late 1960s and 1970s under the leadership of first, Genaro Vázquez, and later of Lucio Cabañas. Later on, after the Zapatistas (EZLN) insurrection in Chiapas in 1994, another, less compromising and more belligerent group, the Ejército Popular Revolucionario started operating, and some of its core support was and remains in Guerrero state. Successive Guerrero governments, particularly under the Figueroa clan and its supporters, have perpetrated massacres against protesters who have tried to fight the egregious inequality and lawlessness in the state.

Likewise, the horrendous massacre of 43 *normalista* students from the Isidro Burgos School in Ayotzinapa, which trains young women and men to become teachers, in the city of Iguala in September 2014, will haunt President Peña Nieto's government and what is written about it in the future. Coordinated activities between municipal, state, and federal police, an organized criminal organization, the Guerreros Unidos, known and protected by the three levels of government, plus the intervention of armed forces, led to the massacre, which has been denounced in many domestic and international forums.[69]

I have been a witness to the transformation of life along the coast in and around the outskirts of Acapulco, as well as parts of the Costa Chica around Copala and parts of the Costa Grande around Zihuatanejo. Land conflict, a perennial problem in the state, has always involved threats about the use of force. However, the situation on the ground was transformed in the course of the 2000s as dozens of small property holders, community representatives, *caciques*, and municipal, state, and federal police forces were forced to take sides and support one or other of several organized criminal cartels, whose aim has been to take over land titles in coveted areas close to or by the coast. The example of Barra Vieja, south of Acapulco and a traditional place where locals and tourists go to eat fresh seafood from the Laguna de Tres Palos, is emblematic.

A low rise area made up of mainly small plots inhabited by locals, as well as many other individuals and families who shun the high-rise, crowded, expensive conditions of Acapulco, their land was targeted by the Beltrán Leyva Cartel and other criminal groups in the course of the 2000s, who aside from speculating about the growing value of land, also chose it as an area where narcotics cargoes could be disembarked to supply Acapulco, Cuernavaca, Mexico City, and then continue their way to the border and on into the USA.

In the course of the 2000s I met at least three community leaders who were later assassinated as a consequence of this land conflict. One of them wanted to improve the quality of life in the Barra Vieja community and demanded education and health services for his people. Unwilling to pay the *derecho de piso* to organized criminals, this individual was killed in broad daylight, his body left battered and unrecognizable on the road between Barra Vieja and Acapulco. Another of these leaders, who once sat down to talk about the problem of endemic violence in the area, and who wore gold rings in all his fingers and several gold chains around his neck, made a point about how he conducted business by putting in front of him on the table where several people sat, including me, four or five cell phones. The phones kept ringing regularly and this individual would interrupt the meeting to mutter a few words as he answered the ringing phones.

"What a busy man, he must control many operations!" said someone after the meeting. Within a year the individual had been assassinated and his henchmen were disappeared. Similar to the case of Coahuila, people from all walks of life have been offered the same *plata o plomo* (silver or lead) bargain and everyone from street beggars to major hoteliers and restauranteurs pay *derecho de piso*. In the meantime Guerrero state continues to be one of the poorest states in Mexico. Aside from tourism, its main revenue comes from the cannabis and white poppy, which have been planted in its mountainous topography since at least the 1940s. The subsistence indigenous farmers in those areas also have to pay *derecho de piso* and are offered the *plata or plomo* bargain. Paid very little for their crops, they continue to be captives of labor-repressive agriculture similar to the system of serfdom, but this in Mexico, a country that claims that every individual is a citizen and has basic civil, political, and social rights, not a feudal polity where serfs are exploited.

After the student massacre in Iguala in 2014, the federal government intervened in Guerrero, although in a less direct way than it did in Michoacán.[70] Many groups from different sectors have continued to ask in 2017 and 2018 for federal government intervention like the one in Michoacán.[71] This has not happened. And while the intervention in Michoacán did not turn around everyday living conditions for a majority of its population, it showed that Mexico is not a failed state. The question is: can conditions on the ground improve overall in Mexico without federal intervention? Likewise, federal intervention is no silver bullet, as evidence since at least the 1980s suggests that such interventions can improve, but also worsen conditions on the ground, as federal authorities have been systematically penetrated by organized criminal groups.

The superficial survey of states reviewed above is not and cannot be taken as social science that in turn allows an analyst to reach general conclusions tested in a systematic way, using objective evidence. They happen to be the states that the author has known and visited dozens of times during the last 40 years. Detractors could easily and fairly ask, what the outcome would be if a given observer had spent a similar amount of time in the states of, say, Yucatán, Campeche, or Querétaro, where organized criminal activity has been significantly less disruptive (at least on the surface) to public life?

My answer is, yes, I concur that, luckily, a collapse of social peace and public order across the board, everywhere in Mexico, has not happened. Law-and-order conditions are weak and precarious, in general, nationally.

However, there is significant variation contained within and between the 31 states (and Mexico City).

Such variation is similar to that observed in the economic sphere. Just like the average national performance of the Mexican economy can be aptly considered sluggish and disappointing, despite the fact that NAFTA was supposed to ramp up growth significantly, the evidence in Chapter 5 suggested very important variations. While some states have been and remain dynamic and fast-growing like Aguascalientes and Querétaro, others like Morelos, Veracruz, and Chiapas have remained relatively static, subject to low growth and, therefore, to substantial emigration of the working age population in search of better opportunities. The national average is that of a country that grows around 2.0 and 2.5 percent annually. The high-growth states do so at between 7 and 9–10 percent, while low growth states have experienced negative growth or growth of less than 1 percent for many years. As observers of this phenomenon have noted, Mexico is made up of many different economic units with significant variation in terms of the evolution of their main macroeconomic indicators.[72] Some can match the high growth of star performers (at least in terms of annual GDP growth) like China. In contrast, others resemble countries with poor, stagnant records.

To this observation, I add that all the Mexican states have suffered as a consequence of the collapse of state authority (at the three levels of government) to different degrees, particularly since the second half of the 1990s. Therefore, some states are much more violent than others. An individual who invokes the record in Yucatán, Campeche, or Querétaro between the 1990s and the 2010s is right when they claim that those states have significantly lower rates of violent deaths per 100,000 inhabitants compared with those I happen to have spent time in, particularly as an insider, meeting family, friends, and colleagues.

This type of immersion in a given context is significantly different compared with that of an interested expert who, nonetheless, is an outsider. In the former case one is immersed into intimate everyday life and local networks where human interaction expresses reality as it is lived, warts and all. In contrast, in the latter case the outsider status of the student or scholar or agent (domestic or foreign) trying to study and understand a complex reality (particularly one dominated by wealth concentration, social animosity, conflict, and growth in common as well as organized crime and violence) tends to shut down intimate channels of communication and lead to outsider experts being fed tailored facts and stories.

Thus, for example, one of the most alarming trends since the 2000s in Mexico has been the sustained attack, suppression, and elimination of journalists who cover law and order, violence, and criminality. Many international organizations have now reported for more than a decade about the violence, disappearance, and murder of Mexican journalists. They tend to be insiders who tow a very fine line, and they are victims of both organized criminal and state authorities' violence. From the insider/outsider perspective, their insider status makes them potentially very dangerous to the criminals, the corrupt authorities, and the crony businessmen and their friends in government and involved in other illegal activities.

As insiders, they know the local reality, warts and all, because they see it, they are told it, and they cross-reference, test, follow the money or other clues, and end up with highly sensitive information that often exposes the rottenness that in places is embedded in Mexico's young, unequal, and violent electoral democracy.[73] Unsurprisingly, the country has been and remains one of the most dangerous places for journalists to live in and do their work anywhere in the world.

The main conclusion I have reached is that Mexico is under the throes of the condition that I initially identified as 'misplaced monopolies' (i.e. extreme wealth concentration, little economic competition, state fragmentation, weakening and high competition from non-state actors to control public peace, and disruption to basic order and stability). However, I also believe that based on all the evidence reviewed, the misplaced monopolies thesis has to be qualified.

For example, far from being a failed state, Mexico's federal government's interventions, when supervised particularly by domestic and foreign impartial observers can make a difference in order and stability—like the case of Michoacán or other interventions that were not reviewed in this work, such as the improvements in basic order and security most notably in the city of Monterrey, which suffered an explosion of organized criminal related activity in 2010–11 and was then 'retaken' with federal, state, and US assistance afterwards.

The Mexican state is present throughout the country's territory, but it does not possess the necessary resources to carry out operations that restore order and stability. In addition, supervision by independent domestic and foreign observers is also limited and cannot be present permanently throughout the country's territory, to hold both criminals and state forces accountable. In many cases authorities openly oppose them because they are with the criminals or their *modus operandi* is violent, ruthless, and similar to that of the main criminals. The Mexican state has access only to relatively few and limited resources. Moreover, as an electoral democracy it tends to allocate those resources in a partisan way. Media that support the government play up and exhibit places where its intervention has helped to stabilize the rise of fear and brutal violence, particularly since the early 2000s, whereas the opposite, that is, censorship or no coverage, is imposed in areas where conditions are deteriorating.

In addition, in the view of local experts who have followed the law and order sphere, Mexican police and military institutions have been forced by governments since the 1990s, but particularly much more intensely and extensively since President Calderón's declaration of the'war on drugs' in December, 2006, to perform actions that are beyond their reach due to the collateral costs in innocent civilians detained, wounded, killed, or disappeared as a consequence of the operations mandated from them by the Mexican federal executive. One of the consequences of the non-synchronized, sometimes confrontational and chaotic relationship between the three levels of government in Mexico's federal structure has been multiple, multidirectional conflicts among the authorities themselves, as local and state forces perceive federal intervention as "occupation." The end result in many cases has been a complex hall of mirrors where no force trusts any other; individuals within each of the forces start mistrusting one another, and it ends up being almost impossible to know who is who: who works for one or another of the main organized criminal organizations; who works for a crooked governor in alliance with one or more of these groups; and whether a federal force that rides to the rescue may actually be tainted by association with one or more of these groups.[74]

It is a situation where the maxim 'each to their own' aptly applies, the end result of this being the evaporation of any source of trust or reliability in state forces, cartels, or Mexican society in terms of the treatment of fellow human beings (except the family, although also with caution). In this sense the Mexican state is weak but Mexican society is even weaker, due to the well-earned, systematic mutual distrust among Mexicans. The political side of the 'misplaced monopolies' therefore might not be so bad in this light: yes, the state is weak and fragmented, but society is even weaker and more fragmented and alienated. This is a horribly defeatist conclusion, but the facts on the ground support it.

Selective Misplaced Monopolies

The bulk of the evidence presented points toward something akin to 'selective misplaced monopolies': a situation whereby, thanks to state authorities' intervention, economic opportunities and political conditions are shaped to produce partisan outcomes at the expense of the general population. Mexico's democratization politicized the country in such a way that partisanship, in general, has become a reliable indicator to estimate how the quality of life of different groups of the population unfolds on a daily basis. State weakening and fragmentation, compared with the years of PRI hegemony, are facts of everyday life in Mexico. However, such weakening and fragmentation remain selective, and they are tied to partisanship, which in turn is a function of more general facts such as personal contacts, networks, and the capacity to appeal to a state and authorities that do exist and can be effective, but only if a supplicant is on their side, not as matter of rule of law, which in 2018 remains patchy if not entirely absent in many parts of Mexico.

Notes

1 Marco Antonio Herrera Toledo, "Ni los veo, ni los oigo", in *SDP noticias*, 7 December 2013, https://www.sdpnoticias.com/columnas/2013/12/07/ni-los-veo-ni-los-oigo, Accessed20 January2018.

2 Alma E. Muñoz, "De 1998 a la fecha han sido asesinados 696 militantes: PRD," in *La Jornada*, 2 November2007, http://www.jornada.unam.mx/2007/11/02/index. php?section=politica&article=013n2pol, Accessed20 January2018.
3 World Bank, "Political Decentralization", http://www1.worldbank.org/publicsec tor/decentralization/political.htm. Accessed 27 October 2016.
4 Ioan Grillo, El Narco: Inside Mexico's Criminal Insurgency, New York: Bloomsbury, 2012.
5 Jorge G. Castañeda and Héctor Aguilar Camín, "Un futuro para México", in *Nexos*, 1 November 2009, https://www.nexos.com.mx/?p=13374, Accessed 20 January 2018; Jorge G. Castañeda and Héctor Aguilar Camín, "Regreso al futuro", in *Nexos*, 1 December 2010, https://www.nexos.com.mx/?p=14042., Accessed 20 January 2018.
6 Frank Ralph Brandenburg, *The Making of Modern Mexico.*
7 The word cacique, used in Spain and in Latin America, refers to a local political leader or chief. That individual, which can be male or female tends to control access to goods such as land, water and other natural resources as well as to jobs, property arrangements and law and order in the territory they claim to preside over. See, *English Oxford Dictionary*, https://en.oxforddictionaries.com/definition/ cacique, Accessed 20 January 2018.
8 Alberto Díaz-Cayeros, "Entrenched Insiders: Limited Access Order in Mexico."
9 "Limited Access Orders in DW -II −2009 May 3-Clean.doc – Limited Access Orders – Rethinking the Problems of Development and Violence.pdf."
10 Frank Ralph Brandenburg, *The Making of Modern Mexico.*
11 Francisco E. González, Dual Transitions from Authoritarian Rule: Institutiona- lized Regimes in Chile and Mexico, 1970–2000, Baltimore: Johns Hopkins University Press, 2008.
12 USA Ibp, Mexico Company Laws and Regulations Handbook, International Business Publications, 2009.
13 Alberto Enríquez Perea, "Aforismos políticos de Jesús Reyes Heroles", in *Nexos*, 1 May 2006, https://www.nexos.com.mx/?p=11879, Accessed 20 January 2018.
14 Reuters, "Factbox: Key Facts about Mexico's Tax System," 6 May 2013. http:// www.reuters.com/article/2013/05/06/us-mexico-tax-facts-. Accessed 7 December 2015.
15 Alberto Díaz-Cayeros, "Entrenched Insiders: Limited Access Order in Mexico."
16 La Razón, "Partida Secreta Presidencial", 27 December 2015, http://razon.com. mx/spip.php?article56649, Accessed 27 December 2015.
17 Carmen Aristégui, "LaFortuna de Raúl Salinas Y La Partida Secreta de Carlos," 1 August 2013, http://aristeguinoticias.com/0108/mexico/la-fortuna-de-raul-salina s-y-la-partida-secreta/. Accessed 27 December 2015.
18 Alberto Díaz-Cayeros, "Entrenched Insiders: Limited Access Order in Mexico."
19 George Grayson, The Cartels: The Story of Mexico's Most Dangerous Criminal Organizations and Their Impact on U.S. Security. Santa Barbara: ABC-CLIO, 2013.
20 Julio Scherer García y Carlos Monsiváis, *Parte de Guerra: documentos del general Marcelino García Barragán, los hechos y la historia*, Mexico, Aguilar (Nuevo Siglo), 1999.
21 Joyful Gypsy, "Tlatelolco Massacre (Mexico City)," CNN iReport, 9 October 2009, http://ireport.cnn.com/docs/DOC-336863, Accessed 16 January 2016.
22 George Grayson, *The Cartels.*
23 Cristian Castaño Contreras and Andrés Poncede León Rosas, *SEGURIDAD NACIONAL EN MEXICO: UNA APROXIMACION A LOS RETOS DEL FUTURO.*
24 Sergio Aguayo Quezada, *La Charola: Una historia de los servicios de inteligencia en México*, Mexico, Grijalbo Mondadori, 2001.

25 Thompson, "Ex-President in Mexico Casts New Light on Rigged 1988 Election."
26 Ibid.
27 Interviews with Cicero (August 2011) and Antony (July 2013).
28 Alan Knight and Wil Pansters, *Caciquismo in Twentieth-Century Mexico.*
29 Ibid.
30 Ibid.
31 Ibid. Pg. 279
32 Ibid. Pg. 356
33 J. Jesús Esquivel, *La CIA, Camarena y Caro Quintero: la historia secreta*, Mexico, Grijalbo, 2014, 51–57; 169–78.
34 George Grayson, *The Cartels.*
35 Ioan Grillo, *El Narco.*
36 Ioan Grillo, *El Narco.*
37 Ibid.
38 Bruce Bagely,"Drug Trafficking and Organized Crime In The Americas: Major Trends – Drug Trafficking and OrganizedCrime in Latin America and the Caribbean.pdf," http://www.issdp.org/conference-papers/2013/2013_papers/Bagley%20B%20-%20%20Drug%20trafficking%20and%20organized%20crime%20in%20Latin%20America%20and%20the%20Caribbean.pdf. Accessed 7 December 2015.
39 George Grayson, *The Cartels.*
40 UPI, "Six killed in disco shootout," 9 November 1992, https://www.upi.com/Archives/1992/11/09/Six-killed-in-Mexico-disco-shootout/5689721285200/, accessed 8 February 2018.
41 Sam Dillon, "Government and Church Reviewers Agree to Disagree on Mexican Cardinal's Slaying," The New York Times, 28 July 2000, http://www.nytimes.com/2000/07/28/world/government-and-church-reviewers-agree-to-disagree-on-mexican-cardinal-s-slaying.html. Accessed 15 January 2016.
42 George Grayson, *The Cartels.*
43 The Brownsville Herald, "Guillermo Calderoni gunned down, Fatal injury: Former Mexican federal officer shot in head," 6 February 2003, http://www.brownsvilleherald.com/news/local/guillermo-calderoni-gunned-down-fatal-injury-fo rmer-mexican-federal-officer/article_40d2a00b-cf6d-50b3-9a3f-0fd0e87aad8a.html, Accessed 8 February 2018.
44 Tim Weiner, "Mexican Drug Agent Crossed the Line Once Too Often", in The New York Times, 18 February 2003, sec. World. http://www.nytimes.com/2003/02/18/world/mexican-drug-agent-crossed-the-line-once-too-often.html, Accessed 12 January 2016.
45 Ioan Grillo, *El Narco.*
46 Bruce Bagely, "Drug Trafficking and Organized Crime In The Americas: Major Trends – Drug Trafficking and Organized Crime in Latin America and the Caribbean.pdf," http://www.issdp.org/conference-papers/2013/2013_papers/Bagley%20B%20-%20%20Drug%20trafficking%20and%20organized%20crime%20in%20Latin%20America%20and%20the%20Caribbean.pdf. Accessed 7 December 2015.
47 United States Institute of Peace, "Legitimate State Monopoly over the Means of Violence," http://www.usip.org/guiding-principles-stabilization-and-reconstruction-the-web-version/6-safe-and-secure-environment/le, Accessed 28 July 2015.
48 Jorge G. Castañeda and Héctor Aguilar Camín, "Regreso Al Futuro."
49 George Grayson, *The Cartels.*
50 Jo Tuckman, "Leading Politician Rodolfo Torre Cantú Murdered in Mexico," The Guardian, 29 June 2010, http://www.theguardian.com/world/2010/jun/29/leading-p olitician-rodolfo-torre-cantu-murdered-mexico. Accessed 12 January 2016.
51 David Luhnow Casey, "Killing Escalates Mexico Drug War," Wall Street Journal, 29 June 2010.

52 Ginger Thompson, "Rival Drug Gangs Turn the Streets of Nuevo Laredo into a War Zone," The New York Times, 4 December 2005. http://www.nytimes.com/2005/12/04/world/americas/rival-drug-gangs-turn-the-streets-of-nuevo-laredo-into-a-war.html. Accessed 7 December 2016.

53 Ibid.

54 Lizbeth Díaz, "Fourth ex-governor from Mexico's PRI arrested on corruption charges," in *Reuters*, 6 October 2017, https://www.justice.gov/usao-sdny/pr/former-governor-mexican-state-sentenced-manhattan-federal-court-131-months-prison-money, Accessed 17 February 2018.

55 Ginger Thompson, "Rival Drug Gangs Turn the Streets of Nuevo Laredo into a War Zone," The New York Times, 4 December 2005. http://www.nytimes.com/2005/12/04/world/americas/rival-drug-gangs-turn-the-streets-of-nuevo-laredo-into-a-war.html Accessed 7 December 2016.

56 Ibid.

57 David Luhnow Casey, "Killing Escalates Mexico Drug War," Wall Street Journal, 29 June 2010.

58 Steven Dudley,"Two Reasons Why Laredo Has Less Homicides than Nuevo Laredo," in *InSight Crime and Woodrow Wilson Center*, https://www.wilsoncenter.org/sites/default/files/Laredo_vs_Nuevo_Laredo_Dudley.pdf, 2013. Accessed 13 January 2016.

59 Ibid.

60 CNN.com, "Los Zetas Called Mexico's Most Dangerous Drug Cartel," 6 August 2009, http://www.cnn.com/2009/WORLD/americas/08/06/mexico.drug.cartels/index.html, Accessed 23 January 2018.

61 Cuernavaca became a paradise for eccentric plutocrats like Peggy Guggenheim and her circle, as well as to great thinkers and intellectuals like Erich Fromm, Ivan Illich, and leading progressive priests and an archbishop, Sergio Méndez Arceo, who followed 'liberation theology' and its claims to support and fight in favor of the dispossessed. The feverish atmosphere of the paradise/hell that was Cuernavaca in the late 1930s was masterly portrayed by Malcolm Lowry, British consul in Cuernavaca in *Under the Volcano: a Novel*, New York, Reynal and Hitchcock, 1947.

62 Denise Dresser, "Tocar un nervio", in *Reforma*, 8 January 2018, http://www.reforma.com/aplicacioneslibre/preacceso/articulo/default.aspx?id=126970&urlredirect=https://www.reforma.com/aplicaciones/editoriales/editorial.aspx?id=126970, Accessed 26 January 2018; Jorge G. Castañeda, "La caravana de Corral", in *El Financiero*, 24 January 2018, http://www.elfinanciero.com.mx/opinion/la-caravana-de-corral.html, Accessed 26 January 2018.

63 Tim Gaynor and Lisbeth Díaz, "Mexico says it killed top Zetas drug lord body snatched," in *Reuters*, 9 October 2012, https://www.reuters.com/article/us-mexico-drugs/mexico-says-it-killed-top-zetas-drug-lord-but-body-snatched-idUSBRE8980ZD20121010, Accessed 24 January 2018.

64 Juan Alberto Cedillo, "Los zetas mataron y quemaron a más de 300 personas en Coahuila: testigo", in *Proceso*, 13 July 2016, http://www.proceso.com.mx/447092/los-zetas-mataron-quemaron-a-300-personas-en-coahuila-testigo, Accessed 24 January 2018.

65 On this village, whose name can be translated as "place of tribute" or "where tribute is paid", and the informal secession from other authorities (local, state, federal) as inhabitants took over and flew a flag with the legend "World Capital of Avocado," see Max Fisher and Amanda Taub, "Building a Mini-State With Avocados and Guns," in *The New York Times*, 18 January 2018, Accessed 3 February 2018.

66 Salvador Maldonado, "Michoacán y las autodefensas: Cómo llegamos aquí?" in *Nexos*, 14 January 2014, https://redaccion.nexos.com.mx/?p=6011, Accessed 25 January 2018.

67 Raymundo Riva Palacio, "La conexión china", in *El Financiero*, 20 March 2015, http://www.elfinanciero.com.mx/opinion/la-conexion-china.html, Accessed 25 January 2018; Dave Graham, "Ventas de mineral de hierro a China provocan choques con cartel de droga mexicano", in *Reuters*, 2 January 2014, https://lta.reuters.com/article/businessNews/idLTASIEA0103D20140102, Accessed 25 January 2018.

68 Arturo Estrada, "Leonel Godoy llama a su hermano Julio César a entregarse a justicia", in *El Financiero*, 4 March 2015, http://www.elfinanciero.com.mx/mundo/leonel-godoy-llama-a-su-hermano-julio-cesar-a-entregarse-a-justicia.html, Accessed 26 January 2018.

69 Manuell aLibardi, "Ayotzinapa three years later: new light, few answers," in *democracia Abierta*, 26 September 2017, https://www.opendemocracy.net/democraciaabierta/manuella-libardi/ayotzinapa-three-years-later-new-light-few-answers, Accessed 25 January 2018.

70 José Luis de la Cruz, "Gobierno federal sale al rescate de Guerrero; anuncia plan emergente de seguridad," in *Proceso*, 31 January 2014, http://hemeroteca.proceso.com.mx/?p=363744, Accessed 26 January 2018.

71 Jesús Guerrero, "Piden intervención federal en Guerrero," in *Reforma*, 10 April 2017, http://www.reforma.com/aplicacioneslibre/articulo/default.aspx?id=1087928&md5=a488eb3ff2ee7bc9531e36b79aa5f20c&ta=0dfdbac11765226904c16cb9ad1b2efe, Accessed 26 January 2018.

72 See, México, cómovamos? "Semáforos Económicos Estatales," which follows and regularly updates general economic performance of all the states in the country and presents variations according to a traffic light system whereby states identified in green color have experienced above national average conditions on a variety of macroeconomic indicators; states identified in yellow color are roughly at the national average in some indicators and under that average in others; and states identified in red color correspond to those that have underperformed in most or all the indicators, http://www.mexicocomovamos.mx/?s=seccion&id=50, Accessed regularly between November 2015 and January 2018.

73 Committee to Protect Journalists (CPJ), "In absence of fresh military conflict, journalists killing decline again," 21 December 2017, https://cpj.org/reports/2017/12/journalists-killed-iraq-crossfire-murder-mexico.php, Accessed 3 February 2018, which highlights Mexico as a global exception due to a continued increase in the murder of journalists which reached a 'historical high' in 2017; Reporters without Borders, "Mexico: Constant Violence and Fear," https://rsf.org/en/mexico, Accessed 3 February 2018, which highlights that Mexico "continues to be the Western Hemisphere's deadliest country in the media." Of 149 countries it follows, this organization ranked Mexico as 147th in 2017.

74 Arturo Alvarado, "Violence and Criminality in Mexico: an Analysis of Recent Trends," presentation at the conference "Mexico at the Crossroads: Learning from History, Facing the Future," 17–18 November 2011, Tulane University, New Orleans.

7 Conclusion: Mexico and Misplaced Monopolies—Comparative Perspective

This book has tried to show that Mexico experienced a dual transition—from authoritarian rule to electoral democracy in the political sphere, and from closed, inward-looking to open production and exchange in the economic sphere; that those transitions took place during a long, protracted, and uncertain process in the course of the 1980s and 1990s; and that the end result was not the establishment of a liberal democracy and an open, competitive economy in Mexico.

Observing the problem of political and economic development from the perspective of the 'violence and social orders' framework created by North, Wallis, and Weingast, I have argued that it is not enough to think about political and economic development, in general, as a function of falling barriers to entry for the free organization of individuals to govern one another in the political sphere, and to produce and exchange in the economic sphere. In my view, the elaboration by these authors of the 'political' and 'economic' spheres is too general, and therefore has to be disaggregated into smaller, more specific components that help us to understand why a general fall in barriers to entry might not be a good thing for a majority of people in any organized society.

Political Sphere: Distinguish the Political Regime from the State

While falling barriers to entry in the competition for public office (the political regime) might help to advance representation and accountability—constitutive elements of liberal democracy—a similar fall in barriers to entry in the competition over the exercise of public persuasion, force, and coercion (the state) might create the Hobbesian world, according to which the absence of a monopoly over their deployment ends up in anarchy and many different individuals and groups exercising violence over one another. Under these circumstances, it is not hard to see why life can become, following Hobbes's dictum, solitary, poor, nasty, brutish, and short.

Therefore, my general conclusion regarding the political sphere suggested that relatively low barriers to entry in the political regime should be combined with high barriers to entry in the state and its vital function of patrolling and keeping law and order without competition (except for the one that patrols the state itself—who polices the police?—which is made up of a combination of legal self-regulation by the state, as well as oversight and accountability demanded by organized civil society and its freedoms of association and expression to enforce such accountability from public authorities).

Economic Sphere: Distinguish the International from the Domestic Sectors

In turn, while a selective (not necessarily general) fall in barriers to entry in the international sector of a given economy—allowing some freedom of movement of raw materials, capital, goods, and human capital—might help to spur growth; allocate resources in an effective, productive way; and incentivize the strengthening of such forces for the economic outlook of a given country to appear positive, this might not be enough to guarantee such growth; nor ensure a good allocation of resources, or a promising future outlook. Excluding from the analysis—or not differentiating—the international from the domestic sectors of a given economy, implies that lowering barriers to entry in the economy (in general) encompasses both sectors.

And this has by no means been necessarily the case. Economies that were opened up to foreign flows of capital and goods, as happened to many emerging market countries in Latin America, Central and Eastern Europe, and Northern and South East Asia in the course of the 1990s, retained heavily concentrated domestic sectors dominated by public and private monopolies and oligopolies. This applies to countries as different as Mexico, Russia, and South Korea, as well as many other countries that liberalized the external sector of their economies during the years of dominance of the so-called 'Washington consensus' paradigm, at the same time that productivity and competition were stifled domestically. The domestic economic structure in these economies remained dominated by a small number of national champions, traditional conglomerates, and transnational corporations and their subsidiaries in these countries.

Therefore, my general conclusion regarding the economic sphere suggested that relatively low barriers to entry in the international component of a given economy might not be enough to produce general growth in productivity, efficient allocation of resources, advantageous exchange, and general well-being for the population of such an economy. Domestic concentration dominated by monopolies and oligopolies tends to lead to underproduction and overpricing, at the same time that a small number of very powerful economic actors can easily become dominant and capture the political sphere to gain favorable legislation, advantageous fiscal terms, and other selective benefits for themselves at the expense of society in general.

I called the end result of countries that have suffered these conditions 'misplaced monopolies': in the political sphere, the state should conserve the monopoly over the legitimate use of persuasion, force, and coercion, while in the economic sphere a variable range of effective legislation and regulation should create some modicum of competition in order that a country can avoid the pernicious economic and political effects that monopolies and oligopolies tend to produce.

My analytical perspective was applied to a wealth of politico-economic data from Mexico's recent history (since the 1980s) and found that the country has suffered from the condition of misplaced monopolies.

More precisely, the application of theory to empirical data helped to qualify the initial proposition. Having concluded my study, I have claimed that Mexico has suffered from a condition of 'selective misplaced monopolies.'

The Mexican state is not as weak and ineffective as the original phrase suggested. When it wants to achieve certain specific aims and goals, it can do so, by intervening in certain states to put a limit on the level of violence and anarchy on the ground; implementing pro-competition policies as happened in 2012–14 under the government of President Enrique Peña Nieto; not to mention managing to empower and enrich its members and crony friends in ways that do not result in any penalties to a majority of them due to the absence of rule of law and predominance of impunity for the rich, powerful, and influential.

Likewise, the injection of some economic competition (even if cronyism underlies some or most of it), as well as the previous integration with the North American economies through the North American Free Trade Agreement have created some sectors that are characterized by high-productivity growth, high innovation, higher share of the world market for their products, and higher wages for those participating in them (the auto industry, electronics, consumer goods from plasma televisions to mobile phones), refrigerators and solar panels, to aeronautics, including large commercial airplanes, smaller private jets, and drones.

The emphasis in the conclusion is therefore on the word 'selective.. It is true that the Mexican state remains relatively weak and fragmented, compared with the years of political regime hegemony under the Partido Revolucionario Institucional (PRI). It is also true that for each of the economic sectors that have grown and managed to become effective competitors in the global market, there are many others—mostly connected to the domestic market as final destination, such as subsistence agriculture, a majority of small and medium-sized firms, as well as, crucially, the approximately 50 percent of the country's economically active population, who perform a variety of jobs and tasks in the informal economy in the non-tradables sector—which have continued to lose ground, and for whom life in Mexico has been increasingly more precarious and difficult. Mexico is indeed a multi-speed economy (like most countries, in the modern world), but where the distance between the large, internationally connected segments and the smaller, inward-looking ones has grown and continues to do so at a rapid rate. Such a growing politico-economic divide is dangerous and has already undermined the type of social peace and political stability Mexico enjoyed for much of the mid-20th century, albeit of course at the very high price of authoritarian rule during the years of PRI hegemony.

Not only Mexico, but also any political economy characterized by extreme inequality among its inhabitants, has a higher inherent probability of social and political conflict, due to economic unfairness and the human indignity such abysmal differences often engender. In my view, this has been and remains the case in Mexico since the onset and entrenchment of the so-called 'selective misplaced monopolies' in the course of the 1980s and 1990s.

The last part of this work extrapolates lessons learnt from the study of the Mexican case. The aim of this comparative perspective is to investigate the extent to which countries from the former Union of Soviet Socialist Republics (USSR—and its largest successor state, Russia), China, and other major emerging market countries (such as India and Brazil) fit in the 'misplaced monopolies' framework.

In turn, the next step is to assess if such placement suggests new observations in the light of the analytical angle I have built, in order to interpret a general problem of political economy. That problem can be stated as the effects that different degrees of barriers to entry in the political and economic realms of life can produce in a given society in the disaggregated political (regime and state) and economic (international and domestic) spheres.

My work has tried to show why electoral democracy (a political regime with relatively low barriers to entry for competition, and relatively free and fair popular voting for public office) and economic liberalization (opening up to financial and trade flows) might not be enough to produce satisfactory degrees of freedom (physical security and economic opportunity). The explanation put forward, according to which 'misplaced monopolies,' or in its revised formulation, 'selective misplaced monopolies' (for the case of Mexico)—that is, authority and power fragmentation coupled with a concentrated domestic economic structure—have thwarted the desirable outcomes of higher physical security and economic opportunity for average citizens in nation-states that have undergone political and economic liberalization, is not necessarily uniform. It does not need to apply to all or no countries. It is reasonable to assume that there is significant empirical variation.

Therefore, concentrating on the two variables responsible for the condition of 'misplaced' or 'selective misplaced monopolies' (i.e. a fragmented state and a concentrated domestic economic structure), it is feasible to construct two axes that can help to assess this 'pathological' condition in a comparative manner.

The vertical axis can represent the continuum between, at one end, a strong monopoly by the state on the use of force and coercion, and at the other end, extreme state fragmentation and a proliferation of non-state actors who can wield power through the exercise of force and coercion in a given territory. In turn, the horizontal axis represents the continuum between, at one end, a highly concentrated economic structure dominated by monopolies and oligopolies (which can be both private, as well as public), and at the other end a fragmented, plural economic structure characterized by high levels of competition.

The recent trajectory of different countries can be plotted to show their approximate movement and the implications given the 'misplaced monopolies' framework. This is an interpretative exercise rather than a formal, positive one. There are no indices, numbers, or statistical methods applied to ascertain the changing placement of the countries the author has in mind. The figures purport to show approximate placing based on reading of qualitative evidence: that is, the political and economic history of these countries, particularly since the beginning of the second half of the 20th century.

The case of Mexico that is described in detail in this work, starts with its trajectory toward misplaced monopolies between the latter years of PRI hegemony (the 1970–82 statist, populist years) and the late 2010s, and is then applied to different countries' political economies in terms of barriers to entry, before finally drawing some general conclusions about this comparative overview.

Figure c.1 shows the changes in direction of Mexico's political economy between the 1970s–2010s, according to presidential periods (sexenios = six years and no re-election), given the interactions of the state/domestic economy spectrums. During the years of PRI hegemony, the state had a relative effective monopoly on the public use of force and coercion thanks to its intimate connection with the President as head of state, government, and of the PRI, as well as the 'no re-election' rule for all public office posts. Likewise, the economy was quite concentrated in terms of many large state-owned enterprises, coupled with highly concentrated private business sectors, of which the concentration and high profits were more often than not the result of an informal alliance between PRI leaders, capitalist tycoons, and the labor leaders, which were controlled by and in fact often became members of the PRI leadership.

The 1982 economic crisis destroyed the state-led model of economic development, and slowly but surely chipped away at and then destroyed the hegemonic party system that dominated Mexico's politics between the 1940s and 1988. President Carlos Salinas (1988–94) carried out significant market-based reforms while family, friends, and partners of the President had privileged access to bids, financing, and the setting of pro-business regulation, which created a new crony system, which instead of being inward-looking (as had been the classic PRI system) was apparently cosmopolitan and pro-globalization. In addition, the President tried to retain PRI 'hegemony-light,' by negotiating support for pro-market reforms from the conservative Partido Acción Nacional (PAN), in exchange for more representation and public power for this party by recognizing some of its electoral victories in governorships and legislatures, while attacking and coercing the newly coalesced left under the Partido Revolucionario Democrática (PRD). Power under Salinas was re-centralized very significantly, in contrast with the weakness and decentralizing features of his predecessor, Miguel de la Madrid (1982–88). Perhaps power needed to be recentralized if the state was to keep or renew its monopoly on the use of force and coercion. The problem is that under Salinas, such concentration of state power ended up being concentrated in the President himself (it was personalized rather than institutionalized), and therefore could not be inherited by his successor.

On the contrary, the economy imploded in one of the early emerging market international financial crises (the so-called 'tequila effect') in 1994–95. As a consequence, the state under President Ernesto Zedillo (1994–2000) was severely weakened and suffered significant fragmentation, as shown in the Figure c.1. Economically, the government retained and in fact extended market reforms, chief among them the internationalization of the banking system, which later on became a major drag on potential growth, given rentier banking practices. Ominously, illegal enterprises that challenged and defeated the state's capacity to preserve in general its monopoly on the use of force and coercion, grew significantly as drug cartels, kidnapping gangs, and Mexican-US smuggling rings (humans, narcotics, vehicles, and weapons) made headlines in the news daily during those years.

Zedillo was forced to give full independence to the electoral authorities, which helped the conservative PAN and the left of center PRD win elections, and ultimately inaugurate an era of party alternation in the presidency. President Vicente Fox (2000–06) despite his good intentions and rapport with the common citizenry, presided over a highly ineffective administration. According to the evidence reviewed in this work, the ultimate collapse of federal authority and capacity to control Mexican territory took place during the Fox years.

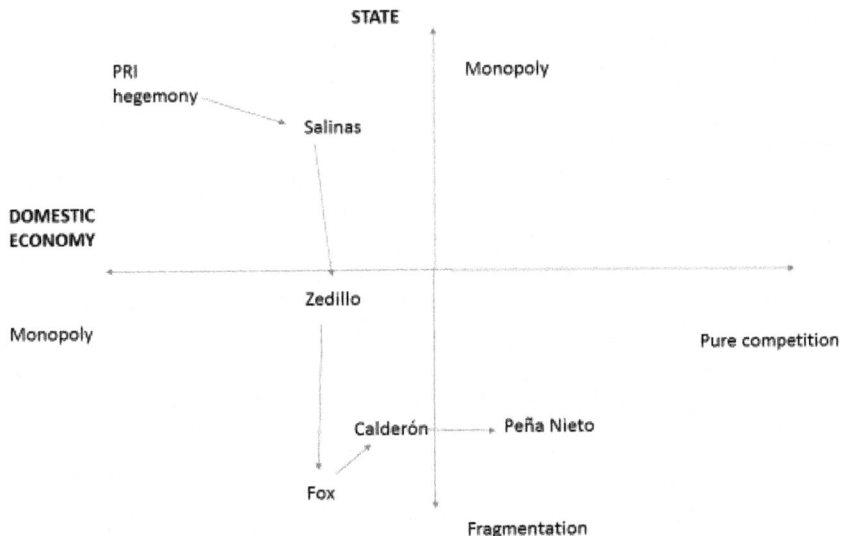

Figure c.1 The Case of Mexico: The Descent into Misplaced Monopolies

Fragmentation of power and authority created the basis for the proliferation of widespread, brutal violence, as the main drug cartels fought for dominance over the most profitable passing points between Mexico and the USA, such as Nuevo Laredo, Ciudad Juárez, and Tijuana. During the Fox years, the 'misplaced monopolies' reached their zenith as the state's capacity to quell violence and stop trafficking collapsed, at the same time that major beneficiaries of the highly concentrated economy, dominated by monopolies and oligopolies in areas like energy, telecoms, visual media, and banking, gained space and resources at the expense of the state and the public interest.

The PAN managed to retain power in 2006 after a controversial presidential election in which less than 250,000 votes separated the winner, who became President Felipe Calderón (2006–12), from the runner-up, the leftist Andrés Manuel López Obrador, of the PRD. Calderón tried, first and foremost, to reverse the fragmentation of authority and power that the country had suffered during his predecessor's term. Calderón's strategy—an all-out 'war on drugs,' later renamed 'war on organized crime'—will remain the subject of both great opposition and support. Calderón, likewise a polarizing figure whose policy tried to kick start a recentralization of authority and power, presided over a failure. The costs in human suffering and loss are incalculable. The consequences since he opened up the Pandora's box of the 'war on drugs' in Mexico remain impossible to quantify, control, or even estimate how long they will continue to negatively affect the daily life of Mexicans.

The two PAN presidencies led to widespread popular dissatisfaction and the PRI subsequently returned to power: President Peña Nieto (2012–) had an incredible honeymoon period he managed early on to craft a multiparty legislative coalition to enact the most significant pro-market reforms since Salinas's presidency. Backed by a supportive media and marketing group in the major broadcaster Televisa, and a group of loyalists that included highly regarded neoliberal economists, as well as seasoned, tough PRI politicians from México and Hidalgo states, Peña Nieto and his team convinced the international financial establishment that Mexico had got its act together; drug-related violence and killings could be controlled; and Mexico could raise its long-term growth potential, thanks to the pro-competition policies the government crafted and enacted in 2013 and 2014.

However, dramatic events in Ayotzinapa (where 43 students were arrested by the municipal police who allegedly turned them over to a drug syndicate who executed them and burned their bodies—an official story discredited by domestic and international forensic experts) and in Mexico's City poshest residential area (where a government contractor to Peña Nieto for many years—and some of his closest collaborators like former Secretary of Finance, Luis Videgaray, and before them to two of Peña Nieto's uncles, both former governors of México state and members of the Atlacomulco political family and power bloc—built the president a US $7m. mansion. The contractor had privileged access to Peña Nieto and was part of a construction consortium that included a large Chinese firm that won the tender to build the government's most expensive infrastructure project, the México-Querétaro bullet train (which was cancelled after the corruption scandal) put a spanner in the works. Since then things for Peña Nieto went downhill. The loss of credibility, the exposure of cronyism and grand corruption, and the return of state repression, violence, and censorship destroyed Peña Nieto's reputation and that of his government and those who served under it.

The structural reforms passed under Peña Nieto could do something to improve the heavy concentration of economic activity in public and private monopolies and oligopolies. Such change will take time, but at least the legal and regulatory changes have been introduced. If implemented impartially and capably, the Mexican economy might become less concentrated in future. By 2018 the state remained weak and fragmented. It is not a failed or quasi-failed state: the state under Peña Nieto managed and pursued objectives (legal and illegal) effectively. But in the realm of security and violence the government remained incapable of shutting the Pandora box opened by his predecessor, President Calderón. Organized criminal groups continue to wreak havoc in hot spots around Mexico. These hot spots are not fixed, but tend to arise in many parts of the country's territory, depending on circumstances. The fragmentation of criminal groups has made it more difficult to track them and apprehend them. In the final two years of the Peña Nieto presidency levels of violence and homicide surpassed the high points of the Calderón years. The Pandora box continues to be open and to yield super-profits to those willing to play the lottery of trafficking, kidnapping, and extorting. US demand for narcotics, particularly the terrifying opioid addiction epidemic, which contributed to reducing the life expectancy of US citizens two years in a row in 2015–16 (something that had not happened since 1962–63 and before that since the 1920s)[1] will continue to be among the strongest drivers of the lethal violence that has dominated in many parts of Mexico since the 2000s.

Having shown Mexico's trajectory, using the categories I cited to identify the problem of 'misplaced monopolies,' I now use the device to place other large countries or groups of countries on this spectrum. The first cases I look at are the largest countries that have experienced totalitarian rule: Russia (part of the former USSR) and China.

Both Marxist regimes were somewhere along the far top left-hand corner, with monopolistic state and command economies. However, the two countries have followed a very different trajectory since the 1980s. In the case of China, Deng Xiaoping's reforms that began in the late 1970s helped to transform the totalitarian system by introducing a commercial economy that replaced the command one. The state has retained a strong and relatively pervasive monopoly on the use of force and coercion, although several peripheral areas under Chinese rule, such as Xinjiang and Tibet, continue to demand autonomy. China's economic opening created the greatest industrial revolution in the world since those in Europe and the USA. The economy remains dominated by the state and despite the degree of autonomy of certain state-owned enterprises, they continue to rely on the state, which controls the banking system and its mighty foreign reserves. This is a case that—in great contrast to Mexico—has experienced very high, long-term economic growth, while its state and regime remain cohesively closed around the leadership of the one-party system.

In great contrast, the dissolution of the Soviet empire and USSR in 1989–91 led to a dramatic weakening of the state and a gold rush by apparatchiks and their henchmen to secure ownership of the newly privatized assets of the bankrupt command economy. The apparatchiks underwent a transformation from bureaucrats into tycoons, or as they are more widely known 'oligarchs.' During Boris Yeltsin's years in power (1991–99) the country experienced the growth of violence, organized crime, and separatist conflicts in the Caucasus. The Kremlin was perceived as very weak, and oligarchs captured the state. The country reached a nadir after the dramatic financial and economic collapse of 1997–98. A major change in the politico-economic landscape took place after Vladimir Putin became President in 2000. An ex-KGB operative and his close colleagues, the *siloviki,* alongside most of the oligarchs, who became pliant and submissive in the face of a strong, no-nonsense president, Russia moved decidedly from a very fragmented state structure and capacity to one of strong re-centralization. President Putin centralized both state force and coercion functions, as well as economic activity, particularly by divesting oligarchs who disagreed with him of their fortunes, and tried to mount challenges in the country's nominally young electoral democracy. The end result has been the return of authoritarian rule and a highly concentrated domestic economic structure.

The state in China and Russia has managed to retain, to different degrees, a solid monopoly over the use of force and coercion in their respective territories. This has been done either through the preservation of centralized rule, and incorporating many features of totalitarianism in social life in China, or in the reintroduction of such type of rule in the case of Russia under Putin. Likewise, in both cases the state remains the dominant force in the economy, and big business is very close to the state. This situation, also prevalent in Mexico, has allowed for a thriving politico-economic system of capital accumulation dominated by cronyism. A crony capitalism index compiled by *The Economist* included China, Russia, and Mexico in the top 20 countries in 2014: Russia ranked as number two, behind Hong Kong, which took first place (the territory has been closely controlled by Beijing since the British handover of sovereignty in 1997). In turn, Mexico was in seventh place, while the People's Republic of China was number 19.[2]

People interested in the possibility of centralized, effective state monopoly on the use of force and violence but under liberal democratic conditions must ask whether countries suffering from fragmentation of authority and power, such as Mexico, can do this without reverting to authoritarian rule, like Russia. Another question concerns the strong state centralization, coupled with control of a highly concentrated economy, that has led to crony capitalism in China, Russia, as well as Mexico, and whose *modus operandi* prizes corruption, impunity, violence if necessary, and a

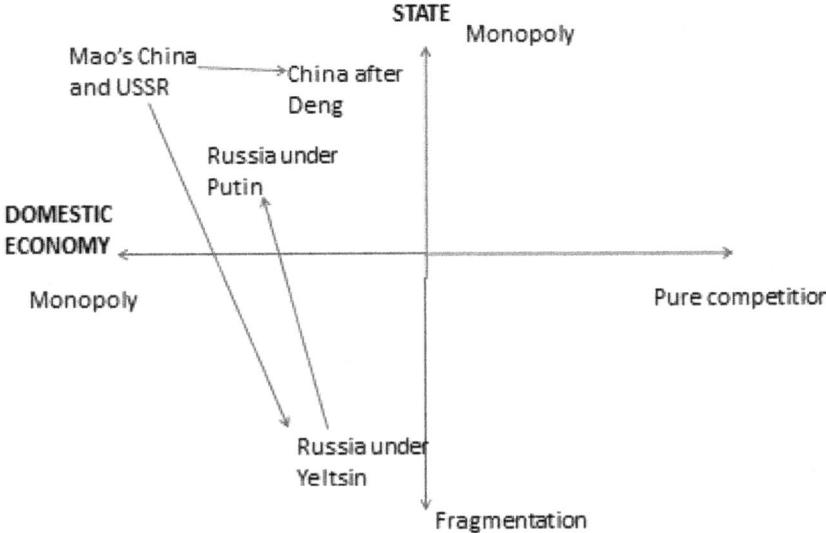

Figure c.2. Totalitarian/Authoritarian Political Regimes in China and Russia

continuation of capital and influence accumulation concentrated among very few individuals, who are very close to the cockpit of power at the expense of the rest of society.

What about large emerging market countries that are not totalitarian or authoritarian but can be considered, although far from perfect, operating electoral democracies? Among these countries we find some of the most high-profile, such as Brazil and India. These countries are characterized by very high levels of inequality, race or ethnically based exclusion, and high levels of violence and criminality, and states that have been relatively ineffective at coping with these conditions. These two countries illustrate examples from two continents, which aside from grabbing the financial and later broader news headlines as members of the so-called BRICS (Brazil, Russia, India, China, and South Africa), are globally significant due to their size, their potential, and the challenges they face in the light of the dual transitions of varying degrees that they have undergone.

The cases of Brazil and India, large federal countries that are electoral democracies, shows a preponderance of relatively strong state monopoly over the use of force and coercion during the years of authoritarian rule in each of them, although to different degrees. Likewise, the two cases show concentrated domestic economic structures under state-led economic policy. Changes since the 1990s pushed the two countries in the opposite direction, specifically less concentrated monopoly over the state's use of force and coercion as authority became decentralized in Brazil and India (compared with the years of military rule in the former and the 'Emergency' years under Prime Minister Indira Gandhi in the latter). Likewise, the countries moved to varying degrees in the direction of economic liberalization and a less concentrated domestic economy, although both remain characterized by very high inequality, a high concentration of capital and wealth, and a high ranking in the crony index: India ranked ninth and Brazil 13th.[3]

Their economies are, likewise, more state-led than the Mexican economy. Neoliberals have had a significantly harder time in both Brazil and India than in many other developing countries. The statist tradition in the economy is strong in both and has deep roots. These roots can be identified in Brazil in the ambitious state-building process initiated by President Getúlio Vargas from the 1930s (although the armed forces embraced positivism, nationalism, and the idea of a national state that would guide modernization since the 1870s–80s). In the case of India, some of the roots can be found in the British and Indian bureaucratic apparatus that ran the Raj (the British colonial empire), but more specifically and in a systematic way since India's independence in 1947 and the state-led socialist economy and secular polity favored by the country's first Prime Minister after emancipation from the United Kingdom, Jawaharlal Nehru.

Federalism has tended to produce stronger centrifugal forces and less central control in Brazil and India than in Mexico during PRI hegemonic rule. Neither Brazil nor India experienced political rule led by civilians under a hegemonic party. The Congress party in India, which aside from forming the backbone of independence, has been a dominant party during various periods, but cannot be described as hegemonic. Brazil's party landscape has been much more fragmented and no party can claim to have been dominant, let alone hegemonic. Therefore, these countries have been more used to significant autonomy for the states that comprise the federation most of the time, and not overweaning power from the center. Periods of authoritarian rule saw such relative state autonomy reversed, but as soon as democracy returned, the *status quo ante* was restored. This is the opposite of what Mexico experienced at least from the 1930s and until the first half of the 1990s. Although a federal polity on paper (the 1917 Constitution defines Mexico as a federal republic), political practice during the years of rule by the PRI centralized power in Mexico City, and federalism, while not dead, was continuously checked and controlled by the national *cacique*, the President of the Republic, in turn. The centrifugal forces that have traditionally characterized Brazil and India in terms of territorial politics are a relatively new phenomenon in Mexico (since the second half of the 1990s).

In summary, in light of the Brazilian and Indian cases, it is possible to identify conditions of relatively fragmented state monopoly on the use of force and coercion, due to the federal framework, but where electoral democracy continues to be viable despite the fact that the quality of democracy, in terms of freedom as considered in this work (basic physical security

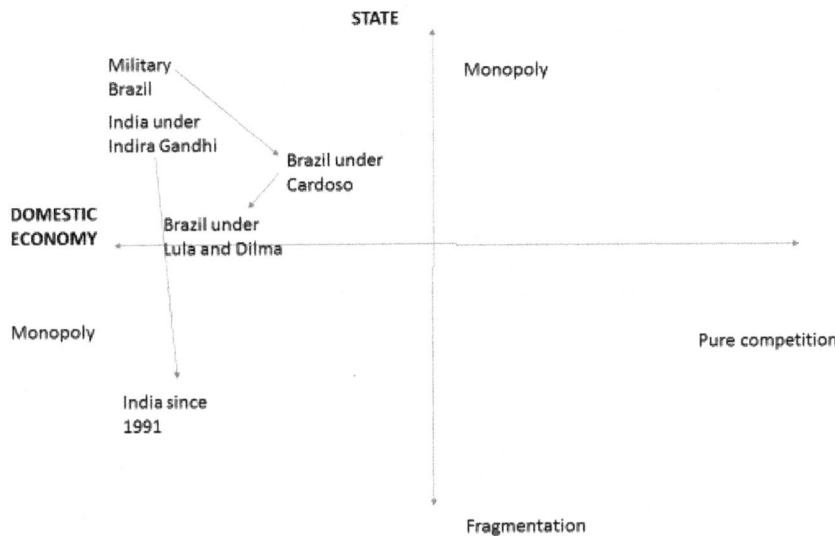

Figure c.3. Big Democratic Federal Countries: Brazil and India

and economic opportunity) remains low, and heavily skewed in favor of those with connections to politico-economic networks of patronage, clientelism, and influences such as wealth and family pedigree.

In all, the placement of different countries in the state/domestic economy axis helps us to think about some of the general implications of the 'misplaced monopolies' framework. Fragmentation of authority without the rule of law can endanger the basic freedom of a population, as the case of Mexico since the 1980s–1990s, and increasingly so in the 2000s and 2010s, has illustrated. Highly concentrated domestic economic structures tend to provide fertile ground for the development of cronyism and the many adverse effects this creates, although this politico-economic relationship also remains alive and well in advanced democratic economies, whose production sectors are less concentrated on average than in large emerging economies.

The combination of fragmented state authority and power in a context with a very defective or inexistent rule of law and a concentrated domestic economic structure, tends to be detrimental to the majority in any given population. Likewise, it does not bode well for democracy and further democratization in countries that face these conditions, because the privileged few tend to capture the state and block reforms that might help to create a less unequal, less unfair society.

Recentralization of authority and power can be achieved, but the danger is that in the light of some of the examples examined briefly above—that is, countries with an authoritarian or a totalitarian tradition—such recentralization can easily reverse into non-democratic rule as in Russia under President Putin. A country like China must walk a narrow tightrope by retaining strongly centralized state and regime control, even though its society has been transformed by the country's industrial revolution, which has urbanized and globalized hundreds of millions of Chinese in the last three decades, creating untold wealth for a few, and made a substantial middle class too. Can political power remain highly concentrated, uncontested by the population, and unaccountable in a society where the income, information, and expectations of growing numbers of the population become more plural and decentralized? This is a question with major implications for global politics in the 21st century.

For Mexico, conditions remain unhelpful for the cause of democracy, fairness, and prosperity, given 'selective misplaced monopolies'. However, there is no 'End of History,' and therefore political and economic conditions will continue to unfold, yielding many outcomes that cannot be forecast, let alone predicted. The same applies, of course, to the other countries briefly mentioned above. The framework presented in this work can hopefully contribute to refine, test, and decide if cross-national comparisons like these, which are the bread-and-butter of academic as well as political work in the continuingly vibrant field of comparative political economy, make sense or not. Looked at through the lens purely of the Mexican case since the 1980s, the conclusion can be summarized as one of the growth of both concentrated wealth and of violence. Do these always go together? Not necessarily, but in Mexico they have done, and with fury.

Will López Obrador and his MORENA's overwhelming victory in the 2018 elections mark the beginning of rolling back 'misplaced monopolies' in Mexico? AMLO won more than 53% of the popular vote (more than any presidential candidate since De la Madrid in 1982, when elections were neither free nor fair in Mexico). His MORENA also won majorities in the federal legislature and also a majority of the nine governorship elections disputed on July 1, 2018. This popular landslide surely reflected the accumulated frustration and anger of a majority of Mexicans whose freedom has been curtailed by official corruption, growing socioeconomic inequality and scant opportunities to develop one's potential at the same time that a majority remain prey to violence and insecurity while the few continue to be able to buy justice through money, influence and power. Chapter 4 of this book was titled 'Looking in vain for exits from misplaced monopolies'. Neither the PAN nor the PRI (or for many they were one and the same, the 'PRIAN') could do it between 2006 and 2018. Might AMLO with his broad, strongly committed and diverse coalition of forces under MORENA manage to reverse the misplaced monopolies? I do not hold my breadth. It is not impossible but it is incredibly difficult. The conditions that weakened and fragmented the Mexican state at the same time that they kept concentrating the production of wealth in the hands of few at the expense of the great majority of Mexicans cannot be fixed by decree from a charismatic, well-meaning leader. Mexico is one of the only countries in Latin America where the left has not had a chance to rule since the so-called 'third wave' of democratization took off in the world in the 1970s. Since the 2000s, leftist governments have been no panacea across-the-board. They have been relatively successful in countries like Chile and Uruguay, have had a mixed record in Bolivia and Ecuador, and have been a tragic disaster in Venezuela. Can 'progressive' politics turn the ship of state away from misplaced monopolies in Mexico? It does not bode well that such a huge amount of hope, dreams and expectations have been placed under the shoulders of a messianic individual. Probabilities of improvement would be higher if such popular energy could be channeled through institutions rather than an individual. However, Mexico's political and economic institutions and those who man them have tended to be particularistic, biased, self-serving, and limited for the well-being of the few 'ins' and against the great majority of 'outs'. It is not up to AMLO and his circle of close collaborators to fix this inherited and living tradition of unfair and unjust rule. It is up to Mexican society to hold AMLO and his group accountable at the same time that society embraces a general rather than a selective well-being mentality. This embrace and change sounds easy on paper but is highly unlikely on the ground. In the meantime concentrated wealth and lethal violence continue to grow in Mexico with fury.

Notes

1 BBC, "Opioid crisis linked to two-year drop in US life expectancy," 22 December 2017, http://www.bbc.com/news/world-us-canada-42452733, Accessed 17 February 2018.
2 *The Economist*, "The new age of crony capitalism,"15–21 March 2014, p. 58.
3 Ibid.

Bibliography

Institutional Sources

Academia Mexicana de los Derechos Humanos.

Centro de Derechos Humanos Miguel Agustín Pro Juárez (Prodh).

Centro de Investigación para el Desarrollo, A.C. (CIDAC).

CIDAC, "Índice de Incidencia Delictiva y Violencia 2009," Centro de Investigación para el Desarrollo A.C., 2009, 10.

Colectivo contra la Tortura y la Impunidad (CCTI).

Committee to Protect Journalists (CPJ), "In absence of fresh military conflict, journalists killing decline again," 21 December 2017, https://cpj.org/reports/2017/12/journalists-killed-iraq-crossfire-murder-mexico.php, Accessed 3 February 2018.

Economic Commission for Latin America and the Caribbean (ECLAC), "Latin America is the world's most unequal region. Here is how to fix it," https://www.cepal.org/en/articles/2016-latin-america-worlds-most-unequal-region-heres-how-fix-it, 25 January 2016, Accessed 6 December 2017.

Economist Intelligence Unit, "Telecoms reform begins to show results," 30 October 2015, http://www.eiu.com/industry/article/673657251/telecoms-reform-begins-to-show-results/2015-10-30, Accessed 11 January 2018.

Energy Information Administration, "Mexico", 16 October 2017, https://www.eia.gov/beta/international/analysis.cfm?iso=MEX, Accessed 19 January 2018.

Equis: Justicia para las Mujeres.

Human Rights Watch, "Mexico," *World Report 2011*, http://www.hrw.org/en/world-report-2011/mexico.

Instituto Mexicano para la Competitividad (IMCO).

Instituto Mexicano de Derechos Humanos y Democracia (IMDHD).

Inter-American Development Bank (IDB), "Latin America and Caribbean register middle class growth. Child poverty and inequality problems persist," 24 October 2016, https://www.iadb.org/en/news/news-releases/2016-10-24/latin-american-middle-class-has-nearly-doubled%2C11611.html, Accessed 7 December 2017.

International Monetary Fund (IMF), "About the IMF: History: Debt and Transition (1982–1989)," http://www.imf.org/external/about/histdebt.htm, Accessed 11 January 2016.

Mexico, Banco de México, "Historia sintética de la banca en México," by Eduardo Turrent, Mexico, 2008, http://www.banxico.org.mx/sistema-financiero/material-educativo/basico/%7BFFF17467-8ED6-2AB2-1B3B-ACCE5C2AF0E6%7D.pdf, Accessed 7 December 2017.

Mexico, Secretaria de Energía, "Ronda Cero", March 2014, https://www.gob.mx/cms/uploads/attachment/file/55590/Ficha_tecnica_R0.pdf, Accessed 19 January 2018.

México, cómovamos? "Semáforos Económicos Estatales," http://www.mexicocomovamos.mx/?s=seccion&id=50, Accessed regularly between November 2015 and January 2018.

México Unido contra la Delincuencia.

MSCI Emerging Markets Index (USD), https://www.msci.com/documents/10199/c0db0a48-01f2-4ba9-ad01-226fd5678111, Accessed 20 January2018.

Oxfam, "Extreme Inequality in Mexico," by Gerardo Esquivel, *Oxfam Report*, July 2015, Accessed 7 January 2018, http://www.pulsamerica.co.uk/2015/07/mexico-wealth-inequality-four-richest-mexicans-worth-same-as-20-million-poorest/

Peterson Institute for International Economics, "Mexico and the United States: Building on the Benefits of NAFTA", conference, 15 July 2014, Washington, DC.

Red Nacional de OrganismosCiviles de Derechos Humanos "Todos los Derechos Humanos – para Todas y Todos".

Red Retoño.

Reporters without Borders, "Mexico: Constant Violence and Fear," https://rsf.org/en/mexico, Accessed 3 February 2018.

USA Ibp, *Mexico Company Laws and Regulations Handbook*, International Business Publications, 2009.

United States Institute of Peace, "Legitimate State Monopoly over the Means of Violence," http://www.usip.org/guiding-principles-stabilization-and-reconstruction-the-web-version/6-safe-and-secure-environment/le., Accessed 28 July 2015.

United States Joint Forces Command, *The Joint Operating Environment 2008: Challenges and Implications for the Future Joint Force*, Norfolk, VA, 2008.

World Bank, Global Development Indicators Database, http://data.worldbank.org/country/mexico

World Bank, "Political Decentralization," http://www1.worldbank.org/publicsector/decentralization/political.htm., Accessed 27 October 2016.

World Bank, Global Financial Development Report 2017/2018, https://openknowledge.worldbank.org/bitstream/handle/10986/28482/9781464811487.pdf.

World Wealth and IncomeDatabase, http://wid.world/world-inequality-lab/.

Woodrow Wilson Center for International Scholars, Mexico Institute, "Mexico: Aztec Tiger – Mexico Institute in the News," in http://www.wilsoncenter.org/article/mexico-aztec-tiger-mexico-institute-the-news.

Yale Center for the Study of Globalization, https://ycsg.yale.edu/about-center-1, Accessed 8 November 2017.

Newspapers, Periodicals, Online Journalism, and General Reference

Adelman, Irma and Edward Taylor, "Is structural adjustment with a human face possible? The case of Mexico," in *The Journal of Development Studies*, 26 (3, 387–407, 1990).

Ahmed, Azam, "Mexico Spends Big on Ads to Tame the News Media," *The New York Times*, 25 December 2017, A1;A10–11.

Ahmed, Azam, "A Scion of Mexico Fights Corruption, and Becomes a Target," in the *New York Times*, 30 August 2017, https://www.nytimes.com/2017/08/30/world/americas/mexico-claudio-gonzalez-laporte.html, Accessed 4 February 2018.

Aristégui, Carmen, "La Fortuna de Raúl Salinas Y La Partida Secreta de Carlos," 1 August2013, http://aristeguinoticias.com/0108/mexico/la-fortuna-de-raul-salinas-y-la-partida-secreta/., Accessed 27 December 2015.

Arte Colonial, "Las castas de la Nueva España", in https://artecolonial.wordpress. com/2011/02/28/las-castas-de-la-nueva-espana/, 28 February2011, Accessed 19 September 2017.

Bagely, Bruce, "Drug Trafficking and Organized Crime In The Americas: Major Trends – Drug Trafficking and Organized Crime in Latin America and the Caribbean.pdf," http://www.issdp.org/conference-papers/2013/2013_papers/Bagley%20B %20-%20%20Drug%20trafficking%20and%20organized%20crime%20in%20Latin% 20America%20and%20the%20Caribbean.pdf., Accessed 7 December 2015.

BBC, "Opioid crisis linked to two-year drop in US life expectancy", 22 December 2017, http://www.bbc.com/news/world-us-canada-42452733, Accessed 17 February 2018.

Robert A. Blecker, "The North American Economies after NAFTA: a Critical Appraisal," in *International Journal of Political Economy*, 33 (3, 5–27, 2003).

The Brownsville Herald, "Guillermo Calderoni gunned down, Fatal injury: Former Mexican federal officer shot in head," 6 February2003, http://www.brownsvilleherald. com/news/local/guillermo-calderoni-gunned-down-fatal-injury-former-mexican-federa l-officer/article_40d2a00b-cf6d-50b3-9a3f-0fd0e87aad8a.html, Accessed 8 February 2018.

Carroll, Rory and Jo Tuckman, "Spotlight falls on Televisa, Mexico's all-powerful TV station," in *The Guardian*, 26 June 2012, https://www.theguardian.com/world/2012/ jun/26/spotlight-televisa-mexico-tv-station, Accessed 12 January 2018.

Casey, David Luhnow, "Killing Escalates Mexico Drug War," *The Wall Street Journal*, 29 June 2010.

Castañeda, Jorge G. and Héctor Aguilar Camín,. "Regreso al futuro", in *Nexos*, December 12010, https://www.nexos.com.mx/?p=14042, Accessed 20 January 2018.

Castañeda, Jorge G. and Héctor Aguilar Camín, "Un futuro para México", in *Nexos*, 1 November2009, https://www.nexos.com.mx/?p=13374, Accessed 20 January 2018.

Castañeda, Jorge G., "La caravana de Corral", in *El Financiero*, 24 January 2018, http://www.elfinanciero.com.mx/opinion/la-caravana-de-corral.html, Accessed 26 January 2018.

Castaño Contreras, Cristian and Andrés Ponce de León Rosas, *Seguridad Nacionalen México: Una Aproximaciónalos Retosdel Futuro*, Mexico, Fundación Rafael Preciado Hernández, 2011. http://info4.juridicas.unam.mx/jusbiblio/juslib/76/37800. htm?s=., Accessed 16 January 2016.

Cave, Damien, "Immigration Upended," in *The New York Times*, 2011–2012, http://www. nytimes.com/interactive/world/americas/immigration-upended-series.html, Accessed 22 February 2018.

Cedillo, Juan Alberto, "Los zetas mataron y quemaron a más de 300 personas en Coahuila: testigo", in *Proceso*, 13 July 2016, http://www.proceso.com.mx/447092/ los-zetas-mataron-quemaron-a-300-personas-en-coahuila-testigo, Accessed 24 January 2018.

CNN.com, "Los Zetas Called Mexico's Most Dangerous Drug Cartel," 6 August2009, http://www.cnn.com/2009/WORLD/americas/08/06/mexico.drug.cartels/index.html, Accessed 23 January 2018.

Cortés, Gabriela, "El zar antidrogas que protegió a un capo," in *Milenio*, http://www.mile nio.com/policia/zar-gutierrez-rebollo-antidroga-muere-senor-cielos-carrillo-fuentes-nar cotrafico_0_211179372.html, 12 December 2013, Accessed 8 November 2017.

Deacon, Robert T., "The Political Economy of the Resource Curse: A Survey of Theory and Evidence," in *Foundations and Trends in Microeconomics*, 7 (2, 111– 208, 2011).

De la Cruz, José Luis, "Gobierno federal sale al rescate de Guerrero; anuncia plan emergente de seguridad," in *Proceso*, 31 January 2014, http://hemeroteca.proceso.com.mx/?p=363744, Accessed 26 January 2018.

Diaz, Lizbeth, "Fourth ex-governor from Mexico's PRI arrested on corruption charges," in *Reuters*, 6 October 2017, https://www.justice.gov/usao-sdny/pr/former-governor-mexican-state-sentenced-manhattan-federal-court-131-months-prison-money, Accessed 17 February 2018.

Dillon, Sam, "Mexico's PRI Party Approves a Primary to Choose Nominee," *The New York Times*, 18 May 1999, http://www.nytimes.com/1999/05/18/world/mexico-s-pri-party-approves-a-primary-to-choose-nominee.html., Accessed 15 January 2016.

Dillon, Sam, "Government and Church Reviewers Agree to Disagree on Mexican Cardinal's Slaying," *The New York Times*, 28 July 2000, http://www.nytimes.com/2000/07/28/world/government-and-church-reviewers-agree-to-disagree-on-mexican-cardinal-s-slaying.html., Accessed 15 January 2016.

Dresser, Denise, "Tocar un nervio", in *Reforma*, 8 January 2018. http://www.reforma.com/aplicacioneslibre/preacceso/articulo/default.aspx?id=126970&urlredirect=https://www.reforma.com/aplicaciones/editoriales/editorial.aspx?id=126970, Accessed 26 January 2018.

Dudley, Steven, "Two Reasons Why Laredo Has Less Homicides than Nuevo Laredo," in In Sight Crime and Woodrow Wilson Center, https://www.wilsoncenter.org/sites/default/files/Laredo_vs_Nuevo_Laredo_Dudley.pdf, 2013, Accessed 13 January 2016.

Economia hoy, "Probable, una tercera subasta petrolera en 2018", 19 October 2017, http://www.economiahoy.mx/empresas-eAm-mexico/noticias/8687385/10/17/Probable-una-tercera-subasta-petrolera-en-2018.html, Accessed 19 January 2018.

The Economist, "The new age of crony capitalism," 15–21 March 2014.

English Oxford Dictionary, "Cacique," https://en.oxforddictionaries.com/definition/cacique, Accessed 20 January 2018.

Enríquez Perea, Alberto, "Aforismos políticos de Jesús Reyes Heroles", in *Nexos*, 1 May 2006, https://www.nexos.com.mx/?p=11879, Accessed 20 January 2018.

Estrada, Arturo, "Leonel Godoy llama a su hermano Julio César a entregarse a justicia," in *El Financiero*, 4 March 2015, http://www.elfinanciero.com.mx/mundo/leonel-godoy-llama-a-su-hermano-julio-cesar-a-entregarse-a-justicia.html, Accessed 26 January 2018.

Excélsior, "Perfil de Joaquín Hernández Galicia, La Quina,"11 November 2013, http://www.excelsior.com.mx/nacional/2013/11/11/928036, Accessed 16 January 2018.

Fineman, Mark, "Zedillo Fires Attorney General, Picks Successor," *Los Angeles Times*, 3 December 1996. http://articles.latimes.com/1996-12-03/news/mn-5284_1_attorney-general, Accessed 13 January 2016.

Fineman, Mark, "Mexico: Savvy New Top Lawman Doesn't Fit the Mold: Antonio Lozano, Named Attorney General, Is Quiet and Studious. As an Opposition-Party Cabinet Member, He Breaks a 65-Year Tradition," *The Los Angeles Times*, 9 December 1994. http://articles.latimes.com/1994-12-09/news/mn-7048_1_antonio-lozano, Accessed 13 January 2016.

Fisher, Max and Amanda Taub, "Building a Mini-State With Avocados and Guns," in *The New York Times*, 18 January 2018, Accessed 3 February 2018.

Focus Economics, "Latin America: the Most Unequal Region in the World," https://www.focus-economics.com/blog/inequality-in-latin-america, 16 June2017, Accessed 6 December 2017.

Forbes: the World's Billionaires, April 2017, https://www.forbes.com/billionaires/list/6/#version:static,Accessed 7 January 2008.

Gaynor, Tim and Lisbeth Diaz, "Mexico says it killed top Zetas drug lord body snatched," in *Reuters*, 9 October 2012, https://www.reuters.com/article/us-mexico-drugs/mexico-says-it-killed-top-zetas-drug-lord-but-body-snatched-idUSBRE8980Z D20121010, Accessed 24 January 2018.

Gómez Hermosillo, Rogelio, "Quién fija el salario mínimo?" in *El Universal*, 8 December 2015, http://www.eluniversal.com.mx/entrada-de-opinion/articulo/rogelio-gomez-herm osillo-m/nacion/2015/12/8/quien-fija-el-salario-minimo, Accessed 19 January 2018.

Graham, Dave, "Ventas de mineral de hierro a China provocan choques con cartel de droga mexicano", in *Reuters*, 2 January 2014, https://lta.reuters.com/article/busi nessNews/idLTASIEA0103D20140102, Accessed 25 January 2018.

Guerrero, Jesús, "Piden intervención federal en Guerrero", in *Reforma*, 10 April 2017, http://www.reforma.com/aplicacioneslibre/articulo/default.aspx?id=1087928 &md5=a488eb3ff2ee7bc9531e36b79aa5f20c&ta=0dfdbac11765226904c16cb9ad1b2 efe, Accessed 26 January 2018.

Haber, Stephen and Aldo Musacchio, "These are the Good Old Days: Foreign Entry and the Mexican Banking System," *Harvard Business School, Working Paper 13–062*, 10 January 2013, https://dash.harvard.edu/bitstream/handle/1/10208236/13-062. pdf?sequence=1, Accessed 8 December 2017, p. 51.

Herrera Toledo, Marco Antonio, "Ni los veo, ni los oigo", in *SDP noticias*, 7 December 2013, https://www.sdpnoticias.com/columnas/2013/12/07/ni-los-veo-ni-lo s-oigo, Accessed 20 January 2018.

Joyful Gypsy, "Tlatelolco Massacre (Mexico City)," *CNN iReport*, 9 October 2009, http://ireport.cnn.com/docs/DOC-336863, Accessed 16 January 2016.

Kwan Yuk, Pan, "Want cheap labor? Head to Mexico, not China," in *Financial Times*, 14 January 2016, https://www.ft.com/content/bddc8121-a7a0-3788-a74c-cd2b49cd3230, Accessed 20 January 2018.

Libardi, Manuella, "Ayotzinapa three years later: new light, few answers," in *demo-craciaAbierta*, 26 September 2017, https://www.opendemocracy.net/democraciaabier ta/manuella-libardi/ayotzinapa-three-years-later-new-light-few-answers, Accessed 25 January 2018.

Loret de Mola, Carlos, "Lo major y lo peor de Felipe Calderón," in *El Universal*, 2 December 2010, http://archivo.eluniversal.com.mx/columnas/87424.html, Accessed 16 January 2018.

Maldonado, Salvador, "Michoacán y las autodefensas: Cómo llegamos aquí?" in *Nexos*, 14 January 2014, https://redaccion.nexos.com.mx/?p=6011, Accessed 25 January 2018.

"Mexican Political Reforms, Something New, Something Old? Woodrow Wilson Center," https://www.wilsoncenter.org/article/mexican-political-reforms-something-new-something-old., Accessed 10 January 2016.

Millman, Joel and Josede Cordoba, "Drug-Cartel Links Haunt an Election South of the Border," *The Wall Street Journal*, 3 July 2009, http://online.wsj.com/article/SB124657442789989017.html.

Moreno, Martín, "Todo el imperio podrido de Carlos Romero Deschamps", in *Sin Embargo*, 25 February 2015, http://www.sinembargo.mx/25-02-2015/1260531, Accessed 16 January 2018.

Muñóz, Alma E., "De 1998 a la fecha han sido asesinados 696 militantes: PRD," in *La Jornada*, 2 November 2007, http://www.jornada.unam.mx/2007/11/02/index.php? section=politica&article=013n2pol, Accessed 20 January 2018.

Nevaer, Luis V., "Mexico and the Myth of the 'Failed State'," *New America Media*, 9 July 2011, http://newamericamedia.org/2011/07/mexico-and-the-myth-of-the-failed-state.php, Accessed 8 November 2014.

O'Neil, Shannon, "Mexico's Voters Have Bigger Problems than Trump," in *Bloomberg View*, 31 January 2018, https://www.bloomberg.com/view/articles/2018-01-31/mexico-s-voters-have-bigger-problems-than-trump, Accessed 4 February 2018.

Open Democracy, "Why does Latin America remain the most unequal region in the world?" https://www.opendemocracy.net/democraciaabierta/why-does-latin-america-remain-most-unequal-region-in-world, 12 June 2017, Accessed 6 December 2017.

"Partida Secreta Presidencial," in *La Razón*, 27 December 2015, http://razon.com.mx/spip.php?article56649, Accessed 27 December 2015.

Preston, Julia, "Raul Salinas Guilty in Killing and Is Sentenced to 50 Years," *The New York Times*, 22 January 1999, http://www.nytimes.com/1999/01/22/world/raul-salinas-guilty-in-killing-and-is-sentenced-to-50-years.html., Accessed 7 December 2016.

Preston, Julia, "Mexican Candidate Plays the Bad Boy," *The New York Times*, 5 November 1999. http://www.nytimes.com/1999/11/05/world/mexican-candidate-plays-the-bad-boy.html., Accessed 7 December 2016.

Proceso, "Azcárraga se declara priísta y soldado del president," 15 May 1982, http://www.proceso.com.mx/133473/azcarraga-se-declara-priista-y-soldado-del-presidente, Accessed 12 January 2018.

Proceso, "En los setenta, Salinas Lozano 'introdujo' a Carlos y Raúl en el tráfico de drogas," 20 January 1999, Accessed 11 January 2018.

Proceso, "Romero Deschamps, historia de un líder menor,"24 September 2002, http://www.proceso.com.mx/245057/245057-romero-deschamps-historia-de-un-lider-menor, Accessed 16 January 2018.

Reuters, "Factbox: Key Facts about Mexico's Tax System," 6 May 2013. http://www.reuters.com/article/2013/05/06/us-mexico-tax-facts, Accessed 7 December 2015.

Rodríguez García, Arturo, "El golpe a Luz y Fuerza, ilegal de principio a fin," in *Proceso*, 26 October 2012, http://www.proceso.com.mx/323571/323571-el-golpe-a-luz-y-fuerza-ilegal-de-principio-a-fin, Accessed 16 January 2018.

Rodríguez García, Arturo, "Los hijos del privilegio", in *Proceso*, 25 May 2013, http://www.proceso.com.mx/343013/los-hijos-del-privilegio, Accessed 17 February 2018.

Sin Embargo, "The Guardian revela que Televisa vendió a EPN plan para posicionarlo y hundir a AMLO; involucra a Fox,"7 June 2012, http://www.sinembargo.mx/07-06-2012/257208, Accessed 12 January 2018.

Solis, Dianne, "U.S. Says Witnesses Boost Drug Probe of Raul Salinas," *The Wall Street Journal*, 23 April 1997, http://www.wsj.com/articles/SB861751952438820500, Accessed 16 January 2016.

SR Srocco Report, "PEMEX: Mexico's State Oil Company on the Verge of Bankruptcy and Collapse," 25 March 2017, https://us-issues.com/2017/03/25/pemex-mexicos-state-oil-company-on-the-verge-of-bankruptcy-collapse/, Accessed 16 January 2018.

Thompson, Ginger, "Ex-President in Mexico Casts New Light on Rigged 1988 Election," *The New York Times*, 9 March 2004, sec. World. http://www.nytimes.com/2004/03/09/world/ex-president-in-mexico-casts-new-light-on-rigged-1988-election.html., Accessed 7 December 2016.

Thompson, Ginger, "Rival Drug Gangs Turn the Streets of Nuevo Laredo into a War Zone," *The New York Times*, 4 December 2005. http://www.nytimes.com/2005/12/

04/world/americas/rival-drug-gangs-turn-the-streets-of-nuevo-laredo-into-a-war.htm l, Accessed 7 December 2016.

Thomson, Adam, "Aztec tiger begins to sharpen its claws" *Financial Times*, 27 June 2013.

Tobar, Hector, "Judicial Overhaul in Mexico OKd," *Los Angeles Times*, 7 March 2008, http://articles.latimes.com/2008/mar/07/world/fg-mexjustice7.

Torres, Joe, Julia Love and Sheky Espejo, "Slim's America Movil wins telecom battle in top Mexico court," in *Reuters*, 16 August 2017, https://www.reuters.com/article/ us-mexico-telecom/slims-america-movil-wins-telecom-battle-in-top-mexico-court-id USKCN1AW2IA, Accessed 11 January 2018.

Tuckman, Jo, "Leading Politician Rodolfo Torre Cantú Murdered in Mexico," *The Guardian*, 29 June 2010, http://www.theguardian.com/world/2010/jun/29/leading-p olitician-rodolfo-torre-cantu-murdered-mexico, Accessed 12 January 2016.

UPI, "Six killed in disco shootout," 9 November1992, https://www.upi.com/Archives/ 1992/11/09/Six-killed-in-Mexico-disco-shootout/5689721285200/, Accessed 8 February 2018.

Villamil, Jenaro, "Va reforma de telecom contra creaciones del propio gobierno", in *Proceso*, 16 March 2013, http://diario.mx/Nacional/2013-03-16_4d5e1fd4/va-reforma -de-telecom-contra-creaciones-del-propio-gobierno/, Accessed 12 January 2018.

Weiner, Tim, "Mexican Drug Agent Crossed the Line Once Too Often", in *The New York Times*, 18 February 2003. http://www.nytimes.com/2003/02/18/world/mexica n-drug-agent-crossed-the-line-once-too-often.html, Accessed 12 January 2016.

"Who Killed Luis Donaldo Colosio?", *The San Diego Union-Tribune*, 16 March 2004, https://www.sandiegouniontribune.com/uniontrib/20040315/news_1e15salinas.html., Accessed 5 March 2016.

Wiktionary, "Narcomanta," https://en.wiktionary.org/wiki/narcomanta, Accessed 4 February 2018.

Wright, Lawrence, "Slim's Time: Who is Carlos Slim, and does he want the paper of record?" *The New Yorker*, 9 June 2009, https://www.newyorker.com/magazine/2009/ 06/01/slims-time, Accessed 11 January 2018.

Zepeda Bustos, Carmen Silvia, "Privatizaciones realizadas durante el sexenio de Ernesto Zedillo", in *El Cotidiano*, 172, March-April 2012, 32–39, http://www.reda lyc.org/html/325/32523118004/, Accessed 16 January 2018.

Primary Sources

Author's interviews with Antony, 19 and 24 August 2011; 5 July 2012, Cuernavaca, Morelos, Mexico.

Author's interviews with Cicero, 16 and 22 August 2011, Mexico City, Mexico.

Alvarado, Arturo, "Violence and Criminality in Mexico: an Analysis of Recent Trends," presentation at the conference "Mexico at the Crossroads: Learning from History, Facing the Future," 17–18 November 2011, New Orleans: Tulane University Press.

Calderón de la Barca, Frances, *Life in Mexico*, original publication, 1843; New York: Doubleday Dolphin, 1960 paperback edition.

Calderón Hinojosa, Felipe, *Los retos que enfrentamos: los problemas de México y las políticas públicas para enfrentarlos (2006–2012)*, Mexico, Grijalbo, 2014.

Carpizo, Jorge, *Anatomía de perversidades. Reflexiones sobre la moral pública en México*, Mexico, Aguilar, 2000.

Casas-Zamora, Kevin, Eric Olson and Celia Toro, "The Future of Security and Border Cooperation," Panel, Inter-American Dialogue, The United States and Mexico in the Trump Era," Conference, Co-hosted by Tulane University, El Colegio de México and Inter-American Dialogue, 6 February 2018.

Castañeda, Jorge G., *La Herencia. Arqueología de la sucesión presidencial en México*, Mexico, Alfaguara, 1999.

Cruz, Francisco and Jorge Toribio Montiel, *Negocios de familia: Biografía no autorizada de Enrique Peña Nieto y el grupo Atlacomulco*, México: Temas de Hoy, 2009.

Giorguli, Silvia, Francisco Alba, Marc Rosenblum, and Andrew Selee, "Migration Dynamics and Policy under Trump," Panel, Inter-American Dialogue, The United States and Mexico in the Trump Era," Conference, Co-hosted by Tulane University, El Colegio de México, and Inter-American Dialogue, 6 February 2018.

Hernández, Roberto and Geoffrey Smith, "Presunto culpable," film, first shown in a documentary festival in Amsterdam in 2008.

Hills, Carla, Arturo Sarukhán, and Michael Shifter, "The State of U.S.-Mexico Relations," Discussion, Inter-American Dialogue, The United States and Mexico in the Trump Era," Conference, Co-hosted by Tulane University, El Colegio de México, and Inter-American Dialogue, 6 February 2018.

Lajous, Alejandra, *Las Razones y las obras: gobierno de Miguel de la Madrid: crónica del sexenio 1982–1988*, Mexico, Fondo de Cultura Económica, 1985.

Lustig, Nora, Gary Gereffi, Doug Nelson, Luis de la Calle, "The Road Ahead for NAFTA," Panel, Inter-American Dialogue, The United States and Mexico in the Trump Era," Conference, Co-hosted by Tulane University, El Colegio de México, and Inter-American Dialogue, 6 February 2018.

López Obrador, Andrés Manuel, *Fobaproa: Expediente abierto. Reseña y archivo*, Mexico, Grijalbo, 1999.

Prud'homme, Jean François and Jesus Silva Herzog Márquez, "Dynamics and Challenges of the 2018 Mexican Presidential Election," Discussion, Inter-American Dialogue, The United States and Mexico in the Trump Era," Conference, Co-hosted by Tulane University, El Colegio de México, and Inter-American Dialogue, 6 February 2018.

Salinas de Gortari, Carlos, "A New Hope for the Hemisphere," in *New Perspectives Quarterly* 8, Winter 1991.

Salinas de Gortari, Carlos, *México. Un paso difícil a la modernidad*, Barcelona, Plaza y Jánes, 2000.

Scherer García, Julio and Carlos Monsiváis, *Parte de Guerra: documentos del general Marcelino García Barragán, los hechos y la historia*, Mexico, Aguilar (Nuevo Siglo), 1999.

Serra Puche, Jaime, "Openness and Growth in Mexico," Keynote Address, Conference "Mexico at the Crossroads: Learning from History, Facing the Future," 17–18 November 2011, New Orleans: Tulane University.

West, Rebecca, *Survivors in Mexico*, New Haven: Yale University Press, 2003.

Zedillo, Ernesto, Interview, "Los saldos del sexenio," in *Proceso*, 26 November 2000.

Secondary Sources

Aguayo Quezada, Sergio, *La Charola: Una historia de los servicios de inteligencia en México*, Mexico, Grijalbo Mondadori, 2001.

Aguilar Camín, Héctor and Jorge G. Castañeda, *Una agenda para México*, México: Punto de Lectura, 2012.

Astorga, Luis, *El siglo de las drogas: del Porfiriato al nuevo milenio*, 3rd edition, Mexico City: Penguin Random House, 2016.

Azaola, Elena and Marcelo Bergman, "The Mexican Prison System," in Wayne A. Cornelius and David A. Shirk, *Reforming the Administration of Justice in Mexico*, Notre Dame: University of Notre Dame Press, 2007.

Baker, Andy, *The Market and the Masses in Latin America: Policy Reform and Consumption in Liberalizing Economies*, New York and Cambridge: Cambridge University Press, 2009.

Barajas Durán, Rafael, "Retrato de un siglo. ¿Cómo ser mexicano en el XIX?", in Enrique Florescano, ed., *Espejo mexicano*, México: Fondo de Cultura Económica, 2002, pp. 116–177.

Bonfil, Guillermo, "México profundo", in Roger Bartra, ed., *Anatomía del mexicano*, México: Plaza y Jánes, 2002, pp. 289–294.

Brading, David A., ed., *Caudillo and Peasant in the Mexican Revolution*, Cambridge: Cambridge University Press, 1980.

Brandenburg, Frank Ralph, *The Making of Modern Mexico*. First Edition, New York: Prentice Hall, 1964.

Carpizo, Jorge, *El presidencialismo mexicano*, México: Siglo xxi, 16th ed., 2002 [1st ed., 1978].

Castañeda, Jorge G., *Sorpresas te da la vida: México 1994*, Mexico, Aguilar (Nuevo Siglo), 1995.

Chávez, Ezequiel A., "La sensibilidad del mexicano", in Roger Bartra, ed., *Anatomía del mexicano*, México: Plaza y Jánes, 2002, pp. 25–45.

Coatsworth, John H., "Obstacles to Economic Growth in Nineteenth-Century Mexico", in *American Historical Review* (February–December 1978), pp. 80–100.

Corchado, Alfredo, *Midnight in Mexico: a Reporter's Journey through a Country's Descent into Darkness*, New York: Penguin, 2014.

Diaz-Cayeros, Alberto, "Entrenched Insiders: Limited Access Order in Mexico," North, Wallis, Webb, and Weingast, eds., 2013, pp. 233–260.

Dixit, Avinash, "Recent Developments in Oligopoly Theory," in *The American Economic Review*, 72, 2, 1982, 12–17.

Esquivel, J. Jesús, *La CIA, Camarena y Caro Quintero: la historia secreta*, Mexico City: Penguin Random House, 2014.

Fernández, Andrés, Luca Flabbi, Juan David Herreño, "Reformas laborales para impulsar el crecimiento económico", in *Online Forum: Rethinking Reforms*, 21 March 2013, http://vox.lacea.org/?q=reformas_laborales_para_crecimiento_2013, Accessed 23 January 2018.

Ferreira, Francisco H.G., et al., *Economic Mobility and the Rise of the Latin American Middle Class*, Washington, DC: The World Bank, 2012, http://elibrary.worldbank.org/doi/abs/10.1596/978-0-8213-9634-6, Accessed 24 October 2014.

Fizbein, Ariel, et al., *Conditional Cash Transfers: Reducing Present and Future Poverty*, Washington, DC: World Bank, 2009, https://openknowledge.worldbank.org/handle/10986/2597, Accessed 6 December 2017.

Fuentes, Carlos, *Nuevo tiempo mexicano*, Mexico, Aguilar (Nuevo Siglo), 1995.

Fukuyama, Francis, *State Building: Governance and World-Order in the Twenty-First Century*, Ithaca, NY, Cornell University Press, 2004.

Gibson, Edward L., *Boundary Control: Subnational Authoritarianism in Federal Democracies*, Cambridge: Cambridge University Press, 2012.

Gilly, Adolfo, *La Revolución interrumpida: México, 1910–1920, una guerra campesina por la tierra y el poder*, Mexico, Ediciones El Caballito, 1971.

Gilly, Adolfo, *El cardenismo: una utopía mexicana*, Mexico, cal y arena, 1994.

González, Francisco E., "Shocks and Social Pressures in the Improvement of the Exercise of Citizenship Rights: Great Britain and Mexico's Different Historical Trajectories", in *Mexican Law Review*, 8, 2, January–July 2015.

González, Francisco E., "Mexico: A Democratic Governance Analysis", in Freedom House, *Countries at the Crossroads*, Washington, DC, 2012.

González, Francisco E., "The War on Drugs in Mexico: a Fatal Distraction?" in *Current History*, Vol.110, February 2011.

González, Francisco E., "Mexico: A Democratic Governance Analysis", in Freedom House, *Countries at the Crossroads*, Washington, DC: Freedom House, February 2010.

González, Francisco E., "Mexico's Bloody Drug Wars," in *Current History*, 108, 715, February 2009, pp. 72–76.

González, Francisco E., "El ciclo de la dominación de un solo partido: México, India y Japón en perspectiva comparada," in *Foro Internacional*, XLIX, January-March 2009, no. 1, pp. 47–68.

González, Francisco E., *Dual Transitions from Authoritarian Rule: Institutionalized Regimes in Chile and Mexico, 1970–2000*, Baltimore, MD: Johns Hopkins University Press, 2008.

Gourevitch, Peter, *Politics in Hard Times: Comparative Responses to International Economic Crises*, Ithaca, NY: Cornell University Press, 1986.

Grayson, George. *The Cartels: The Story of Mexico's Most Dangerous Criminal Organizations and Their Impact on U.S. Security*. Santa Barbara: ABC-CLIO, 2013.

Grayson, George. *The Politics of Mexican Oil*, Pittsburgh, PA: University of Pittsburgh Press, 1980.

Grillo, Ioan, *El Narco: Inside Mexico's Criminal Insurgency*, New York: Bloomsbury, 2012.

Haber, Stephen, Armando Razo, and Noel Maurer, *The Politics of Property Rights: Political Instability, Credible Commitments, and Economic Growth in Mexico, 1876–1929*, Cambridge: Cambridge University Press, pp. 29–40.

Hanson, Gordon H., "Why is Mexico not Rich," University of California, San Diego and National Bureau of Economic Research (NBER), September 2010, http://irps.ucsd.edu/assets/001/500330.pdf, Accessed 18 October 2014.

Hernández, Anabel, *Los señores del narco*, Mexico, Grijalbo Mondadori, 2010.

Hirth, Kenneth G., *The Aztec Economic World: Merchants and Markets in Ancient Mesoamerica*, Cambridge: Cambridge University Press, 2016.

Holden, Steinar, "Avoiding the Resource Curse: the Case of Norway," in *Energy Policy*, 63 (December 2013, 870–876).

Humphreys, Macartan, Jeffrey D.Sachs, Joseph E.Stiglitz, eds., *Escaping the Resource Curse*, New York, Columbia University Press, 2007.

Terry Lynn Karl, *The Paradox of Plenty: Oil Booms and Petro-States*, Berkeley: University of California Press, 1997.

Ibarra, David, *La crisis inacabada*, México: UNAM, 2013.

Ibarra, David, *Paradigmas monetarios en México*, México: UNAM, 2010.

Ibarra Palafox, Francisco, *La privatización bancaria en México*, México, Siglo XXI, 2014.

Knight, Alan, *The Mexican Revolution*, 2 vols, Cambridge: Cambridge University Press, 1986.

Knight, Alan and Wil Pansters, eds., *Caciquismo in Twentieth Century Mexico*, London: Institute for the Study of the Americas, 2005.

Krauze, Enrique, *La presidencia imperial*, Barcelona y México: Tusquets, 1997.

Krauze, Enrique, *Biografía del poder: caudillos de la Revolución Mexicana, 1910–1940*, Mexico, Tusquets, 1998.

Siglo de caudillos: biografía política de México, 1810–1910, Mexico, Tusquets, 1999.

Kurtz, Marcus J., *Latin American State Building in Comparative Perspective: Social Foundations of Institutional Order*, Cambridge: Cambridge University Press, 2013.

Kuznets, Simon, *Economic Growth of Nations: Total Output and Production Structure*, Cambridge, MA: Harvard University Press, 1971.

Levy, Santiago and Michael Walton, eds., *No Growth without Equity? Inequality, Interests, and Competition in Mexico*, New York: Palgrave, 2009.

Linz, Juan J., *The Breakdown of Democratic Regimes: Crisis, Breakdown, and Reequilibration*, Baltimore, MD: Johns Hopkins University Press, 1978.

Linz, Juan J. and Alfred Stepan, eds. *The Breakdown of Democratic Regimes*, 4 vols. Baltimore, MD: Johns Hopkins University Press, 1978.

Linz, Juan J. and Alfred Stepan, eds. *Problems of Democratic Transition and Consolidation: Southern Europe, South America, and Post-Communist Europe*, Baltimore, MD: Johns Hopkins University Press, 1996.

Lohse, Jon C. and Fred Valdez, Jr., eds., *Ancient Maya Commoners*, Austin: University of Texas Press, 2004.

Lowry, Malcolm, *Under the Volcano: a Novel*, New York: Reynal and Hitchcock, 1947.

Lynch, John, *Caudillos in Spanish America, 1800–1850*, Oxford: Oxford University Press, 1992.

MacLeod, Dag, *Downsizing the State: Privatization and the Limits of Neoliberal Reform in Mexico*, University Park: Penn State University Press, 2004.

Mahoney, James and Dietrich Rueschemeyer, eds., *Comparative Historical Analysis in the Social Sciences*, Cambridge: Cambridge University Press, 2003.

Meyer, Lorenzo, *Mexico y los Estados Unidos en el conflicto petrolero, 1917–1942*, Mexico, El Colegio de Mexico, 1981.

Meyer, Lorenzo and Isidro Morales, *Petróleo y nación: la política petrolera en México, 1900–1987*, Mexico, Fondo de Cultura Económica, 1990.

North, Douglass C., John Joseph Wallis, and Barry R. Weingast, *Violence and Social Orders*, New York and Cambridge: Cambridge University Press, 2009.

North, Douglass C., John Joseph Wallis, Steven B. Webb, and Barry R. Weingast, eds., *In the Shadow of Violence: Politics, Economics, and the Problems of Development*, New York and Cambridge: Cambridge University Press, 2013.

O'Donnell, Guillermo, Philippe Schmitter, and Laurence Whitehead, eds. *Transitions from Authoritarian Rule*, 4 vols, Baltimore, MD: Johns Hopkins University Press, 1986.

Pansters, Wil G., ed., *Violence, Coercion, and State-Making in Twentieth-Century Mexico: the Other Half of the Centaur*, Stanford, CA: Stanford University Press, 2012.

Pérez, Ana Lilia, *Camisas azules, manos negras: El saqueo de PEMEX desde Los Pinos*, Mexico, Grijalbo, 2010.

Pérez, Ana Lilia, *El Cártel Negro: Cómo el crimen organizado se ha apoderado de PEMEX*, Mexico, Grijalbo, 2011.

Piketty, Thomas, *Capital in the Twenty-First Century*, Cambridge: Harvard University Press, 2013.

Ramos, Samuel, "El complejo de inferioridad", in Roger Bartra, ed., *Anatomía del mexicano*, México: Plaza y Jánes, 2002, 109–120.

Ravelo, Ricardo, *Narcomex: Historia e Historias de una Guerra*, Mexico, Vintage, 2012.

Reveles, José, *Las historias más negras: de narco, impunidad y corrupción en México*, México, Grijalbo, 2009.

Reyes Heroles, Jesús, "Fiscal and Energy Issues in Mexico in a Presidential Election Year," Presentation at The Johns Hopkins University School of Advanced International Studies (SAIS), 5 April 2012.

Riva Palacio, Raymundo, "La conexión china", in *El Financiero*, 20 March 2015, http://www.elfinanciero.com.mx/opinion/la-conexion-china.html , Accessed 25 January 2018.

Ros Bosch, Jaime, *Algunas tesis equivocadas sobre el estancamiento económico de México*, Mexico: El Colegio de México, 2014.

Scarborough, Vernon L. and John E. Clark, eds., The Political Economy of Ancient Mesoamerica: *Transformations during the Formative and Classical Periods*, Albuquerque: University of New Mexico Press, 2007.

Scheidel, Walter, *The Great Leveler: Violence and the History of Inequality from the Stone Age to the Twenty-First Century*, Princeton: Princeton University Press, 2017.

Scott, James C., *Against the Grain: A Deep History of the Earliest States*, New Haven, CT: Yale University Press, 2017.

Sen, Amartya, *Development as Freedom*, New York: Oxford University Press, 1999.

Sierra, Justo, *The Political Evolution of the Mexican People*, Austin: University of Texas Press, 1969 [1900–1902].

Silva Herzog, Jesús, *Breve historia de la Revolución Mexicana*, 2 vols, Mexico, Fondo de Cultura Económica, 1960.

Smith, Adam, *An Inquiry into the Nature and Causes of the Wealth of Nations*, first published in 1776, Vol. II, Books IV and V of The Glasgow Edition of the Works and Correspondence of Adam Smith, edited by R.H. Campbell and A.S. Skinner, Oxford: Oxford University Press, 1976.

Steinmo, Sven, Kathleen Thelen, and Frank Longstreth, eds., *Historical Institutionalism in Comparative Analysis*, Cambridge: Cambridge University Press, 1992.

Stiglitz, Joseph E., *Globalization and its Discontents*, New York: W.W. Norton, 2002.

Suárez Dávila, Francisco, *Crecer o no crecer: Del estancamiento estabilizador al nuevo desarrollo*, Mexico: Taurus, 2013.

Thelen, Kathleen, "Historical Institutionalism in Comparative Politics," *Annual Review of Political Science*, 2 (June 1999, 369–404).

Tilly, Charles, "War Making and State Making as Organized Crime," in Peter Evans, Dietrich Rueschemeyer, and Theda Skocpol, eds., *Bringing the State Back In*, Cambridge: Cambridge University Press, 1985.

Tollison, Robert D., "Rent Seeking," *The Encyclopedia of Public Choice*, 2004, 820–824, 820, http://link.springer.com/chapter/10.1007/978-0-306-47828-4_179, Accessed 11 November 2014.

Weber, Max, "Politics as a Vocation," published originally as a lecture in Munich in 1921 and translated and edited by H.H. Gerth and C. Wright Mills, *From Max Weber: Essays in Sociology*, New York: Oxford University Press, 1946, 77–128.

Index